THE ANGLO-NORMAN NOBILITY
IN THE REIGN OF HENRY I

The ANGLO-NORMAN NOBILITY in the REIGN of HENRY I

The Second Generation

CHARLOTTE A. NEWMAN

upp

UNIVERSITY OF PENNSYLVANIA PRESS
Philadelphia

University of Pennsylvania Press
MIDDLE AGES SERIES
Edited by
EDWARD PETERS
Henry Charles Lea Professor
of Medieval History
University of Pennsylvania

A complete listing of the books in this series
appears at the back of this volume

Portions of this material appeared in an earlier form in
articles by the author:
 "Family and Royal Favor in Henry I's England" *Albion* 14 (1982), 292–306
 "Chris Given-Wilson and Alice Curteis, *The Royal Bastards of Medieval
England*. Review Essay" *Medieval Prosopography* 7 (1986), 87–97.

Library of Congress Cataloging-in-Publication Data

Newman, Charlotte A.
  The Anglo-Norman nobility in the reign of Henry I : the second generation /
Charlotte A. Newman.
    p.   cm.—(University of Pennsylvania Press Middle Ages series)
  Bibliography: p.
  Includes index.
  ISBN 0–8122–8138–1
  1. Great Britain—History—Henry I, 1100–1135. 2. Normans—England—
History. 3. Great Britain—Nobility—History. I. Title. II. Series: Middle
Ages.
DA198.N48   1989
942.02'3—dc19
                                                    88–20817
                                                    CIP

For my parents
Herbert, of blessed memory, and May Newman

CONTENTS

ACKNOWLEDGMENTS

As a child, I spent many hours poring over photo albums of ancestors I never knew and asking relatives for stories of our family's past. I knew the pictures and stories by heart, but somehow hoped for new knowledge with each repetition. As an adult, I became a historian of a group of people very different from my own ancestors, but when I used my training to research my own ancestors' era, I found what I had been searching for as a child. I could never know more about them as individuals or hear them speak, but I could learn about the world in which they lived and about others like them who also inhabited that world.

This professional and personal search taught me to be a social historian. We are all affected by our environments—the climate, the landscape, the technology, the politics, the way we earn our living, and the people with whom we live (both familially and socially). To understand any one aspect of a person or of a society, we need to look at all of them. The more aspects of the Anglo-Norman nobility I examined, the more I was convinced that studying them as a group clarifies many questions of medieval and specifically English history.

This book has evolved over time. It began in a very different form as my dissertation, and, as such, it is justifiably the termed the "second generation" of my work. At each stage of its (and my) development, a long list of people helped in a variety of ways.

The first generation of this work owes much to my adviser, Robin S. Oggins, who taught me the basics, showed me how to see people within structures, and let me work on a topic of my choosing so that it would hold my interest.

Special thanks go to Bert Hansen, for asking cogent questions in spite of protests that he knew little of the period; to the late Stanley Ferber, for asking me about social mobility; and to Virginia Oggins and her red pen.

The second generation took a long time to gestate. From this time of my life, I owe unquantifiable thanks to C. Warren Hollister, who generously adopted this non-Santa Barbarian and in so many ways is responsible for my being an active professional. Thanks go to the Haskins Society for support and criticism, especially to Victoria Chandler and David Spear, and to Constance Bouchard and Paul Hyams, who asked the right question at the right time. A different type of acknowledgment must be made of the intellectual help and personal support of my Albany colleagues, especially my dear friends Henry Brownstein (who taught me to respect sociology), Willie Marlowe (who helps me see form and substance), and Peggy Walker (who epitomizes the idea of family). An indefinable thank you goes to Dr. Stefanie Isser.

Miami University has been the midwife. The Faculty Research Committee gave me tangible support, while my colleagues in the History Department, especially Thomas Coakley, David Fahey, and Allan Winkler, have provided the intangible kind. Special thanks must be given to my "coaches": Elliot Gorn for interest and advice; Jeffrey Kimball for computer help; graduate students Mary Brennan and V. Padmavathy; "the group," Jilda Aliotta, Judith deLuce, Ann Fuehrer, and Emily Murphree; and my friend and colleague Chris Africa. The brunt of the labor pains have fallen on my husband Rabbi Dr. Robert Goldy, who now has my thanks as well as my love.

A new class of thanks and a new definition of generosity must be created for Joel T. Rosenthal. Though drafted into serving on my dissertation committee, he has been there ever since, well beyond the call of professional duty, whether feeding me in Kalamazoo or reading drafts of my manuscript.

Throughout my life I have been given the gift of family. Whatever I have been able to include of myself in this work is due to the love and support of my parents, to whom this work is dedicated, my sister Joan C. Knutsen and her family, my "other parents" Lillian and Herman Cohen, and all of the spouses and children of my Albany family.

In my heart, this book is a "family" endeavor. My mind knows that all errors are mine.

Oxford, Ohio 1987   Charlotte A. Newman

ABBREVIATIONS

Anglo-Norman Studies	*The Battle Conference on Anglo-Norman Studies. Proceedings.* Edited by R. Allen Brown.
B. L.	British Library
CDF	Round, J. H. (ed.). *Calendar of documents Preserved in France A.D. 918–1206.*
EYC	Farrer, William and Clay, Charles T. (eds.). *Early Yorkshire Charters.* 12 vols.
FE	Round, J. H.. *Feudal England: Historical Studies on the XIth and XIIth Centuries.*
GP	William of Malmesbury. *Willelmi Malmesbiriensis monachi de gestis pontificum Anglorum.* Edited by N.E.S.A. Hamilton.
GR	William of Malmesbury. *Willelmi Malmesbiriensis monachi de gestis regum Anglorum.* Edited by William Stubbs. 2 vols.
GS	*Gesta Stephani.* Edited and translated by K. R. Potter.
Heref.Dd.	*Herefordshire Domesday.* Edited by James Tait and V. H. Galbraith.
HN	William of Malmesbury. *Historia Novella.* Edited by K. R. Potter.
Leic.Surv.	Slade, Cecil F. (ed. and trans.) *The Leicestershire Survey c. A.D. 1130.*
Liber Winton	Biddle, Martin, ed. *Winchester in the Early Middle Ages.* vol. 1.
Lind.Surv.	Foster, Charles W. and Longley, Thomas (eds.). *The Lincolnshire Domesday and the Lindsey Survey.*

Mon. Ang.	Dugdale, William. *Monasticon Anglicanum.* 6 vols. in 8.
Nhants. Surv.	"Northamptonshire Survey." Edited by J. H. Round.
OVB	Orderic Vitalis. *The Ecclesiastical History of England and Normandy.* 4 vols. Translated by Thomas Forester.
OVC	Orderic Vitalis. *The Ecclesiastical History of Orderic Vitalis.* Edited and Translated by Marjorie Chibnall. 6 vols.
PL	*Patrologia cursus completus, serie Latina,* ed. J.-P. Migne. 221 vols.
PR	Great Britain. Record Commission. *Magnum rotulum scaccarii, vel magnum rotulum pipae.*
RB	*Red Book of the Exchequer.* Edited by Hubert Hall.
Reg. I–IV	*Regesta regum Anglo-Normannorum, 1066–1154.* 4 vols.
Worc.Cart.	*Cartulary of Worcester Cathedral Priory.* Edited by R. R. Carlington.

INTRODUCTION

It is easy to forget that the Anglo-Norman nobility who lived in the first half of the twelfth century were people. After all, they lived at a time when various institutions and cultural tastes were developing, and we tend to study these trends rather than the group of individuals who participated in them. Besides, we do not have enough particulars to write many individual biographies. Yet they were people who lived within families and were part of a generation; they also lived within a country and were part of an estate. In fact, they are the perfect candidates for a fully developed social biography.

Within the general scope of medieval history, the Anglo-Normans give us perspectives on several crucial developments. They are an example of nobles in the transition from a functioning military group to an aristocratic class, from what Bloch calls the "First Feudal Age" to the "Second." They lived at the beginning of the Twelfth-Century Renaissance; like their contemporaries in other countries, they exhibited certain interests in the patronage of the written word (whether for administrative or cultural reasons) and of the new religious orders. The new emphasis in this period on inheritance laws illustrates changes in families caused by external pressures.

Within the specific world of the Anglo-Norman kingdom, this period marked the beginning of the royal government based upon the new administrative and legal techniques that would change the relationship of the nobles to the crown. Furthermore, this was the first generation of *Anglo*-Norman nobles born in England and into a family with noble status. The relationship between the men of this generation and the crown sets the stage for both the politics of the Anarchy (1135–54) and the important legal developments of Henry II's reign (1154–89).

The twelfth century has long been recognized as an era of important demographic, political, institutional, and intellectual change.[1] The metaphor of the Wheel of Fortune was used by Anglo-Norman chroniclers, indicating that they were as aware of the uncertainty or possibility of change in social status and in individual fortune as were fifteenth-century Italians.[2] By this time, population levels had increased perceptibly. With more children living, parents throughout society found it more difficult to provide for their children. For the nobility it was especially important to make provisions commensurate to their status, that is, to acquire for the children land held by feudal tenure. Traditionally, this land had been acquired by participating in military ventures but, as fewer military conquests occurred within Europe, other types of royal service or indirect methods of gaining land, such as marriage to an heiress, became more important.

Feudal land was of course held for military service, and the vassal ruled it for the lord. Therefore, since tenure was linked to the defense and government of the kingdom, economic and social changes always had political consequences.[3] That was the case in early twelfth-century England. Henry I began experimenting with royal administration, expanding it beyond these families by using the increased number of literate lower clergy, and nobles who were more dependent for their wealth on the king's patronage than on their inherited land. Since these lesser nobles obtained a new, nonmilitary access to land and marriages, and therefore to power, this administrative experiment not only benefited the king but also provided the social mobility so needed by the growing noble population. Yet this royal patronage necessarily created tension between the older feudal families and those newer ones whose wealth and social status were increasing.

The Anglo-Norman nobles, of course, like people throughout history, had many different roles in life, places in society, identities as they saw each other. Historians, however, have tended to compartmentalize their lives. Usually we have looked at the nobles as political beings who held land by feudal tenure, fought on horseback, and were involved in a power struggle with the king. In recent years we have become aware of the private noble, who had a family and emotions. In addition there was the social noble, affected by a place in time and culture. Yet in reality, these were the same men and women, and their various roles were intertwined and complex.

This book looks at this group of nobles as a group within society, combining questions of time and place with those of family and estate in the hope of gaining a better understanding of the interrelationship of a social group with its society. These men and women were individuals affected by their gender, their birth order, their family, and their generation (in its many definitions); they were also members of a noble "class" whose opportunities were perceptibly changing due both to royal administrative changes and to larger demographic ones.

This book is also designed to look at all possible nobles. I would like to reinstate membership in the family for those who were not inheriting sons. For too long, our studies have dealt with women, younger sons, and illegitimates only as pawns of a "family" defined by its senior males, pawns used to build the "family" fortune. Certainly, during this period as throughout history, the less economically or politically powerful had less control over their lives, but they did have lives and they deserve recognition. We must also recognize that while they were less powerful, they were not powerless.

While individuals were located in families, these families in turn moved through time. People are affected by being members of generations. In a 1974 article,[4] David Herlihy proposes using the tool of the study of generations in our investigation of medieval society. The approach has been used effectively for other periods and in other disciplines, most notably and fully in sociology,[5] but there has as yet been little follow-up by medievalists. I have found that the generational approach and the questions raised by it are particularly useful for looking at Anglo-Norman history. In many ways, as the subtitle of this book indicates, I find it crucial to understanding these nobles.

Before applying this approach, though, we must define a "generation." Three senses of the word will be introduced here because of their proven usefulness with this material. The first has been called variously "biological," "generation-set," or familial (father-son-grandson); by this definition all fathers are of one generation, all sons of another.[6] The starting point here is a chronological age or a period of years in which the fathers were born. This definition is most useful when looking at an individual's life and actions, or at a particular family's history. It raises questions of family relationships and of tensions between individuals.[7] As a tool, though, it is of limited use outside a lineal family. Within a larger population, biological generation is far from easily determined, especially without complete age records or a structured age for passing on power. Indeed, preliterate societies generally lack a "conceptualization of absolute age," instead, shifts in roles result from relative ages and physical capability.[8] This would seem to describe the medieval world, which lacked birth records and even definite limits of life stage.[9]

Two other definitions, each of which is more flexible, can also be applied to the group to be studied. Both define a generation as a group with a particular orientation based upon shared experiences and expectations. The first identifies a generation with an era or a period of time; for example, the "generation of the Conquest" labels those who experienced the Conquest together, although many of the knights were of different ages. While individuals would respond somewhat differently because they were of different life stages or ages at the time, the shared experience nevertheless separated them from others who did not share it.

The second alternative applies the term "generation" to those who shared an experience regardless of time. For example, studies of American immigration show that "first generation" or "second generation" Americans have experienced a series of very similar responses although at different points in time, and age, and in combination with other historical experiences.[10] In the Anglo-Norman world, a second-generation magnate (the first born or reared to that status) exhibited a different behavior and attitude from that of his father, and with political and social consequences.

Each of these definitions presents only part of the historical picture, because everyone is a part of many different generations at the same time. Generational questions add a new dimension of our understanding of the Anglo-Norman period—one especially important in understanding the mechanisms of change. The generational approach will be applied to the Anglo-Norman nobility in a variety of ways throughout this book.

The various written sources available the time have let us identify approximately 250 families, though only a small number of these families left enough information for full family studies. These families formed a social estate separate from others, but it was far from a uniform one. There actually were many types of nobles. In order to understand them as a group, I have organized them into categories based on ties to the court, titles, service, and heritage in England. Seven categories in all have been used. Category 1 includes people known to have been retainers of nobles and ecclesiastics, episcopal staff, and a small group of unidentified men who attested royal documents. Category 2 is the general group of lesser nobles, untitled and not associated with royal office, but holding land in chief. Category 3 is the service families, those already identified with royal office in 1100. Category 4 is the "new men," those having no noticeable status in England before 1100. Category 5 is the magnates, most having titles. Category 6 is the royal family, while category 7 is the upper clergy.

These categories have proven to be highly flexible and useful. My research used court attendance as a starting point, including people in the study because they attended court. Surprisingly, this criterion also proved to include most of the landholders who appear in other documents. Nobles were, however, added to this core group if they left no evidence of court attendance but appear in other sources as holding some land in chief. Also added were any identifiable members of holders' families. On the other hand, a number of people attended court at least once, because they witnessed one document in Henry's reign, but who could not be identified through other evidence. Since most holders appear in a variety of documents, it would seem highly improbable that a *major* noble's records of existence would entirely disappear. I conclude that these men were not very high in rank, but they will be considered in the section regarding court attendance.

These categories are simply tools for analysis. Twelfth-century nobles did not categorize themselves or define their world so precisely. There can always be discussions about the placement of an individual in a particular category. Other historians, especially C. Warren Hollister, have attempted to obtain a more objective categorization through quantitative analyses of landholding. While not ignoring this approach, I have placed less emphasis on it, in part because of the incomplete nature of the sources, which prevents any absolute quantification, and in part because what is possible has been done well elsewhere.[11] In spite of their different approaches to categorization, quantification and my system agree on the general power of individuals within the nobility. There are some differences. The placement of noble illegitimates who performed royal service is an issue. I include some of them in the "new men" category, when the evidence does not show them acting with a parent or sibling.[12] I have separated lay and ecclesiastical "magnates," though they often held comparable amounts of land, because church titles themselves provided status, mobility, and a relationship to the court. The same is true of the royal family, who have their own category although their income and lifestyle differed little from those of the magnates. The categories of lesser nobles, service families, and new men separate other tenants-in-chief of comparable wealth by their behavior in relation to the court. While this approach creates a greater number of categories than those based on quantification, some seemingly more subjective as well, my categorization works well for the questions of family, strategies, "lifestyle," and the interchange of the nobles with the court in ways which affect them as a group—the questions that are the focus of this work. No categorizations can be expected to be scientifically accurate. They are intended and should function as a historian's tool.

The question of how to categorize or stratify the nobility would never arise if the Anglo-Normans had precisely defined the terms they used for themselves. However, this was not a world of rigid distinctions.[13] Though the textbook depiction of the Middle Ages is that of a rigid society composed of three groups—those who fought, prayed, or worked—most re-searchers find much evidence of fluidity within each group and little agreement among contemporary authors on the definitions of "class" terms.[14] Since these authors did not define their terms, some introductory definitions of common words such as "baron," "magnate," "noble," "class," and "family" are necessary.

Several of these terms give medieval historians particular trouble because contemporaries either used them more flexibly than we might wish or did not think to define them. Stenton pointed out fifty years ago that while historians fight over the precise legal definition of the word "baron," chancery scribes and authors in early twelfth-century England applied the term to a great variety of nobles. Indeed, the term *barones* was applied to both tenants-in-chief and rear vassals.[15] Since terms like baron were not yet specialized, any titles used become especially important;[16] hence my designation of a "magnate" as belonging to a titled family—the magnates were seen by contemporaries as having a special status. Furthermore, I have chosen to use the more general term "noble" throughout, since "baron" tends to be associated by medievalists with Magna Carta definitions, and "aristocrat" with an estate more defined by birth than was the case in the early twelfth century. For this work, "noble" refers to anyone holding land by feudal military or serjeanty tenure or a member of his/her family.[17]

An even more debated, but unavoidable, word is "class." Again, the broadest definition is used in this work, and only because of its familiarity to the reader. Obviously, terms like "estate" or "social group" avoid the connotations that "class" has acquired since Marx, but they are cumbersome and less familiar. Here the term is applied to a group of individuals and families within the society having comparable amounts of power, wealth, and status and a shared attitude toward other groups in the society. The noble class in a feudal society generally held some land as tenants-in-chief through either military or serjeanty tenure, and owed certain feudal dues for the land. H. A. Cronne[18] provides a useful definition of the class as composed of men having office, birth, tenure, and a common outlook. He takes his definition of the upper class from the address of the royal charters issued to the "realm as a whole"—"earls, justices, sheriffs, barons, officials (*ministri*) and all the king's faithful men (*fideles*) French and English." This includes the upper clergy since they overlap with the nobles through shared attitudes and interests as landholders.

The most common words are the most troublesome academically. "Family" is the worst. Again, for lack of contemporary definitions, the broadest definition of family is used to allow its application throughout.

In it I include the extended family, various generations, and affinal ties. The question of family structure will be dealt with in chapter 2.

Since I have already complained about the lack of complete data, let me briefly describe the sources available and how I used them. Compared to the reign of Henry II, relatively few documents dating from Henry I's survive.[19] The period offers a marvelous balance between just enough material upon which to draw conclusions and not too much to be able to work through it all. There is a bit of everything—surveys, charters, financial accounts, narratives, and a dash of theoretical musing. There are only two extant treatises—the "Constitutio Domus Regis"[20] and the *Leges Henrici Primi*. Both are literary works concerned with government and were written shortly after Henry's death. The *Leges* provides a more abstract statement of the nobles' relation to the society, and especially, the developing attitudes toward land. The "Constitutio" mentions a few household officers and is invaluable as a record of the relative importance of particular offices within the royal household.

The chronicles provide both the meat and the spice of the narrative sources, especially the works of two contemporaries, Orderic Vitalis and William of Malmesbury.[21] In the course of presenting the chronology of the period, the chronicles often place individuals at certain events or remark on their reputations, often when recording a death. Usually, the nobles who appear in any detail are those whose reputations were either particularly saintly or especially sinful. The chronicle of the gossipy Orderic is especially filled with personalities of the times. The other chronicles of the period[22] provide additional details about a few nobles who were special patrons of a monastery or who attended great events, or note people's reputations. Beyond the usual warnings, Emma Mason[23] has reminded us that chroniclers often were younger, noninheriting sons who were placed in the clergy. They therefore might have a different perspective on the "rapacity" of the nobles than their older brothers or might be "temperamentally unsuited to normal, that is, aggressive behaviour." We must keep this bias in mind when our sources discuss the nobles.

The sources most useful for this prosopographic study are governmental records and private charters. The governmental records fall into three categories: (1) surveys made as the result of special inquests; (2) exchequer records; and (3) chancery records. There are nine extant surveys.[24] They vary in content, extent, and time, but they provide information as to how much land was held in given areas by certain families, who were their neighbors, and who were their feudal connections. As in all the sources, many names were followed by epithets such as *fratre* which indicated relationships to others.

Only one exchequer account, the Pipe Roll of 31 Henry I (1130),[25] is extant for the reign. For this work, the miscellaneous topics were of the most interest. For example, among the items recorded in 1130 were payments of reliefs from which we can determine relationships, dates of death, holders of guardianships, and relative sizes of holdings. Various types of royal favor and nobles' actions can be seen in the variety of payments. Also noted in this Pipe Roll are the collections of and exemptions from assessments. These lists present the most complete record available of landholding in most shires. The Pipe Roll is also to some extent a record of offices held, since justices, sheriffs, and other officials were accountable to the Exchequer.

As rich in information as the Pipe Roll is, it is a snapshot, providing such information for one year only. Chancery documents, mostly royal charters and writs, survive for the entire period. More than 1500 were preserved by their recipients, 90 percent of these latter being religious houses.[26] The royal charters give direct evidence of royal patronage and service, and provide information about property held, though usually in the context of that land being granted to religious houses (alienated). Their witness lists are rich in material, giving evidence of attendance at court and noting family relationships or feudal bonds.

While most documents available for Henry I's reign are royal, some private ones have survived, once again because most of their recipients were religious houses interested in preserving them. Most of the surviving private documents are found in cartulary form, and are grants of land and records of court cases similar to those listed in the *Regesta*.[27] While most of the private charters duplicate the material of their royal confirmation, they have been witnessed by the people most directly connected with the donor and extend our knowledge of the group.

Previous studies of Henry I's reign have for the most part concentrated on a few families and individuals,[28] on church-state relations,[29] on administrative developments,[30] or on a particular source.[31] There is, however, a danger of staying with one family or source. Mooers' fine work on the Pipe Roll of 31 Henry I has shown the variety of patronage available at that time, but it suffers from a lack of comparison to patronage at other times in the reign. Omissions are sometimes surprising. Crouch's groundbreaking work, which looks at the Beaumont twins as brothers rather than two important nobles, all but ignores their sisters except when they were "used." Most studies concerned with social change during this period have centered on Henry's needs and innovations rather than on the nobles as a class.[32] Henry's early life, to 1107, has been the subject of a dissertation,[33] but Professor Hollister's projected biography in the University of California English Kings series will present the first complete picture of the man and the reign. Judith Green's excellent book, *The Government of England Under Henry I*, investigates both the royal and local administration and the men who composed it, though she also concentrates on the year 1130. Yet for all the excellent work being done, no one has attempted to synthesize the individual aspects into a whole, nor looked at the social questions of family.

That synthesis is the goal of this work. Some of the material will seem familiar to the specialist, but is necessary to provide the context in which this group of nobles lived, the world that formed their political and economic needs and informed their minds. By bringing the material together and focusing on the group, some old questions can be answered and some new discussions stimulated. Ultimately, an understanding of the complex, rich reality of the Anglo-Norman world will come from our combining the individual, the family, and the institutional, the technological and the cultural.

Notes

1. Charles Homer Haskins, certainly coined the phrase "Twelfth-Century Renaissance" in *The Renaissance of the Twelfth Century*. Besides Haskins' own earlier work on the Normans, twelfth-century science and the creation of universities, however, work had already been done on the growth of common law, on courtly love literature, on the monarchies, and on Gothic art.

2. E. Mason, "Magnates, Curiales and the Wheel of Fortune."

3. Lally ("Secular Patronage," p. 169) writes that "sociologists have isolated in society the three dimensions of wealth, status and power—economic, social and political dimensions—as motives of action." Within the nonspecialized medieval world, if one gained one type of power, then one was able to pursue others through court and royal patronage. One could achieve social status through marriage, and through intangibles such as presence at court.

4. Herlihy, "The Generation in Medieval History."

5. A year before Herlihy's article, Alan Spitzer in "The Historical Problem of Generations" analyzed certain aspects of recent history to illustrate the utility of the concept. Herlihy points to Millard Meiss' *Painting in Florence and Siena After the Black Death* as an application of the generation approach to cultural history, and to the fourteenth-century Ibn Khaldun's application of it to political history. In the *Muquaddimah*, Ibn Khaldun examined the cycle of Muslim dynastic power lasting one hundred and twenty years and defined the taking of power by a new generation every forty years as an argument that political creativity exhausted itself in the third generation. For discussions of his idea and its more general applications from two different points of view, see Constance B. Bouchard, "The Structure of a Twelfth-Century French Family," p. 51 n.39, and Julián Marías, *Generations*, pp. 198–207. Herlihy gives a good overview of the large bibliography of sociological applications starting with the "father of sociology," Auguste Comte. More recent and pertinent to historical sociology are Marías, and Yves Renouard, "La notion de génération en histoire."

6. Foner, *Ages in Conflict*, p. 24. There is another common definition, "age-

set system," in which people of a similar age are grouped together at some point of their life cycles. This definition is less useful for our population.

7. These tensions are commonly termed a generation gap. Such gaps between old and young arise when the economic advantage of one interferes with that of the other, in property control (inheritance), work, marital state, or living pattern (Foner, *Ages in Conflict,* pp. 40–46). This analysis has been applied to twelfth-century history, to Henry II's reign. T. M. Jones ("The Generation Gap of 1173–74," p. 40), described the rebels of 1173–74 as "young, aggressive aspirants eager to seize power under the old rules, but shut out by their elders because the rules had substantially changed."

8. Foner, *Ages in Conflict,* pp. 9–16.

9. While the *Leges Henrici Primi* defines the age of discretion and inheritance as 15 (59,9; 59,9a; 59,9b), it was neither universally accepted nor universally used. Where did one generation end and the next start? When did one come of age, and how much time separated these "biological cohorts" in the holding of power in society? There is no consensus of opinion. Estimates of a generation range from fifteen (Renouard) to forty years (Ibn Khaldun) for two reasons. First of all, the average life span and age of marriage varied even within a generation much less the Middle Ages. While many fathers may have been twenty years older than their eldest child, many others were thirty. In the absence of complete records, how is an average determined? Second, the historians defined a generation's "coming of age" differently. What percentage of a group had to hold power before the "generation" did?

10. Marcus L. Hansen, *The Problem of the Third Generation Immigrant* and *The Immigrant in American History.* Most recently, Robert G. Goldy combines philosophy, sociology, and history in "The Question of Jewish Theology in America Since the Second World War."

11. Arguments about the relative merits of the quantitative approach are found in Newman, "Family and Royal Favor in Henry I's England," p. 297 n.14. C. Warren Hollister has published the most complete attempt at a quantitative approach to land holding, using the figure £750 per annum to designate a magnate ("Magnates and *Curiales* in Early Norman England," p. 63). The figures are based on Domesday Book and the classification devised by Corbett ("The Development of the Duchy of Normandy," pp. 502–20). There is no complete record of land-holdings for the first half of the twelfth century, so any attempt at total figures for land held by an individual during Henry I's reign must be inexact (Hollister, "Magnates and *Curiales,*" p. 75, n.3). Hollister continues the analysis in "Henry I and the Anglo-Norman Magnates," with the warning that "the methodology, though admittedly precarious, does provide a valuable general picture—blurred yet not seriously misleading" (p. 99). A magnate is "a very wealthy landholder," with the distinctions becoming more "fuzzy at the boundaries" (pp. 99–100). Judith Green (*The Government of England Under Henry I,* pp. 134–53) has categorized people simply as "king's servants" (total 104) and others. Her "servants" category combines most of the people in my categories 3 and 4, and serves her scholarly intent of studying government. She includes a nice discussion of the problems of ranking the nobility of the time, as well as the problems of determining social or geographic origins and amounts of land.

12. Mooers ("Patronage in the Pipe Roll of 1130," p. 285) argues that Brian fitz Count should be considered a magnate because of his father's status.

13. Paul Hyams makes this argument clearly in two articles, "The Common Law and the French Connection," and "Henry II and Ganelon."

14. Rogozinski ("Ennoblement by the Crown," p. 274) noted that even by the fourteenth century, a far more legalistic time than the twelfth, one cannot write

of a "fixed and unvarying class" in France, and the term "*noble* itself had no fixed signification and connotations—or none that historians have been able to get at."

15. Stenton, *First Century of English Feudalism 1066–1166*, pp. 83–114 gives a full discussion of the various terms. Marjorie Chibnall discusses Orderic's use of terms for knights in "Feudal Society in Orderic Vitalis," pp. 35–48.

16. Stenton, *First Century*, p. 88.

17. For a discussion of the changing definition of the word "noble" see Genicot,"La Noblesse au Moyen Age," pp. 52–59. More recently, Barlow (*William Rufus*, p. 159) gives a practical working definition of noble based upon the work of Genicot. A noble is someone with "direct subordination and access to the ruling prince," in "possession of jurisdiction over subordinates," with "ownership of a fortified centre to one's estate," and "freed from general tax and common duties." This is obviously a very broad definition, but probably as accurate as we will ever get.

18. Cronne, *Reign of Stephen*, pp. 135–36.

19. Clanchy, *From Memory to Written Record*, pp. 116–47 has a good section on the "preservation and use of documents" for the reigns.

20. "Constitutio Domus Regis," pp. 128–35.

21. Most references to Orderic are taken from the excellent dual translation edition by Marjorie Chibnall (hereafter cited as OVC). Occasionally it is still necessary to make reference to the older editions *Historiae Ecclesiasticae,* edited by Auguste le Prévost, and *The Ecclesiatical History of England and Normandy,* translated by Thomas Forester. For William of Malmesbury we have the *Chronicle of the Kings of England,* translated by J. A. Giles; *Historia Novella,* edited by K. R. Potter (hereafter cited as *HN*); *Willelmi Malmesbiriensis monachi de gestis pontificum Anglorum,* edited by N. E. S. A. Hamilton (hereafter cited as *GP*); and *Willelmi Malmesbiriensis monachi de gestis regum Anglorum,* edited by William Stubbs (hereafter cited as *GR*).

22. The chroniclers are too numerous to cite here. Most of the ones useful for a prosopographic study are cited in the bibliography; Gransden, *Historical Writing in England,* pp. 136–37 has provided an excellent discussion of contemporary chroniclers.

23. E. Mason, "Magnates, Curiales and the Wheel of Fortune," p. 121.

24. The nine surveys are The Bayeux Inquest (*The Red Book of the Exchequer,* edited by Hubert Hall, [hereafter cited as *RB*], II, pp. 645–47. See also Tabuteau, "Definitions of Feudal Military Obligations in Eleventh-Century Normandy," pp. 21–25 for a discussion of the Bayeaux Inquest as a source); the feudatory of Canterbury (Douglas, ed., *The Domesday Monachorum of Christ Church Canterbury*); the feudatory of Peterborough ("Descriptio militum de Abbatia de Burgo," edited by Thomas Stapleton, pp. 168–75); the Winchester survey (Martin Biddle, ed., *Winchester in the Early Middle Ages* [hereafter cited as *Liber Winton*]); the Worcestershire survey (Round, *Feudal England* [hereafter cited as *FE*], pp. 169–80), the Lindsey survey (Lincolnshire), (*The Lincolnshire Domesday and the Lindsey Survey,* edited by C. Foster and T. Longley [hereafter cited as *Lind.Surv.*]); the Leicestershire survey (*The Leicestershire Survey,* edited by C. F. Slade [hereafter cited as *Leic. Surv.*]); the Northamptonshire survey ("The Northamptonshire Survey," edited by J. H.Round [hereafter cited as *Nhants Surv.*]); and the Herefordshire "Domesday" (*Herefordshire Domesday,* edited by J. Tait and V. H. Galbraith [hereafter cited as *Heref.Dd.*]). Where values of lands were listed they appear to have been merely Domesday value, (P. Sawyer, "Domesday Book"), but the surveys, especially the hidages, give us the relative holdings in an area as well as feudal relations.

25. Great Britain. Record Commission. *Magnum rotulum scaccarii,* edited by

J. Hunter (hereafter cited as *PR*). The Pipe Roll as a source is described and discussed by Judith Green in "Praeclarum et Magnificum Antiquitatis Monumentum," and her more recent work *Government*, pp. 51–94.

26. *Regesta regum Anglo-Normannorum, 1066–1154*, 4 vols. (hereafter cited as *Reg.* I, *Reg.* II, *Reg.* III, *Reg.* IV).

27. Most of the major cartularies, manuscript and printed, with appropriate documents, are listed in the bibliography, and in G. R. C. Davis, ed., *Medieval Cartularies of Great Britain. A Short Catalogue*. Some newer works on individual families have more reliable texts than the older printed ones, most notably Greenway, ed., *Charters of the Honour of Mowbray;* D. Walker, ed., "Charters of the Earldom of Hereford"; and R. B. Patterson, ed., *Earldom of Gloucester Charters*. Recently, a number of British theses have been written on families: Atkin, "The Bigod Family," Bearman, "Charters of the Redvers Family," and Charlton, "A Study of the Mandeville Family."

28. In addition to the introductions to the charter texts cited above, see Alexander, "Herbert of Norwich, 1091–1119"; Altschul, *A Baronial Family in Medieval England, the Clares;* Chandler, "Ada de Warenne, Queen Mother of Scotland," and "Family Histories: An Aid in the Study of the Anglo-Norman Aristocracy"; Cronne, "Ranulf de Gernons, Earl of Chester, 1129–53"; Crouch, *The Beaumont Twins;* Kealey, *Roger of Salisbury;* J. F. A. Mason, "Roger de Montgomery and His Sons (1067–1102)"; Meisel, *Barons of the Welsh Frontier;* Nicholl, *Thurstan, archbishop of York (1114–1140);* Powley, *The House of De La Pomeroi;* Reedy, "Were Ralph and Richard Basset Really Chief Justiciars of England in the Reign of Henry I?"; Vaughn, "Robert of Meulan and Raison d'Etat in the Anglo-Norman State, 1093–1118,"; D. Walker, "Miles of Gloucester, Earl of Hereford"; Ward, "The Estates of the Clare Family 1066–1317"; G. H. White, "The Career of Waleran, Count of Meulan and Earl of Worcester (1104–1166)"; Wightman, *The Lacy Family in England, 1066–1194*.

29. Barlow, *The English Church, 1066–1154;* Brett, *The English Church Under Henry I;* Cantor, *Church, Kingship and Lay Investiture in England, 1089–1135;* Crosby, "The Origin of the English Episcopate under Henry I"; Vaughn, "St. Anselm and the English Investiture Controversy Reconsidered," "St. Anselm of Canterbury: The Philosopher-Saint as Politician," and "Saint Anselm: Reluctant Archbishop?".

30. Farrer, "The Sheriffs of Lincolnshire and Yorkshire, 1066–1130"; Haskins, *Norman Institutions;* Hoyt, *The Royal Demesne in English Constitutional History, 1066–1275;* Kimball, *Serjeanty Tenure in Medieval England;* E. Mason, "The Mauduits and Their Chamberlainship of the Exchequer"; W. A. Morris, "The Sheriffs and the Administrative System of Henry I"; Painter, "Castle Guard"; R. L. Poole, *The Exchequer in the Twelfth Century;* Prestwich, "War and Finance in the Anglo-Norman State"; Reedy, "Origins of the General Eyre in the Reign of Henry I"; H. G. Richardson and G. O. Sayles, *The Governance of Mediaeval England;* Southern, "Ranulf Flambard and Early Anglo-Norman Administration"; T. F. Tout, *Chapters in the Administrative History of Mediaeval England;* C. Walker, "Sheriffs in the Pipe Roll of 31 Henry I"; West, *The Justiciarship in England, 1066–1232;* G. H. White, "Financial Administration Under Henry I," "The Household of the Norman Kings"; Young, *The Royal Forests of Medieval England*.

31. Stephanie Mooers' work on the Pipe Roll ("Networks of Power in Anglo-Norman England," and "Patronage in the Pipe Roll,") employs computer analysis. Marjorie Chibnall intensively mines Orderic Vitalis in a different way in *The World of Orderic Vitalis*.

32. Southern, "The Place of Henry I in English History"; B. Walker, "King Henry's 'Old Men'."

33. Wootten, "A Study of Henry I: King of England, 1068–1107."

CHAPTER 1

The Anglo-Norman World During the Reign of Henry I

What was the world inhabited by the Anglo-Norman families like? It had its share of dramatic events—wars, sudden deaths, disputed crowns, economic troubles—and long peaceful periods in which there were less dramatic administrative changes, some of them necessitated by the generation of nobles being governed. Culturally, what historians would later call "the Twelfth-Century Renaissance" had begun. The Anglo-Norman kingdom was not the center of these cultural changes, but it certainly participated in them, especially in the practical "experiments," in medicine and technology. Most of all, this generation included the first Anglo-Normans. The most interesting and innovative aspects of their world show the merging of the two cultures, as seen in their literature, arts, and politics.

Henry I's long reign (1100–35) was characterized by great activity, both in war and in government. Comparative peace in England allowed the king to experiment and enlarge royal government, beginning many of the developments that his grandson completed. These developments inevitably affected the lives of the nobility.

Henry's reign began in uncertainty. Following William II's death in a hunting accident in 1100, Henry rode to Winchester, secured the treasury, and was elected king.[1] His first and most important task was to secure his rule, as seen in the steps he took to do so: issuing a Coronation Charter of Liberties;[2] various general ecclesiastical confirmations;[3] a conciliatory letter to the exiled archbishop of Canterbury;[4] and marriage to Edith/Maud of Scotland, ensuring peace on his northern border as well as a symbolic union with the Anglo-Saxons.[5]

The real threat to Henry, however, was to the south, in Normandy. A rebellion began almost immediately after his accession, led by a group of powerful nobles who supported Henry's brother Robert of Normandy's claim to the throne. England was invaded by these men in 1101, but a settlement was reached quickly with the Treaty of Alton and there was no actual fighting on English soil. However, the years that followed were far from peaceful. Civil wars occurred mainly because of the desire by some (including the king) to reunite England and Normandy.[6] A series of military encounters on Norman soil culminated in Robert's defeat and capture at Tinchbrai (1106) and the disinheriting of many of the Anglo-Norman nobles. Though Robert spent the rest of his life as Henry's prisoner, his son, William Clito, was released and would continue until 1128 to provide a rallying point for dissatisfied nobles, usually with the backing of Philip I and Louis VI of France, Fulk, count of Anjou, and the pope.[7] Henry probably rarely felt secure on the throne.

However threatening these disputes were, they were different from the typical feudal ones of an earlier era. In the late eleventh and early twelfth centuries, the political situation evolved from one in which the king was predominantly threatened by "baronial rebellions" to one of "international relations between kingdoms." After 1106, Henry's continental wars were ways of seeking secure borders, while his relations with the nobility were by and large secure. However, because of the wars and because he was governing Normandy, Henry spent over half of his reign in Normandy.[8]

While Henry and the nobles were most occupied with Normandy, there were also two northern border lands to deal with. Henry sent three expeditions (1106, 1114, and 1121) into Wales to put down rebellions. He used the first of these (1106) to resettle many of the Flemish who had come to England with Matilda of Flanders and had become a problem.[9] However, the Flemish were not the only settlers in Wales. Indeed Henry, like his father, used trusted *curiales* and *familiares* (both clerical and noble magnates) as personnel to settle the rebellious area. Though rebellions would continue, Wales was becoming more integrated into European society during this reign.[10]

Henry was even more successful with his other Northern neighbor, Scotland, which as Kapelle put it, he conquered "by proxy."[11] Henry's marriage to Edith/Maud had meant that the reign began with a peaceful border; in addition, Edith/Maud's brother David was reared at the Anglo-Norman court and he returned home a Norman. David was Norman in administration, in feudal relations, in royal policy on matters like coinage, and in that he encouraged the migration of Anglo-Norman nobles. Many nobles moved north during the reign, both to Scotland and to the now peaceful northern England.[12] Thus the Anglo-Norman noble lived in a world with a frontier into which he could move.

Henry I's reign also coincided with the Gregorian reform, which had given continental nobles an antiroyal focal point.[13] Like his wars, however, the religious issues of his reign were small in comparison to those of other kings. On the international scale, the basic question of the Investiture Controversy was settled for England in 1107, and Archbishop Anselm, who had led the papal cause in England, died in 1109. Other ecclesiastical problems arose, such as the revival of the York-Canterbury disputes in 1114–21,[14] and the opposition to a particular appointment,[15] but none was so serious a threat to the royal-ecclesiastical relationship as those faced by either Rufus or Henry II. Indeed, the Anglo-Norman clergy were often only reluctant supporters of Gregorian reforms, especially clerical celibacy.[16] This attitude can be seen even in the way they recorded the reforms. Henry of Huntingdon omitted the important Council of 1108 from his history because it was Anselm's attempt to enforce celibacy for deacons. Henry of Huntingdon was not only not a Gregorian, but had a "wife," was the son of an archdeacon and even had succeeded his father as archdeacon in 1110.[17] Henry I's handling of ecclesiastical matters has been seen as part of a conscious plan. The clergy remained his allies during his unification of England and Normandy and his problems with William Clito.[18]

The only other threat to the royal peace was the question of dynastic succession, especially while William Clito, the Norman claimant, lived. Henry had two legitimate children, William and Matilda. Matilda was betrothed to the future Emperor Henry V when she was eight years old (1109), and lived in the Empire until her return to England as a widow in 1125. Meanwhile, Henry had his vassals swear fealty to the young heir William in 1115. Then, in 1120, William did homage to Louis VI of France for Normandy to ensure his continental succession. It was on his return to England that William and many young nobles were drowned when the White Ship was wrecked. Since Queen Edith/Maud had died two years before her son, Henry announced his intention to marry Adeliza of Louvain only six weeks after the White Ship disaster. Later that year or early in the next, Robert, the most loyal and capable of Henry's illegitimate sons, was created the earl of Gloucester. His elevation possibly reflects Henry's fear that his nephew Stephen of Blois was in a position to designate himself the next king. Earl Robert was a powerful male counterbalance to Stephen, and could be counted upon to support any young son he would leave. Unfortunately, the marriage to Adeliza did not produce the hoped-for new male heir.[19] In 1127, Henry had the nobles swear fealty to his widowed daughter, the Empress, and five months later he betrothed her in semisecrecy to Geoffrey, heir of his enemy Fulk of

Anjou.[20] It was hoped that the marriage would not only prevent Fulk from supporting William Clito but would secure another border of the duchy. William Clito died childless in 1128 and his father, Robert, died in 1134. Ultimately, it was the succession question which would revive the royal-noble tensions.

Henry died in 1135. Robert of Torigni cites his epitaph:

> Here lies the late King Henry, one to be respected for his intellect, his riches, his conditions toward the injured, and his decent severity towards the oppressor; he was excellent, wealthy, and easy of access. He was the peace and glory of the earth.[21]

Not all contemporaries shared Robert's high opinion. Most praised Henry for his peaceful reign, especially in comparison to Stephen's, that in which they were living while writing, and for his love of family. Henry was also praised for his justice, though the severity of his punishments was noted. The picture of Henry has continued to shift. Often it focuses on his justice and the portrait is of a cruel and greedy ruler. However, as the accusations of extreme judicial cruelty (mutilation) have been analyzed within the context of both the sources and the harsh reality of medieval justice, the picture has been refocused and Robert of Torigni's opinion that Henry showed "decent severity" has been reinstated.[22]

Another aspect of Henry's reign that historians have tried to bring into focus is his governmental style and its effects on the nobles. One judgment of his reign made by Orderic is often quoted:

> [Henry] brought all of his enemies to heel by his wisdom and courage, and rewarded his loyal supporters with riches and honours. So he pulled down many great men from positions of eminence for their presumption, and sentenced them to be disinherited for ever. On the other hand, he ennobled others of base stock who had served him well, raised them, so to say, from the dust, and heaping all kinds of favours on them, stationed them above earls and famous castellans.[23]

From this statement arose the argument of whether he unjustly alienated men who had traditionally ruled, replacing them with men of humble origins. However, even Orderic says that the men who were "pulled" down were being justly punished for their "presumption," and the new men were rewarded for their service, not just their loyalty. He did not make this distinction when he described Rufus' government. Rufus replaced those Conquest nobles who died during his reign with "certain underlings whom he exalted by the grant of extensive honors as a reward for their flattery."[24] Orderic's observation can be said to point to a major change in governmental policy begun during Henry's reign—the use of professional administrators more dependent on royal favor than on their patrimony for power.

The Conqueror had had no need for such men. His government consisted of handpicked nobles whose loyalty had been proven at Hastings.[25] Rufus' thirteen-year reign was characterized by a lack of a clear-cut governmental policy, and though there were some professional administrators, it appears that no effort was made by the king to form an administration based on such men or to experiment on any broad scale in governing with professional administrators.[26] Whether Henry actually governed through "new men" whose social origin was middle or lower class or "old men" whose families came to England with the Conqueror[27] becomes a hollow argument when studied in depth. Obviously, few men rose "from the dust" to hold a barony, and many magnate families continued to gain during the reign. What is evident is that, even while at war, Henry took a personal interest in governing, developing "administrative kingship."[28] He experimented with various methods of administration, often centralizing power, broke some monopolies on power, and allowed many lower ranking nobles to gain additional power and wealth through their roles in royal government.

On the other hand, these actions were also influenced by a generational change in the nobility. When the generation is defined by era, the Norman Conquest of 1066 presents historians with a case study of centralized feudal rule. Most of the nobles who came with the Conqueror were noninheriting sons of major nobles or were fathers seeking to acquire land for noninheriting sons. The Conquest provided William with the opportunity to distribute almost an entire country by feudal tenure to men of proven military loyalty who also needed him for their status. As Hollister has termed it, William had a *tabula rasa* upon which to create his kingdom.[29] The men who were trusted received the best and/or greatest amount of land, so that William's "administration" coincided with the greatest level of nobility. As early as William II's reign, however, "magnates" and *curiales* began to separate into two groups. Most of the rebels against William Rufus were sons and heirs of the Conqueror's most rewarded followers.[30] By the 1101 civil war, this fact is even more evident. Time and again, "English" supporters of Duke Robert and other rebels against Henry were heirs of Domesday magnates.[31] Henry I needed to build a new type of administration if he wished to keep the power centralized. He was clearly confronting the textbook problems of inheritance in a feudal society.

However, the emphasis is not on just the "coming of age" of the second generation from the Conquest—obviously, by 1100 everyone, rebel or not, was of this era-defined generation, even the king. Defining the generation by the event of the Conquest has led others to a dead end.[32] In some situations, such as their attitudes toward the Anglo-Saxons, perhaps they did form a generation, but in most other ways, they did not.

Yet it can be argued that a generational pattern emerges if we use a different type of generation, if the members of the first generation, the starting point, are defined by their achievement of magnate wealth (whether defined by quantity or quality of land) and status, not by their gain of English land. Like American immigrants, they do not have to be defined by a set period of time but rather by a common experience. Following this experience, the son and heir to this status had a vastly different expectation than did his father who had achieved it. The father had *done* something, *served* somehow, to acquire his reward. The son had not. With a different set of experiences, he had different expectations. He expected to be consulted and to receive patronage commensurate to his status without necessarily fulfilling administrative duties.[33] When his expectations were not fulfilled, rebellion sometimes occurred. More often, the behavior was more passive. The magnate son was rarely a curial figure. His witnessing at court was limited to state occasions, crown-wearings, or major treaties. As described, this generational pattern is based on the gain of status. Whether we define the first generation as having achieved status by gaining land (as was the case under William I) or by gaining a title (as was more often the case under Rufus), there was an evident, if not quantifiable, stage at which status was reached.[34] This status in turn affected the behavior of the nobles. This pattern was repeated in the actions of many of the heirs of those who were Henry I's most rewarded *familiares*. The sons of these men who built their wealth on curial service were rarely curial figures.[35]

The impetus for Henry I's (and to a lesser extent William II's) building of a curial administration based upon *familiares* rather than magnates may have been royal politics, but it is vital to our understanding to recognize that the second generation magnates created the political situation of the period. These men do not appear to have wanted to continue the relationship between noble and crown by which they had won their status originally, but rather were concerned only with the perpetuation of that status through rewards. Henry I's government and, as we will see, patronage policy had to deal with this situation.

Henry not only changed the personnel but increased governmental activity as reflected in the number of surviving chancery documents.[36] The editors of the *Regesta* listed approximately 490 charters for the thirty-four years of the two Williams, but approximately 1520 for Henry's thirty-five years. Additionally, though only one Exchequer account, the Pipe Roll of 31 Henry I, is extant, internal examination shows that it was already one in a series, and the Exchequer as a functioning body undoubtedly took form in Henry's reign.[37] The Treasury also was developing at this time around particular court officials.[38] Indeed, as the "Constitutio Domus Regis" describes, Henry had a growing household in which can be recognized the origins of later governmental departments. Though the offices were still only vaguely defined, some of them were already considered hereditary (e.g., that of the *dapifer* or steward) and were held by Conquest families associated with royal service. Henry's reign is part of the "formative period" for the household which would last into Henry II's reign, as much of the actual governing was conducted through this still flexible group of servants.[39] In addition to relying on this informal group to aid him in governing, Henry increased both the number of great councils of the realm and the regularity with which they were called.[40]

For out-of-court administration, Henry continued to rely heavily on the sheriffs, who accounted for most of the royal income within the developing Exchequer system. The group as a whole did, however, undergo changes during Henry's reign which underline the royal concern about inherited offices. As we will see, the king seems to have tried to prevent the shrievalties from becoming automatically hereditary and therefore independent of his control.[41] It is possibly in this part of the administration that one can most clearly see royal experimentation and changes in methods of governing.

In addition to this established group of royal, out-of-court officials, Henry made increased, perhaps original, use of justices, both to investigate royal rights and to hear complaints.[42] Their courts are in evidence in the 1130 Pipe Roll,[43] while royal *missi* with local representatives held special inquests, such as that of 1106 into the customs of York Minster[44] and landholding in Winchester.[45] Regular visitations of the demesne took place during the reign—made perhaps by the justices in eyre.[46]

Henry needed help in running the growing royal administration in a cross-channel kingdom, especially when the court was in Normandy. In the first half of the reign, members of the royal family most often acted as regent: Queen Edith/Maud until her death in 1118, and Prince William in the following year. During the balance of the reign, however, Henry's trusted *familiares*, Roger, the bishop of Salisbury, seems to have acted as regent; and this role was later to become associated with the office of justiciar. Indeed, until recently historians marked the beginning of this formal office with Roger of Salisbury.[47] Now, however, the argument surrounding the formalization of the job has been reopened. Henry may have been following a procedure set by William I—a flexible delegation of regency powers with some special powers, usually to a family member but not without precedent to a prominent *familiaris*.[48] Whichever the case, Henry I continued to centralize his administration around *curiales*.[49] The evolving office of justiciar, whether formalized or not, was a necessity in a cross-channel kingdom populated by second generation nobles.

These newer developments in administration did not usurp the role the clergy had played since the Conquest. Henry continued to rely upon the bishops, who were unique in their combination of great wealth and non-hereditary appointment. Like his father and brother, Henry used his household clergy for daily governmental tasks. The household was the training ground for bishops, as these men, known personally to the king and lacking any conflict of interests, often were elevated to bishoprics. With the exception of his three coronation appointments, Henry's major clerical appointments were not members of magnate families.[50] Generally, Henry was able to continue clerical policies already established, without serious opposition or change.

Norman administration grew along the same lines as the English, though at a slower rate.[51] There was probably only one household for both realms, that which traveled with the king, but a group of Norman justices formed a separate core of administration for the duchy.[52] In some areas of administration, developments began on the English side of the Channel. The famous English writ may not have been used in Normandy until Henry I's reign, as the first verifiable one is dated 1107.[53] The formalization of knight service in Normandy occurred under Henry I's rule, not before.[54] Though historians today still argue over which direction the intellectual fertilization took across the Channel, we are seeing increasingly that it occurred in Henry I's reign, not in 1066.

The fact that the Anglo-Norman kingdom was divided by the Channel cannot be ignored in describing the world of the Anglo-Norman noble. Historians have been Anglocentric, however. The late John Le Patourel's work was dedicated to correcting this view by showing the connections of the two parts of the Anglo-Norman realm. He and others have succeeded. David S. Spear's work on the Norman clergy has shown the currents of personnel going both ways across the Channel to fill positions, as well as back and forth between service to cathedrals or abbeys and royal service.[55] From studies such as these, it is obvious that the Anglo-

Normans did not see the Channel as a political or emotional border.[56] We must not forget, however, that it *was* a physical barrier. The Anglo-Normans were fully aware that once they crossed the Channel, there was a mandatory stay on the other side until they could return. This fact would seem to necessitate some division of administration and political ties. In our zeal to embrace the concept of the Anglo-Norman Empire, we are in danger of minimizing this need. We see, on one hand, that ideas (such as organizational ones) were increasingly shared, and personnel traveled from one section to the other. However, in some ways the two parts of the realm were separating. Cross-channel landholding in Henry I's reign shows an increasing tendency toward a concentration of landholding in one part or the other. There also were behaviorial differences connected to land tenure. Norman rear tenants tended to follow their immediate lords in rebellion, while Anglo-Norman ones stayed with the king and, as a result, became the tenant-in-chief when the lord forfeited.[57] Thus, in some ways, there was a growing regionalism.

More than land tenure, politics and government were changing during this time, and the Anglo-Norman nobles lived in a world that encompassed more than politics. Europe had been experiencing population growth since about 1000, growth that would continue until about 1300. This growth was evidenced by the greater survival of children, and greater density of settlement—land was cleared and new towns founded—and by conquests such as the Drang nach Osten and the Reconquista. Its effects were evident by 1100, but Henry I's reign apparently also included a time of low fertility.[58] The chronicles have also recorded low crop yields in the years 1103, 1105, 1110–11, 1116–18, and famine in 1124–25. Epidemic diseases are reported in the Anglo-Norman realm in 1103, 1111–12, 1115, 1125 and 1131. The years are sequential, perhaps because the drop in nutrition levels lowered resistance to disease or perhaps because disease limited the number of people available to farm.[59] Nevertheless, towns continued to grow throughout the reign, both because of the long-term population trends and because the Anglo-Norman kings used towns as administrative and ecclesiastical centers.[60] Problems typical to medieval towns occurred at this time which actually benefited London. A great fire in 1133 probably led to its being granted a royal charter reducing its farm, thus giving it a needed economic boost and a new measure of independence.[61] Generally, trade was encouraged, especially through Henry's standardization of coinage and measurement and his support of fairs and guilds. During his reign, commercial building increased—especially that of bridges and the new technological wonder of windmills. All presents a picture of an economically growing world.[62]

The Anglo-Norman noble world was still to some extent an immigrant society, though less of a Conquest one. During Henry's reign, new "noble immigrants" continued to arrive from Flanders and regions of France, and Normans were still arriving for the first time in the English part of the kingdom.[63] However, this generation was mixing the Norman and Anglo-Saxon cultures especially through the use of language and visual arts. The Anglo-Norman cultural world was both part of the pan-European trend and a unique merger of these two northern cultures.

The nobles' use of the Anglo-Norman language presents an example of what has been termed "linguistic colonization." Knowledge of Anglo-Norman was a social and professional necessity even among the clergy. Any native Englishman in the upper class had to be bilingual. Furthermore, the nobles encouraged not only the use but the growth of the language. It was in this generation that the works in England written in Anglo-Norman French were commissioned by the nobles—we know of none commissioned between 1066 and 1100. Yet the language already shows separation from other forms of French; it is "one seen as decadent," and the adoption of English words is evident. That is, the languages were influencing each other as the governments were merging.[64]

We know far more about the written than the spoken languages of the period. There must have been many daily problems for an elite who spoke a different language than the subjects. However, although every other aspect of the Conquest was discussed, no contemporary discussed bilingualism. As usual, the commonplace is not described. There are later (but only occasional) references to all nobles speaking French, and we know English was not as "acceptable" until the fourteenth century. Yet some bilingualism must have been necessary. By the twelfth century, many Anglo-Norman nobles had Anglo-Saxon wives or mothers, and most probably had had Anglo-Saxon nurses. Orderic Vitalis' autobiographical account tells us that he had a Norman father and an Anglo-Saxon mother but that his first language was English. Presumably, many of the Anglo-Norman nobles (male and female) had at least a working knowledge of English. An additional problem is the bilingual knowledge of French and Latin, the governmental language. Clanchy argues that Latin charters might have been read aloud in French or in English because the "disjunction" between spoken and written languages was wide. Yet it appears that more nobles understood Latin than read it.[65] Again with this generation, we see the mixture of cultures, a "transition." No longer were clergy being killed by their abbots for using English, but neither was Anglo-Norman as artificial as it later would become. It was still a flexible vernacular.[66]

Indeed, bilingualism indicates other changes which were basic to this society. The Anglo-Saxon and Norman cultures were mixing in various ways. In one direction, we see evidence of English families giving their sons Norman names,[67] which would be expected in order to help one's child advance.[68] More women's than men's names retained the Anglo-Saxon heritage.[69] There were exceptions, however. The Pomeroy family used mainly continental names, but around 1100 an unmistakably English Ethelwerd is included in their records.[70] In addition, we also see both Anglo-Saxon and Norman families using more neutral, biblical names such as Samson and Adam.[71] Under the definition of generation by era, (second generation from the Conquest), the second generation after the Conquest appear to be accepting the role of *Anglo*-Norman. We see this in the language and the names within a family, and will see it especially in the art. The nobles still believed themselves superior to the English, but they were less conquerors, and could accept more from the conquered. Much of this change must be due to the role of women. If Orderic's language skills were so influenced by his mother, other aspects of development must have also been. Most likely, Anglo-Saxon women influenced the upper class in spite of obvious prejudices against things Anglo-Saxon.[72]

As noted at the beginning of this chapter, the second generation of Anglo-Normans lived during what historians call the "Twelfth-Century Renaissance." England's place in these cultural developments is still given little space in texts, and even then is associated with the second half of the century, with Henry II's reign. However, though the Anglo-Normans did not live in the center of this renaissance, an English cultural renaissance did begin in the 1090s, and accelerate in the reign of Henry I, due in large part to royal patronage. Many writers associated with the latter part of the century returned to England during Henry I's reign after studying abroad, creating "une société de philosophes" in London. Gilbert Crispin was there; by 1130, Adelard of Bath; by 1135, Gaimar and Geoffrey of Monmouth.[73] Furthermore, although most of the cultural trends in England throughout the century had begun in France, this was not always the case. Beginning in Henry I's reign, Anglo-Normans were particularly creative in the "literature of secular government," the development of secular schools, the writing of history, and an interest in nature.[74]

The increased reliance on the written word for governmental records and historical memory was an important part of twelfth-century culture. Not only was the quantity of writing increasing but a "literate mentality" was growing along with it. In England, in many ways, Henry I's reign was critical in establishing the trend both in numbers of documents and regularity of the *scriptoria*.[75] Again, as in the literary developments, historians' focus has been on Henry II and the latter half of the century. In variety and sheer numbers of documents and histories, Henry I's reign cannot compare to his grandson's. However, the literary growth of the second half of the century could not have occurred without the foundations set in the peaceful first thirty-five years.[76] Both the numbers of written orders and records, and the numbers of historians actively writing were increasing.

The emphasis on writing had to go hand in hand with an increase in education. Anglo-Norman schools were primarily for clergy, but there were literate nobles who had to have been educated somewhere.[77] It was in this generation that a noble who could read became "not uncommon." Writing perhaps was a "specialized craft," but a literate (reading) laity (nobles or *clericus* without vows) was necessary for Henry I's use of lay administrators.[78] As this argument would lead one to expect, most of the verifiably educated, or even those who are "major suspects," are associated with the royal court, where there was a demand for literacy. In addition, very often these people generally show an interest in writing, being patrons of various forms of literature.[79]

The intellectual world of the Anglo-Normans was less philosophical or theological than the continental one, and more oriented to the "natural," whether the latter was historical, practical, or "marvelous." This interest runs through all cultural forms—medicine, law, secular literature, and art. There was much support of practical medicine in this reign. There are only eleven identifiable physicians in the period 1066–1100 but there are ninety in the next fifty years. A similar growth is seen in numbers of "hospitals," from twenty-one to 113.[80]

While medicine was perhaps in its adolescence, Anglo-Norman law was in its infancy. "The new nobility that followed William across the water brought over its own law, from Brittany and Flanders as well as Normandy—wherever they had grown up and lived."[81] However, one tradition began to evolve. There was a gap between the practice and the theory or treatise "law." In practice, beginning during the reign of Henry I law was slowly changing to rely upon written proof.[82] While the emphasis was still on the practical not the theoretical, the theory of the next generation came from the practice in this one. The great political-legal theorist, John of Salisbury (1115–80), wrote under Henry II but was a friend of Robert, earl of Leicester. Robert's father, Robert of Meulan, may have influenced John's theory. Robert of Meulan helped to formulate policies of William Rufus and Henry I which are expressed abstractly in John of Salisbury's work.[83]

The practical nature of these developments shows the cultural emphasis of this world. Other books produced during Henry I's reign show the generation's interest in nature. Natural treatises and bestiaries were created, both new ones and copies of old ones with additional beasts. Not just animals and plants but stones caught people's interest. In the 1130s, the first vernacular lapidaries were produced, and Anglo-Norman works by Gaimar and the *Voyage of Brendan* both used imagery of gems. The generation's eyes were also turned to the stars. The copies of manuscripts produced at Hereford show an interest in astrology. Obviously few of these were "scientific" works, but the quantity produced and range of amateur interest show a new awareness of the natural world.[84]

It is perhaps in the visual arts of the time that we see all these trends—the mixing of the cultures in the second generation, the interest in nature, the creativity—clearly reflected. This was a new development. Between 1066 and 1100, much monumental building was begun in England, all showing distinctly Norman features but being even less decorated, more severe than the Norman buildings. Few of the Anglo-Saxon traditions of decoration were continued, or Anglo-Saxon style manuscripts produced.[85] Because of the size and numbers of the first generation buildings still under construction, few buildings were begun during Henry I's reign.[86] After 1100, however, the style and amount of sculptural decoration changed and manuscript production increased. This second generation of Anglo-Norman Romanesque builders revived the Anglo-Saxon workshops and styles, and merged them with the Norman and with styles from places where the Normans had contact. In doing so, they created a genuine Anglo-Norman style.[87]

By 1066, Anglo-Saxon styles were already known on the continent and the Norman style known in England. Indeed, some adaptation between them occurred before the political conquest. Norman sculpture generally was adaptive; for instance, it included capitals which were well-executed combinations of different types of continental ones, especially from the Loire Valley. One important building, however, Jumièges (*ca.* 1040–67), shows the influence of the artistic style so characteristic of Anglo-Saxon manuscripts. Artistic influences also had moved in the other direction. In England, the recently excavated York minster site has shown pre-1066 Norman columns similar to those at Bayeux. Much but not all of this cross-fertilization pauses at 1066. After 1066, in spite of the stated prejudices against the English and the severity of the building style, the first generation continued to use Anglo-Saxon builders. These local builders are credited with including the Anglo-Saxon cushion capitals found in many first generation Anglo-Norman buildings.

It was in the second generation, however, that both styles reemerged and merged. Geometric decoration, which was definitely Norman, shows up especially in those parts of the church, like the tympana, which had not been decorated in Anglo-Saxon times. This fact suggests that the builder might have an easier time accepting new ideas where they could be added on an existing style rather than replacing an older one. For the first time, however, the patrons accepted acanthus sculpted borders, from Anglo-Saxon manuscript style, on the same buildings. The passage of books across the Channel was of utmost importance in this procedure. Norman books went to England as well as Anglo-Saxon ones to Normandy. Manuscript styles from both cultures were adapted to architecture. The Norman style of historiated initials had been used on the eleventh-century Fécamp capitals and on the Knook (Wiltshire) tympanum (dated as first decade of the twelfth century). *Scriptoria* at Christ Church and St. Augustine's Canterbury, traditionally Anglo-Saxon in style, began using "Norman-type initials from the 1090s onwards" and, by about 1100, these show up as well in cathedral crypts.[88]

The new Anglo-Norman style shows this generation's openness to influences, and also its political contacts. Various manuscript schools and styles flourished. Indeed, from 1100 onward, a mixture not just of Norman and Anglo-Saxon but also of Scandinavian styles was used in illumination and sculpture. Along with the Anglo-Saxon Winchester style was the Ringerike style from Scandinavia. This style probably had been important during Cnut's reign but continued even beyond the Norman Conquest. The Kilpeck (Herefordshire) jambs (*ca.* 1140), as well as the sculpture found at Ipswich, St. Bees, Norwich, and Southwell, show it and thus reflect the many heritages of Angles, Saxons, and Normans. The art it produced was unique, not just eclectic. A new school of sculpture and architecture, the Herefordshire school, existed in the 1130s.[89] The variety of twelfth-century art goes beyond the kingdom: wherever the Normans had contacts, they brought back some artistic detail and adapted it. In Anglo-Norman works of the early twelfth century, we see the influence of crusading, and of Cluny with its continental style. The new continental theme of the tree of Jesse appears in England then. The Winchester Psalter and the art in York (especially in the images of Mary) show Byzantine influence probably picked up by the Normans while on crusades and visiting the cosmopolitan Norman court at Sicily.[90]

The increase in both production and variety of sculptural styles were in many ways directly related to Henry I's court. Cluniac styles were due to Henry I's patronage of the order and building of Reading. Pilgrimages increased due to the peace of the reign, and pilgrims brought back styles from the Cluniac pilgrimage "hotels" of Europe.[91] Since Anglo-Norman sculpture was limited to smaller areas or pieces attached to buildings (as opposed to the High Romanesque style on the continent), little remains undamaged, much less in situ. One capital from Reading is an early Coronation of the Virgin (Reading being dedicated to Mary), and points to England's being at the forefront of the Mariology movement usually associated with France.[92] Some artistic influence also can be linked to Empress Matilda's connections to the Holy Roman Empire, including Lombardy. A rare wooden head of Jesus (*ca.* 1130 Gloucestershire) shows a resemblance to the Holy Roman Empire's wooden crucifixes, possibly based on items brought back by the Empress.[93]

Variety is the key word for this generation's art, especially in comparison to that of the previous one. In the early twelfth century there was an increase in patterned surfaces, giving plasticity to them, and even in variety of form. For example, the Chapter House of Worcester was polygonal and possibly covered with a vault emanating from a central column—a major variation from the uniformity of the first generation buildings.[94]

In the minor arts, England was perhaps not experimenting, but it was not lagging behind either. The Transitional Style is evident. The numbers of ivories, and metalwork (such as the Gloucester candlestick) increased by mid-century, paralleling continental development. Also by mid-century, a Mosan artist was probably in England. As with the other arts, the Anglo-Norman workshops were adapting styles to different media. The champlevé style is seen in manuscript illuminations.[95]

Furthermore, the motifs used by the artists reflect the same interest in nature which we saw in the subject matter of the codices. The specific motifs in manuscripts from 1120 on show an "increasing emphasis on individualized flowers—as opposed to undifferentiated acanthus scrolls" of the Anglo-Saxon pre-1066 workshops.[96]

So the art reflects the world at large both in themes and in Anglo-Norman acceptance of the various cultures in their world. All becomes blended into the new Anglo-Norman style, and much is related to the royal court. This was the world in which the second generation Anglo-Norman noble lived.

Notes

1. His possible responsibility for his brother's death was for a long time the subject for debate among modern historians, although the consensus now is that the death was a fortuitous accident. Freeman, *The Reign of William Rufus,* vol. 2, pp. 321–38, 345–52; Barlow, *William Rufus,* pp. 408–32; Hollister, "The Strange Death of William Rufus"; and J. C. Russell, "Death Along the Deer Trails" are especially useful.

2. *Reg.* II, #488 (unspecified); Riess, "The Reissue of Henry I's Coronation Charter" (full text).

3. For example, *Reg.* II, #490, 492, 493.

4. *Reg.* II, #491. Archbishop Anselm was a self-imposed exile over Investiture disputes with Rufus.

5. *GR*, pp. 470–71; Kapelle, *The Norman Conquest of the North,* pp. 191–97. The most common female name in the royal family was Matilda. To avoid confusion, I use the original Anglo-Saxon name of Edith with the older form of Matilda (Maud) for Henry I's queen, for whom Matilda was a foreign name; Matilda of Flanders for William I's wife; the Empress for Henry I's daughter; and Queen Matilda for Stephen's wife.

6. For the supporters of Curthose, as well as his sad history see C. W. David, *Robert Curthose;* Hollister, "The Anglo-Norman Civil War of 1101"; and Mooers, "Stabbers and Backers."

7. David, *Robert Curthose,* pp. 120–71 is still the most complete summary of events. For an analysis of the events, see Hicks, "The Impact of William Clito upon the Continental Policies of Henry I of England." Clito was a child in 1106. Hicks, "The Anglo-Papal Bargain of 1125: The Legatine Mission of John of Crema" describes the rare case of Henry compromising royal power.

8. Hollister ("International War and Diplomacy in the Anglo-Norman World: The Reign of Henry I") convincingly demonstrates the connections between the domestic rebellions and the international politics. He also shows that Henry did not pursue an expansionist policy but rather sought to secure his borders. Once Normandy was "reunited" with England, Henry did not add any territory on the continent. *Reg.* II, pp. xxix-xxxi gives Henry's itinerary.

9. *GR,* p. 477.

10. D. Walker, *The Norman Conquerors,* though a survey, includes the regional prosopography. See also D. Walker, "The Norman Settlement in Wales;" I. W. Rowlands "The Making of the March: Aspects of Norman Settlement in Dyfed." Bartlett's "Rewriting Saints' Lives: The Case of Gerald of Wales" indicates that Bernard (1115–48), bishop of St. David's, Normanized the church, leading, among other things, to its becoming part of the organized Roman Church.

11. Kapelle, *Norman Conquest of the North,* p. 191.

12. Barrow, *Kingship and Unity: Scotland 1000–1306.* In *The Anglo-Norman Era in Scottish History,* Barrow argues that Scottish land was used for younger sons; as with all such arguments, examples are few since family identifications are tentative. He backs off a bit in *Kingship.* The same analysis of David was used by Stringer (*Earl David of Huntingdon 1152–1219*) who went so far as to call David "Henry's creation," bound to "the Anglo-Frankish world by upbringing, marriage and tenurial ties" (p. 2). Kapelle, *Norman Conquest of the North,* pp. 191–236, shows the increased movement of curial families to the now peaceful North and Scotland that led to the *real* Conquest.

13. For a complete discussion of the Investiture Controversy in England, see Cantor, *Church, Kingship and Lay Investiture in England,* and Barlow, *The English Church,* pp. 104–14. For Anselm see the works of Sally N. Vaughn listed in the bibliography.

14. Nicholl, pp. 41–74.

15. Henry met opposition when he tried to appoint Faritius, abbot of Abingdon, to the archbishopric of Canterbury. *GP,* pp. 125–26.

16. For Norman and Anglo-Norman resistance to celibacy, see C. Brooke, "Gregorian Reform in Action: Clerical Marriage in England, 1050–1200." Roger of Salisbury is the best known married Anglo-Norman cleric; see Kealey's biography, *Roger of Salisbury: Viceroy of England.*

17. Partner, *Serious Entertainments. The Writing of History in Twelfth-Century England*, pp. 41–48. The strength of his opposition is seen in Anselm's obituary in the *Historia Anglorum*, in which Henry calls Anselm simply "philosopher of Christ," whereas his own father received a longer eulogy.

18. Brett, *The English Church Under Henry I*, p. 4.

19. Southern, "Place," p. 135 n.1.

20. Malmesbury wrote (*HN*, p. 5) that only Robert, earl of Gloucester, Brian fitz Count, and the bishop of Lisieux knew of the betrothal, and that this secrecy, as well as the choice of an Angevin, led to the alienation of some nobles. For discussions of the marriage and the politics around it see Hollister and Keefe, "The Making of the Angevin Empire," and Bachrach, "The Idea of the Angevin Empire." Hicks, "England's King Henry I and the Flemish Succession Crisis of 1127–1128," details the double crisis of the time—Henry's handling of the marriage and his attempt to prevent William Clito from becoming count of Flanders.

21. Robert of Torigni, *King Henry I*, p. 28. "Rex probat Henricus Rex vivens pacis amicus / Exstiterat; siquidem prae cunctis ditior idem, / Occiduae genti quos praetulit ordo regendi. / Quippe pater populi, rex et tutela pusilli, / Dum pius ipse ruit, furit impius, opprimit, urit. / Anglia lugeat hinc, Normannica gens fleat illinc. / Occidis, Henrice, tunc pax, nunc luctus utrique. / Quo dum dura febris prima sub nocte Decembris / Mundum nudavit, mundo mala multiplicavit. / Sensu, divitiis, aditu, feritate decenti, / Mire, plus dictu, vim perpessis, scelerosis, / Excellens, locuples, haud difficilis, reverendus, / Hic jacet Henricus rex, quondam pax, decus orbis." *Chronicle of Robert of Torigni, Abbot of the Monastery of St. Michael-in-Peril-of-the-Sea*, p. 126. For a discussion of the chronicle sources and eulogies for Henry's death see Lohrmann, "Der Tod König Heinrichs I. von England."

22. Hollister, "Royal Acts of Mutilation: The Case Against Henry I"; Green, *Government*, pp. 95–117. The same revisionism has been occurring for Rufus. E. Mason ("William Rufus: Myth and Reality") and M. T. Clanchy (*England and Its Rulers, 1066–1272*) each effectively argue for a balanced reputation but go too far in reducing Henry I's character. For example, Clanchy overuses the Anglo-Saxon Chronicle as evidence of rebellion under which "Henry's power collapsed" (pp. 72–73). Clanchy generally is more suspicious of the motives of clerical writers criticizing William than of equally suspect ones criticizing Henry. For an analysis of this revisionism, see Chandler, "Historical Revision and the English Monarchs: The Case of William II and His Barons."

23. OVC 6:16–17. "Omnes inimcos suos sapientia uel fortitudine sibi subiugauit, sibique seruientes diuitiis et honoribus remunerauit. Unde plerosque illustres pro temeritate sua de sullimi potestatis culmine precipitauit, et haereditario iure irrecuperabiliter spoliatos condemnpauit. Alios e contra fauorabiliter illi obsequentes de ignobili stirpe illustrauit, de puluere, ut ita dicam extulit, dataque multiplici facultate, super consules et illustres oppidanos exaltauit."

24. OVC 5:202–03. "Multi sub ipso patris sui proceres obierunt, qui proauis suis extraneum ius belicose uendicauerunt pro quibus nonnullos degeneres in locis magnatorum restituit, et amplis pro adulationis merito datis honoribus sullimauit." Note the two descriptive phrases—Rufus' new men were *adulationes* while Henry's were *servientes*. Orderic's criticism appears to be similar to that which the nobles throughout medieval English history leveled against the kings' *familiares*. However, Orderic's criticism takes on a greater significance because Henry's reign was the first period of administrative activity, and it was followed by an "anarchy."

25. White, "Household of the Norman Kings," pp. 129–30. White points out that the Conqueror's reign was the only period of medieval English history when even the household offices were held by major nobles, men who had proven them-

30   THE ANGLO-NORMAN WORLD

selves militarily. Hollister ("Magnates and *Curiales*," pp. 63–81) has conclusively demonstrated that the Conqueror's magnates were also *curiales*. As he goes on to point out, however, this situation was "predictable" since William had created their wealth because of their proven loyalty and capability.

26. West (*Justiciarship in England*, pp. 10–13) believes that Flambard and a few others could be considered to have been professional administrators. Barlow (*William Rufus*, primarily pp. 99–213) has a higher opinion of William II's government, though too often his evidence dates to Henry I's reign and is being read back. Hollister believes that Rufus' major attempt to organize government was made between 1096 and 1100, concentrating on the viceregency, a necessity of the cross-channel kingdom (Hollister and Baldwin, "Rise of Administrative Kingship").

27. B. Walker ("King Henry I's 'Old Men'") argues that most of the Domesday families retained power, and that therefore Henry did not change any traditions of governing.

28. The phrase "administrative kingship" belongs to Hollister and Baldwin ("Rise of Administrative Kingship"), who provide a good summary of the developing government. Another such overview is found in Chibnall, *Anglo-Norman England, 1066–1166*, pp. 105–34. The most complete analysis to date is found in Green, *Government*.

29. Hollister, "Henry I and the Anglo-Norman Magnates." pp. 94, 98

30. Hollister, "Magnates and *Curiales*," p. 72, table C, and "Henry I and the Anglo-Norman Magnates."

31. Hollister, "The Anglo-Norman Civil War: 1101," pp. 315–34, and "Henry I and Robert Malet."

32. Holt ("Presidential Address. III. Patronage and Politics," p. 4) has dismissed the idea that there was a male generational pattern of behavior in the twelfth century because he was limiting the first generation to one defined by its relation to an event, the Conquest.

33. The development of these expectations is included in the sociological theory of Julián Marías. Marías, a disciple of Ortega y Gasset, developed a rigid four-generation cycle of historical forms and ideas, in which the first generation fights to create a form or idea; the second receives it as a "given" and develops a consciousness of its role; the third begins to question and test it which leads to a weakening; the fourth is alienated from it and sometimes begins to create a new one (*Generations: A Historical Method*, pp. 177–79). While most historians would reject this formula as being simpler than historical reality, the attitudes of the first and second generations occur quite often and fit the evidence of the inheritors of magnate status.

34. Hollister, "Magnates and *Curiales*," p. 72.

35. Examples of the curial patterns are developed in chapters 2, 4, and 7.

36. During Henry's adminstration both the actual production of documents and the preservation of records increased. For a very different view of the administration under Henry I see Warren, "The Myth of Norman Administrative Efficiency." Warren argues that the Normans did not understand Anglo-Saxon administration and that it broke down during Henry I's reign mandating that a new system to be formed.

37. Richard fitz Nigel, *Dialogus de Scaccario*, p. 58. R. Poole, *The Exchequer in the Twelfth Century* discusses the development of the Exchequer.

38. Hollister, "Origins of the English Treasury."

39. See Tout, *Chapters in the Administrative History of Mediaeval England*, vol. 1, and Richardson and Sayles, *The Governance of Mediaeval England*, for the development of the household departments.

40. Adams, *Councils and Courts in Anglo-Norman England,* pp. 100–22.

41. Morris, "The Sheriffs and the Administrative System of Henry I," pp. 168–70. A fuller discussion will follow in chapter 4. Barlow (*William Rufus,* pp. 187–89) shows the continuity in shrievalty tenure from William I to William II.

42. Reedy, "Origins of the General Eyre."

43. For example, *PR,* p. 10 has an account for pleas heard before Geoffrey de Clinton.

44. Leach, ed., *Visitations and Memorials of Southwell Minster,* pp. 190–96.

45. *Liber Winton.*

46. Hoyt, *The Royal Demesne,* p. 93; *PR,* pp. 131, 133.

47. West, *Justiciarship in England,* pp. 13–23; Kealey, *Roger of Salisbury,* pp. 37, 56–57; Hollister and Baldwin, "Rise of Administrative Kingship," pp. 874–77.

48. Bates, "The Origins of the Justiciarship."

49. *Curialis* is another term which is important to this study. This too was not precisely applied at the time. Hollister ("Magnates and *Curiales,*" p. 64) tries to delineate the curial group by defining a *curialis* as one of the top fifteen of the lay witnesses. E. Mason ("Magnates, Curiales and the Wheel of Fortune," p. 118) gives the broadest definition by juxtaposing the "baronial" non-curial noble with the person who associates with the court in order to gain a reward. This would include a whole range of servants but imposes the motivation I was looking for. Boston ("The Territorial Interests of the Anglo-Norman Aristocracy c.1086–1135," pp. 30–32) argues that what constituted an important family was the combination of "lands, wealth, proximity to the king." Again, I will opt for the most open definition, seeking curial behavior rather than labelling someone a *curialis* unless he bases his career on the court.

50. The three coronation appointments were William Giffard as bishop of Winchester, Robert of Chester as abbot of Bury St. Edmund's, and Richard de Clare as abbot of Ely.

51. Haskins, *Norman Institutions,* pp. 85–122.

52. White, "Household," p. 141; Haskins, *Norman Institutions,* p. 89.

53. Bates, "The Earliest Norman Writs."

54. Tabuteau, "Definitions of Feudal Military Obligations."

55. Spear, "Les archdiacres de Rouen au cours de la période ducale," "Les Doyens du Chapitre Cathédral de Rouen durant la période ducale," "Membership in the Norman Cathedral Chapters During the Ducal Period: Some Preliminary Findings," and "The Norman Empire and the Secular Clergy, 1066–1204."

56. For John Le Patourel, see especially "The Norman Conquest, 1066, 1106, 1154?," *The Norman Empire,* and *Feudal Empires* which collects many of his important essays. Bates, *Normandy Before 1066;* Spear, "Une famille ecclésiastique Anglo-Normande."

57. Boston, "Territorial Interests," pp. 10–11, 38–49.

58. For a general introduction to the developments of the time see Cipolla, ed., *The Fontana Economic History of Europe. Vol. 1, The Middle Ages.* Picardy is one of the few areas providing enough data for statistics for these years, and these show low fertility for 1100–50. Russell, *Late Ancient and Medieval Population Control,* p. 181.

59. Kealey, *Medieval Medicus,* p. 4.

60. Rowley, *The Norman Heritage, 1055–1200,* puts post-Conquest town growth into perspective, replete with aerial photography and town plans showing the upsurge by 1100.

61. For the dispute over the charter see C. N. L. Brooke, G. Keir, and

S. Reynolds, "Henry I's Charter for the City of London" which argues that it was either a forgery or a mislabelled charter of Stephen's. In "London's First Charter of Liberties," Hollister effectively answers this charge and places the charter squarely in the later part of Henry's reign, probably in part resulting from the fire.

62. The commercial changes have been described in Kealey's excellent article, "Anglo-Norman Policy and the Public Welfare." For windmill technology see Kealey, *Harvesting the Air.*

63. R. H. C. Davis, *The Normans and Their Myth.* Davis uses the continued movement of Europeans into the Norman areas to argue against a Norman "race."

64. Clanchy, *From Memory to Written Record,* p. 168; Short, "On Bilingualism in Anglo-Norman England," pp. 467–74.

65. Legge, "Anglo-Norman as a Spoken Language"; Clanchy, *From Memory,* pp. 154–74, 186; Searle,"Women and the Legitimisation of Succession at the Norman Conquest."

66. Short, "On Bilingualism," p. 468. Orderic (OVC, 2:270) reports that Thurston of Glastonbury ordered his retainers to shoot monks who refused to substitute a Norman chant for an Anglo-Saxon one. Another Conquest abbot, Paul of St. Albans, destroyed the tombs of his Anglo-Saxon predecessors and called his English monks illiterates (Newman, "Anglo-Norman Romanesque Architecture and the Conquest," p. 273). S. J. Ridyard ("*Condigna Veneratio:* Post-Conquest Attitudes to the Saints of the Anglo-Saxons") has shown that this second "generation" of Norman abbots and bishops also were more accepting of Anglo-Saxon saints. She credits the change to the Normans' new understanding of the usefulness of these cults to their churches. While I agree with this conclusion, I would add that it would not have been possible if the general elite attitude towards Anglo-Saxon culture had not changed.

67. The tendency to use Norman names extends as far as the peasants in the Burton Abbey surveys (B. L. Loan No. 30 fols. 28–36; transcribed by Bridgeman, ed., "The Burton Abbey Twelfth Century Surveys," pp. 209–300), "B" *ca.* 1114–1118, "A" *ca.* 1116–1133. Godrics and Wulfrics still dominated, but a Richard fitz Godit (p.214) is found in "B" and "A" has a William fitz Godwin (pp. 234, 235).

68. Swain fitz Ailric was the adult male heir of a lower Anglo-Saxon noble who survived the Conquest. Swain made the family fortune in the time of Henry I, and gave his sons names to help them in the future. The eldest had a "neutral" name, Adam, while his younger son was named Henry and his daughter Matilda. I thank Hugh Thomas for the reference from his work on this family, "A Yorkshire Thegn and his Descendants After the Conquest."

69. Clark, "Women's Names in Post-Conquest England: Observations and Speculations." Anglo-Saxon names continued to be used for women.

70. Powley, *The House of De La Pomeroi,* genealogy.

71. Examples of biblical names include Adam fitz Swain, from an Anglo-Saxon family, and Samson, bishop of Worcester, son of Normans.

72. Clark, "Women's Names," and Searle "Women and the Legitimisation of Succession." Some Anglo-Saxon families "retained" their land through their daughters who were married to Normans.

73. Legge, "L'influence littéraire de la cour d'Henri Beauclerc," pp. 681–82.

74. Southern, "The Place of England in the Twelfth-Century Renaissance."

75. Clanchy, *From Memory,* traces the beginning of the "literate mentality" to the Norman Conquest and details its growth until Edward I's death.

76. Clanchy, *From Memory.* For historical writing specifically see Gransden,

Historical Writing in England, c. 550–c.1307, and Partner, *Serious Entertainments.*

77. Barlow, *The English Church,* pp. 217–67. Southern, "The Place of England in the Twelfth-Century Renaissance," p. 163, lists schools in Huntingdon, Gloucester, Winchester, Bath, London, and Warwick established by the time of Henry I's death. While it is unclear whether some of them were founded between 1066–1100 or 1100–35, their activity certainly increased substantially after 1100.

78. Turner, "The *Miles Literatus* in Twelfth- and Thirteenth-Century England: How Rare a Phenomenon?"

79. Legge ("L'influence littéraire," pp. 683–85) postulates a Caen network ("un réseau Caennais") of Roger of Salisbury, Alexander of Lincoln, and Robert of Gloucester—all from Caen, and possibly educated there, all patrons of literature, all with similar political views (supporters of the Empress). Education will be examined in chapter 2, specific patronage in chapter 3. See also Green, *Government,* pp. 158–59.

80. Kealey, *Medieval Medicus,* pp. 2–3.

81. Hyams, "The Common Law and the French Connection," p. 78.

82. Hyams, "Trial by Ordeal: The Key to Proof in the Early Common Law."

83. Vaughn, "Robert of Meulan and Raison d'Etat," p. 366. The relationship between the practical and the literary would continue. Hyams, "Henry II and Ganelon," pp. 23–35, writes: "Certainly we ought not to draw sharp lines between law and culture of the period." He goes on to show the similarities of the court and the "real" law to the romances as late as Henry II. Certainly no greater distinction was made earlier.

84. Kealey, *Medicus,* pp. 5–14; David Bernstein, in conversation (question session following "The Englishness of the Bayeux Tapestry"); Southern, "Place of England." Examples of the variety in the manuscripts include: B.L. Sloane 2839, ca. 1100 medical; B.L. Cotton Tib.C.I./Harley 3667 astrological (Peterborough, 1122) with a map of the world on fol. 8v.; and those reproduced in Zarnecki, Holt, and Holland, *English Romanesque Art 1066–1200* canon law (Christ Church, Cants. c. 1120, p. 107/B.L. Cotton Claudius E.V.); natural science (Ramsey, 1080–90, p. 104); herbal (Bury St. Edmunds, 1100, p. 105); medical and astrological (Durham and Peterborough, 1100–20, pp. 105–106); and in Kauffmann, *Romanesque Manuscripts 1066–1190* Josephus (catalogue #83).

85. Newman, "Anglo-Norman Romanesque Architecture and the Conquest." Gem ("The Romanesque Rebuilding of Westminster Abbey"), however, argues for Anglo-Saxon decoration in Westminster Abbey in the 1090s.

86. Clapham, *English Romanesque Architecture After the Conquest,* pp. 41–48. Those begun in the time of Henry I were Reading/Cluniac, Selby/Benedictine, Peterborough/Benedictine, Chertsey, Romsey/Benedictine nuns, a wing of Old Sarum, and Rochester. Most were Benedictine, most had apsidial and radiating chapels, and ambulatories.

87. Newman, "Anglo-Norman Romanesque Architecture," p. 272; Zarnecki, *English Romanesque Sculpture 1066–1140,* p. 20; Zarnecki, Holt, and Holland, *English Romanesque Art,* pp. 36–37. Clapham (*English Romanesque Architecture,* p. 19) used the term "first generation" when describing the 1066–1100 building, but did not follow through with the metaphor.

88. Zarnecki, "Romanesque Sculpture in Normandy and England in the Eleventh Century," pp. 168–89.

89. Zarnecki, Holt, and Holland, *English Romanesque Art,* pp. 18–22; Thurlby, "Romanesque Sculpture at Tewkesbury Abbey," pp. 89–94.

90. Zarnecki, Holt, and Holland, *English Romanesque Art,* pp. 22–25.

91. Ibid., p. 147.

92. Ibid., p. 159, #113.
93. Ibid., p. 160, #115.
94. Ibid., p. 36.
95. For example, the Henry of Blois champlevé, (Zarnecki, Holt, and Holland, *English Romanesque Art*, pp. 261–63, #227). Additionally, an Augustine commentary on the psalms dated 1115–24 from Rochester (B.L. Royal 5.D.II) has historiated initials, Norman in form though Anglo-Saxon in color and style. The initial C on folio 1r has feeling of champlevé in its use of white.
96. Ibid., p. 85.

CHAPTER 2

The Anglo-Norman Family

In addition to living within a world of politics, trade, and art, the Anglo-Norman noble lived within a family. As far as scholars of various fields can discover, people have always lived within families, but the structure and dynamics of this amazing institution have varied. Therefore it is necessary to outline the structure of the Anglo-Norman noble family before examining the relationships within it.

The Anglo-Norman family, like other medieval institutions, was flexible. It appears to have been composed of relatives by blood from both sides as well as those related by marriage, with these blood and marriage ties providing a pool of people from which to choose for various types of support. From what we can glean without literature that was written by the subject, the family structure was perceived by the Anglo-Norman noble[1] to vary by situation or function. Who functioned as family or could call upon others depended on the circumstances. In most situations, the family was bilateral and cognatic—extending at least through uncles, aunts, and their children, as well as to the first degree of affinity. Yet when the transmission of land already within the family was at issue, agnatic, that is male, lines usually were stressed.

Various forms of the Anglo-Norman noble family continued to fill six of the functions that recent scholars have suggested were basic to the European family—reproductive, religious, judicial, protective, economic, and socializing.[2] The nuclear family was the functioning unit of reproduction; in addition, in Anglo-Norman society it was the religious unit as well, as evidenced by information regarding oblature, patronage descent, and especially prayer requests. Each nuclear unit seems to have attempted to have an oblate—one did not serve to pray for the extended family. The patronage of endowed religious houses passed through the line of inheritance—heirs patronized the houses that their parents had.[3]

In the votive clauses of the time, the family was usually defined narrowly, as a legitimate, nuclear family. For example, Miles of Gloucester requested prayers for his wife, his eldest son, and "other sons" although he had three daughters, a sister and nephews living.[4] In a typical clause, Fulk de Lisures (a forester) gave land for the love of God, the safety of the souls of himself, his wife, and his ancestors.[5]

The family served judicial functions such as witnessing each other's documents, especially land transfers. This was not exclusively a familial function since members of both the family and feudal networks witnessed, but the importance of the family connection is seen by the common usage of the terms of relation to identify the witness. Feudal associations were not noted except for a rear vassal. Some of the relatives witnessed because they had a claim on the land being transferred in the document. However, the donor does not appear to have gathered together all possible claimants—only the immediate heir appears to have *had* to witness—yet many family members including collateral kin witnessed. For example, a land transfer by Earl Roger of Hereford was witnessed by a son-in-law Herbert whose children eventually would be the donor's heirs, but also by a first cousin, Elias Gifford.[6] Judicially then, the family was cognatic, that is, almost any blood relative could function.

The family functioned militarily, but usually only as a tie which could validate the feudal one. Here both cognatic and affinal ties could be used, though none automatically created a military obligation.[7] Later we will see examples of military blocs which show a broadly defined family, especially including in-laws (like the Beaumont bloc in the Anarchy) and maternal uncles (like the Empress's uncle, David of Scotland).[8]

More important to this generation, the family served an economic function by providing for children and siblings[9]—through acquired land, marriages, clerical positions, and family subinfeudation. This function is omnipresent in this book because of its importance to the nobles, and examples will be seen throughout, especially for Henry I's family. When looking at this broad question of provision, we see most blood ties being called upon. However, when we look at inheritance of land, we see the emergence of agnatic structure in primogeniture, and with it a narrow agnatic definition of family.[10]

The family also served an educational or socializing function; family members were often called upon to train, protect, and provide for younger members. Here there was an alternative in that children could also be sent for education to the clergy or to the court of the feudal lord. As with political functions, the family was not the imperative but an alternative.

Who from among the available sources provided the best potential benefit? Again, Henry I's family will show clear examples.

Coincidentally, it was during the Anglo-Norman era that the church was attempting to define the family by passing marriage and incest regulations. What emerges is that the clerical definition differed somewhat from that of the nobles. The church had the broadest definition of family found at the time. Councils held in England in 1075, 1102, and 1127 forbade marriage within seven degrees of blood. In addition, affinity lines were within the definition of family. Marriage was banned to the seventh degree of the spouse's blood relatives; to the fourth degree of the spouse's blood relatives' spouses; and even to the second degree of the spouse's blood relatives' spouses' relatives.[11] In addition, there were regulations against those related by spiritual affinity, that is, godparents.[12] Unfortunately we do not have the specific evidence of Anglo-Norman godparentage, so it is difficult to determine if in general godparents were considered to be part of the family. Both the Anglo-Saxon and Norman nobles set limits to inheritance at the seventh degree of blood, which seems to indicate partial agreement with the church. Yet at the Lateran Council of 1215, the church "retreated" to the fourth degree of blood and a far more limited degree of affinity;[13] the nobility successfully had resisted this regulation. In other words, the nobles had at least two definitions of family, one pertaining to claims of inheritance (to the seventh degree) and the other to marriage (to the fourth degree).

This Anglo-Norman structure fits into the current scholarly views of the European family generally. For many years, scholars argued that the family went through evolutionary stages, from a primitive cognatic structure to the more modern agnatic one. Now family historians and sociologists are discarding this view and replacing it with recognition that most families were a mixture, mainly cognatic with a stress on patrilineage for some aspect of their structure, usually inheritance.[14] Alexander Murray and others have recently published studies which show this "mixed" cognatic system in Germanic Europe, including in Anglo-Saxon England,[15] and in Early Modern Europe.[16]

It would be convenient for us, of course, if the Anglo-Normans had a precise word for family, but they did not. A rare use of "familia" to indicate blood relatives appears in a confirmation by Earl Simon of St. Liz of a grant within the bishopric of Lincoln, 1094–1107; the document included the phrase "aliis quam pluribus de familia comitis."[17] Anthropologist Jack Goody[18] cites the Anglo-Norman use of the French word "cousin" for all collateral relatives beyond siblings, stressing both the bilateral family and the differentiation of the elementary family from the rest. They also adopted the term "in-law" to separate the affinal family from the birth one. But little can be said beyond this.

Naming, usually used as an indicator of family, presents special problems for the student of the Anglo-Norman nobles but also demonstrates the flexibility of the family. The Anglo-Norman nobles were beginning to use surnames of various types. Such names indicated the important elements of a noble's identity—family heritage, land, and, to a lesser extent, office. Patronymics were common, occasionally even being used to designate members of the lower classes. These patronymics not only help the historian trying to determine family connections, but are often the only actual evidence we possess of any relationship between individuals. However, more often they cause confusion because of the use of common names and the repetition of names in successive generations. Matronymics were used, though less frequently. The choice of a matronymic was indicative of the relative status of the parents. However, toponymics, indicating their holdings, were just as common. The majority of toponymics are French and usually provide us with evidence of the location of these patrimonial lands.[19] They also indicate the noble's opinion of the importance of his land, and the relative importance of his English and Norman lands. These names are further evidence of the *Anglo* quality of the generation. During this period, some of the newer families or younger sons of established families began to use toponymics derived from their English lands rather than the Norman ones. In general, while names may give some indication as to upper class status or as to location of an individual's holdings, when we look for evidence of attitude toward family, they are often more confusing than enlightening.

Certainly these names, especially toponymics, show that these nobles were attempting to connect the land to the family, but it does not necessarily follow that they were trying to define the boundaries of their family.[20] Neither does the name necessarily reflect the attitude of the individual to the family. Even where a surname was adopted, it was not universally applied within the family (where brothers and cousins, like the Basset/Ridels or the Redvers, were known by different "surnames")[21] or even by the individual (as names varied in the records).[22] Some of the toponymics, like Vesci and Mowbray, were chosen from the maternal side, indicating that the choice was bilateral, not agnatic.[23] In addition, there is the persistence of identification by patronymics beyond the Anglo-Norman period. The "Fitz Alan" family alone seems to incorporate most of the naming techniques. Alan fitz Flaad's sons were known as fitz Alans. The eldest line continued using noninherited patronymics (fitz Jordan) in the next generation; the second son kept fitz Alan as a surname; the third son's line took the office name of Stewart. Women's names as recorded in the documents show the same variations, sometimes being linked to one or another husband (not necessarily the current one) or to her family of origin.[24] We cannot, then, connect the name to a precise view of family when agnatic cousins, sometimes brothers, certainly sisters, were known by different names, even at the very moment of choosing the name and even though they all had claims on the land. Names reflected this breadth and flexibility of relationships, feudal as well as familial ones, and were applied accordingly in different situations.

The Anglo-Normans were far from unique. Naming patterns varied through twelfth-century Europe. Freed has found a situation similar to the Anglo-Norman one in the family of the counts of Falkenstein. Their names provided an identity associated with land and status but were chosen from both sides of the family and not just the paternal.[25] Some geographic areas provide better resources for study. Bouchard has found that the Seignelay nobles also used geographic nicknames and matrilineal names, and were beginning to pass along fixed names. However, they sometimes changed their names when marriage brought land, or did not use a name until they entered their patrimony. Furthermore, sometimes unrelated people used the names.[26] In Seignelay, however, Christian names were used consciously to define groups.[27] I cannot find evidence of this practice for the Anglo-Normans. The Anglo-Normans were very fond of a few names—William and Matilda leading all others. Perhaps they used specific Christian names to link themselves to a particular familial group or godparents or feudal lord, but, because of the small pool of common names which they used, we cannot define *which* group.[28]

Ultimately, we are left frustrated. Our modern sensibilities and historical knowledge tell us that people's names mean something. However, in the Anglo-Norman world, they meant many things. If we look for precision, we lose the reality. Names show the Anglo-Norman nobles' many identities. Furthermore, they show the flexibility of the institution of the family and of its relation to the other institutions of Anglo-Norman society.

The creation of a family is symbolized by marriage.[29] There is no evidence that the Anglo-Normans veered from the medieval norm, with the marriages arranged by male relatives and lords and the bride a minor at the time of her first marriage. After all, marriages were the way to perpetuate the legitimate families, and a young bride would ensure begetting legitimate heirs.[30] In addition, though, marriage was the means for social climbing, for provision for younger children, and for alliances. Marriage could build a political alliance. An obvious case of this is that of Waleran Beaumont, who arranged the marriage of his sisters to his political allies—Hugh de Montfort, Hugh fitz Gervase, and William Louvel—just prior to their rebellion against Henry I. They were led in rebellion by Amauri de Montfort, the head of this new extended family.[31]

There are also many cases of marriages which created political opposition rather than unity. Robert Marmion and Walter Beauchamp each married a d'Abetot heiress. However, disagreement over the land division between the heiresses led to their husbands' choosing opposing sides in the Anarchy, and led to a dispute not settled until their heirs married one another late in the century.[32] Marriage into a family could even mean acquiring a family enemy as one's own. Gilbert de Laigle, a supporter of Henry, was given the English land that had been forfeited by his Norman neighbor, Geoffrey, count of Mortain, as well as Mortain's daughter in marriage; but this brought Gilbert into conflict with Mortain's enemy, his neighbor, Robert de Bellême. Mortain had disputed a land claim with Bellême in the Domfront area which had yet to be settled.[33]

Beyond the direct impact of marriages, remarriages by heiresses added complications to the political world. The story of Countess Lucy's heirs demonstrates this. Though her first marriage was childless, her second, to Roger fitz Gerold de Roumare, resulted in a son, William de Roumare. When Lucy's third husband, Ranulf, became earl of Chester, Henry I forced him to surrender some of his patrimony and possibly some of Lucy's land. Her elder son, William de Roumare, claimed a filial right to some of the land his stepfather had surrendered, and when his claim was denied joined Clito's forces.[34]

The primary benefit however, was usually not direct political action, but rather economic alliance[35] or the social prestige of linkage to another family.[36] Nobles especially tried to "marry up." This important aspect of noble life, and the strategies used, will be examined later.

The importance of arranged marriages and the little influence which women had in this decision suggest strict gender divisions and control of women. However, the family which the marriage created shows more variety than we would expect. Our glimpses of the personal side of marriage show that the relations between husbands and wives in this period varied greatly, ranging from abuse to partnership. Agnes de Bellême was beaten and imprisoned until her chamberlain helped her to escape to the sanctuary of her overlord's court.[37] There is one chronicle story of Henry I disseising a noble because of his mistreatment of the wife which Henry had given him.[38] Another noblewoman, Maud de Laigle, although not "abused," was obviously treated like a marriage pawn. Her marriage was annulled when her husband of three months rebelled. The king "gave" her her ex-husband's land to take to her new husband, Nigel, a *curialis* whom the king had chosen. Nigel treated her at best with cold respect while her male relatives lived, but shortly after their deaths he annulled the still childless marriage. With royal consent, however, Nigel kept the first husband's land.[39]

Evidence of partnership defined by respect and shared responsibility is more common.[40] Most of the known Anglo-Norman women had their own households, and several issued charters in their own names from their own *scriptoria*.[41] The majority of women are visible to us because they appear in the records governing land, acting as political and military partners, or acting as regents for the sons. There are numerous examples of women being relied upon while the men fought elsewhere. Adela of Blois ran the duchy while Stephen was on crusade, and later, as regent for her son, raised an army for Louis le Gros.[42] Mabel of Gloucester and Queen Matilda were responsible for negotiating and implementing a major treaty during the Anarchy.[43] Juliana de Breteuil defended the *caput* while her husband fought elsewhere.[44] These women, none of whom had a say in the formation of their marriage, were each given control of the family's destiny.

Most of what we know about women within the family comes from monastic chroniclers. A survey of the three contemporary chroniclers who provide us with the most details about many families—Orderic Vitalis, William of Malmesbury (*GR, GP,* and *HN*), and the anonymous author of *Gesta Stephani*—leads us to the conclusion that they, if not a large part of traditional male society, recognized and praised (or at least accepted) the role of the Anglo-Norman noblewoman as helpmate in most male jobs. Indeed, they appear to have expected the pious, meek woman to step in to save the castle or the duchy. She was expected to act swiftly and effectively. However, the chroniclers credit good women's actions to their love for their husbands and their Christian duty as wives, and they condemn those women who acted from their own political or emotional motives, even when these motives were understandable. Orderic provides fine examples. Women of course were tangential to Orderic's topic. He recognized them as necessary to family succession and as such he noted them by their father, husband, and number and sex of their children, but he often omitted their first names. The women who were most praised were those who took the veil, not a surprising attitude to find in a monk's work.[45] However, many of these women were applauded precisely because they had led wanton, unfeminine lives and were now repenting. Orderic did not expect all women to become nuns, but neither did he condemn

every woman who entered the male sphere of life. Rather his opinion was
determined by the motivation for the act. He lavishly and romantically
praised Sybil de Bordet, for example, for wearing armor and guarding the
castle of Tarragona.

> She was as brave as she was beautiful. During her husband's ab-
> sences she kept a sleepless watch; every night she put on a hau-
> berk like a soldier and carrying a rod in her hand, mounted on
> to the battlements, patrolled the circuit of the walls, kept the
> guards on alert, and encouraged everyone with good counsel to
> be on the alert for the enemy's stratagems. How greatly the
> young countess deserves praise for serving her husband with
> such loyalty and unfaltering love, and watching dutifully over
> God's people with such sleepless care![46]

The motive for her military action was lofty in part because it was against
Saracens, but Orderic praised Sybil because she was motivated by uxorial
duty.

   However, repeatedly Orderic displayed a lack of understanding or sym-
pathy toward women's individual motivations or an individual woman's
actual sentiments. For one example let us look at his description of Juliana
de Breteuil, one of the many illegitimate daughters of Henry I. While
Juliana's husband was in rebellion against the king in 1118, an exchange
of hostages was arranged. Juliana's two daughters were exchanged for the
son of one of Henry's men. However, Juliana's husband broke the truce
and mutilated the boy he was holding. The boy's father petitioned Henry
for justice. With their grandfather's acquiescence, the girls lost their eyes
and noses. During this time, Juliana was holding the keep at Breteuil. On
hearing the news of her daughters, she wanted to attack the king's forces,
but the burgesses feared Henry's strength and sided with him. So Juliana
arranged a meeting with her father and attempted to assassinate him.
Although Juliana was desperate, was suffering, and had been violent in
an acceptable way, that is, she had led an armed force and held a besieged
castle, Orderic notes that Henry was taken totally by surprise by this
action. Orderic goes further and blames it on her female deceit. Henry is
said to have been "ignorant of the woman's trick (*fraudia feminae*)," that
is, he never expected a woman to be violent or to attempt revenge. It was
this personal act, not her participation in the treasonous rebellion, which
drew Orderic's strongest criticism. While the military actions were credited, seemingly by both Henry and Orderic, to her obligation as a wife

and her duty to her family, any personally motivated violence was unacceptable in a noblewoman. Her punishment was gender appropriate. Henry allowed her to return to Eustace but condemned her to jump into the freezing moat, where she "fell shamefully, with bare buttocks" and the water numbed "the tender flesh of the woman." Eventually forgiven, she entered Fontevrault.[47]

The only female behavior routinely condemned by Orderic and other chroniclers was sexual—either adultery or a widow taking a lover instead of a new husband.[48] Of course, this view is consistent with the moral and religious views of the culture, but it was held even when the husband previously had been condemned by the chronicler for his cruel behavior. Again, there is a lack of concern for the individual. The husband became the poor mistreated victim whenever the wife rebelled sexually. William de Pont de l'Arche's wife was not even named by the author of the *Gesta Stephani,* yet he related how she was seduced by a soldier of low birth. They imprisoned William in the dungeon while they lived together above. Since William was a servant of Henry I and had switched allegiance in the Anarchy, the chronicler did not consider him of noble character, yet he treated him sympathetically in relating this episode.[49] Indeed, the chroniclers do not judge individual women's actions solely on the basis of political or religious biases even when they do so for the men. Our insights from the chronicles into women's roles are more limited than they are for men.

The chroniclers do reflect what we have seen in behavior, that is, an acceptance of a *virtuous* female leader. Let us compare two Matildas. The Empress Matilda was Henry I's legitimate daughter and designated heir. Only one chronicler, William of Malmesbury, fell short of condemning her, and it is obvious that this generosity was a result of her ally and brother's being his patron. Nowhere however, did any contemporary chronicler condemn her for fighting for the throne in her own right; rather she was condemned for her arrogance, her so-called German haughtiness. Even Malmesbury's use of the word virago (*viraginis*) was in an account of the Empress alienating the Londoners through her arrogance.[50] The second Matilda, Stephen's queen, received the universal praise of contemporary chroniclers. This Matilda led a "powerful force" to besiege Dover while, in answer to her personal appeal, her *maritagium* subjects from Boulogne blockaded it from the sea. For all of her military exploits, her considerable part in governing both England and Boulogne,[52] no chronicler, not even in the partisan time of the Anarchy, labeled her a virago. Seen in this light, the Anglo-Norman chroniclers appear to reflect a more open acceptance of the practical demands which Anglo-Norman society made on noblewomen, though the writers themselves showed neither understanding nor acceptance of the women's actual sentiments.

Women also appear both in chronicle admonitions and in reported behavior serving as the religious conscience of the family. The clearest examples occur in the royal family and will be dealt with later, but Orderic describes such a woman, Aubrée de Cravent, in an almost comic account. When her son robbed a monk, Aubrée's husband refused to act, but Aubrée wrung her hands, tore at her hair, groaned and cried that he would kill his mother and lose his soul with this evil deed. Then her husband listened and the monk regained his property.[53]

Again, in the absence of reflective literature and of chroniclers' lack of direct knowledge of individual women's actual sentiments, it is difficult to gauge the feelings that lay behind the wives' participation in a family "partnership." Was it merely survival, or duty to or "employment" by a husband for whom she never developed feelings? We have but a few glimpses of noblewomen who did develop tenderness for their husbands. Votive clauses in donation charters are so formulaic that when there is a variation, it jumps out at the reader. Margaret, countess of Warwick, added to her donation to Kenilworth Priory the description of her late husband as "my man" (*viri mei*) although feudally he was not.[54] In another charter, the dowager Queen Adeliza, who had been married to a much older Henry I for the sole purpose of giving birth to a replacement heir, gave candles to light his tomb, adding the phrase "my most noble lord" (*domini mei nobilissimi*).[55]

As has been the case in most European societies, widowhood—especially for a woman who was a mother—brought the most freedom of behavior to Anglo-Norman women. It is as widows that they most often appear in the records as governing territory or taking control of their own lives and marriages. Adeliza, widow of Roger of Gloucester, appears to have served as sheriff in her late husband's stead. She used the feminine form of the title for sheriff, *vicecomitissa*, in a grant well after his death.[56] Gaining control of one's own life was not easy, though, because it often set the woman against the king even if she was accepted by the men in her family. The practice of widows' buying their freedom from guardianship or remarriage from the king—a practice John later found so profitable—is evident in the 1130 Pipe Roll and will be treated in detail in the discussion of royal favor. From this evidence we see the acceptance of the free woman, the desire for control, and the need to deal with the king as well as the men in her family affected all levels of noble women.[57]

The outstanding example of a woman's use in marriage as well as her fight to be able to act on her own behalf is that of Lucy, countess of Chester. Lucy was a Lincolnshire heiress who was married and widowed three times.[58] The chronicle evidence is clear that she had been given no choice in marriage, nor much time between remarriages. In 1130, after her third husband had died, Lucy was entered in the Pipe Roll as accounting for her patrimony and owing 500*m*. for permission not to marry for five years. She owed an additional sum (45*m*.) for the same concessions to be paid to whomever the king named—that is, to compensate whomever the king would have chosen to give her to in patronage as her new guardian or husband. Furthermore, she owed yet another 100*m*. for the right to hold court cases between her vassals in her own name.[59] Perhaps more interesting than what this demonstrates about royal control is what it shows of Lucy's relationship to her family. Lucy's early marriages appear to have been controlled by the men of her generation or that of her parents'. We cannot accurately determine her age, but she appears to have been very young at her first marriage.[60] Her relative youth would have made her closer in age to her eldest sons than to any of her husbands. By 1130, her sons were grown and would have been her guardians. They must have agreed to their mother's move for self-control, her choice not to remarry. Furthermore, they must have agreed to her choice to run her lands. Therefore they must have recognized her ability actively to run their future inheritance.

But what was the actual freedom of choice allowed widows? After Robert of Meulan died, his widow married William of Warenne, a *curialis* and magnate who then became partial guardian of her twins. Recently, this marriage has been characterized as a love match. In other words, Elizabeth chose to marry. The evidence is found in Henry of Huntingdon's *Contemptu Mundi* description of Robert's death. Henry said that Robert died in mental torment partly because of his guilty conscience over damage done to clerical lands, but also because his wife was having an affair. The inference drawn is that Elizabeth and William were having an affair in Robert's lifetime, and happily married after he died.[61] Even if we accept Henry of Huntingdon's statement, the affair and the marriage may be unconnected: the lover may not have been William. All evidence points to arranged marriages being the norm. The choice of William of Warenne as a partner for Elizabeth makes sense within this context. It is just as feasible, if not more probable, that Henry I chose to have this heiress and mother of important landholders married quickly to one of the few *curiales* (i.e., trusted man) of magnate status who were not already related to the Beaumonts. There is no evidence of Elizabeth's making the choice.

Most of our evidence of family—both from chronicles and from land transfer charters or surveys—deals with the father and his heir. It is in analyzing this relationship that we see the benefits of the generational approach. It is here that we are examining issues which concern the passing on of responsibility, property, and power, "the manner in which [a society] consequently assures its own survival. [They] will affect its internal structure, the relationships of its members, and the style of its culture."[62]

Most of the nobles appear to have had close relations with their male heirs. Since these sons were available to be witnesses to their fathers' charters, and since they were being trained to follow their fathers as knights, we can infer that they spent time with their fathers from a young age. Time spent together could have allowed a personal relationship to have been established. The heirs' childhoods varied, even in length. While the *Leges Henrici I* defined the age of discretion and inheritance as 15,[63] this age does not appear to have been a fixed idea. William the Aethling and the Beaumont twins came of age at 16.[64] During this childhood they were educated to be noblemen. We can glimpse the education of noble heirs at the royal court where relatives' and *familiares'* heirs were sent.[65] Although father and son may have been close, there was a crucial difference. Many of the fathers were part of the generation who had come with William I to conquer England or were benefiting from the new administration to gain status; this experience was different from that of the next generation.

As already described, the son who was born to this status had different experiences and hence expectations from those of his father who had worked to acquire it. The son expected to be consulted and to receive patronage because of his birth status. Administrative duties were not necessarily part of his lifestyle. Nor was regular court attendance, especially among the magnate sons, who were witnesses to state occasions, crown-wearing times, or major treaties, but little else. This development helped to create a separation between the royal bureaucracy and the more self-conscious aristocratic nobles.[66] Furthermore, in the Anglo-Norman world, a number of nobles married later in life, and this affected their relationships with their heirs. Nigel d'Albini and Richard de Redvers left minor heirs, but had had long, productive careers and can be assumed to have been "older" and well-established when their heirs were born. Robert of Meulan was seventy-five at his death in 1118, and his twin heirs were minors.[67] What is important here is not so much the age as the "life-stage." Marriage was linked with adulthood—either coinciding with coming into one's inheritance or, if marriage was to an heiress, gaining one's land. This was especially true for those who gained new status. The heir was the tangible symbol of having survived youth and an uncertain early manhood and now having "made it."

This relationship seems to have led to the phenomenon of doting on the heir, sometimes to the extent of spoiling him, perhaps to the extent of creating in him this expectation of status. One example is Waleran Beaumont; in him we see the heir who formed his own court at sixteen when he came into his inheritance. When the royal court went back to England, he remained in Normandy with this newly formed household who would soon help him rebel.[68] The most obvious example in this period, though, is Henry's legitimate son William and his court of young heirs who will be described later.

The relationship between the noble mother and the heir differed from that between her and her husband or between him and the heir. This difference may have been a product of a difference in ages. Herlihy has argued that the age gap between husband and wife may have placed her in an arbiter's position between father and heir. In age, she was, after all, approximately half-way between their generations.[69] This was the case for some of the Anglo-Norman women, the most flamboyant example being Matilda of Flanders, who indeed, served in this intermediary position between the Conqueror and the rebellious Robert Curthose.[70] However, more commonly these noblewomen demonstrated a close relation with the heir as a minor or after he had attained his majority. Adela of Blois and Agnes Giffard served as guardians for their sons and continued to influence them as adults—Adela even continued to advise Count Theobald from her convent retirement.[71] Neither Gundrede de Gournai nor Mabel of Gloucester served as guardians, yet each was active in the running of her son's lands after his majority was attained, indicating a strong, personal relationship that would have been established during the father's lifetime. Gundrede de Gournai, who survived her husband Nigel d'Albini by about twenty-five years, was particularly active in her son's early majority and was usually first witness to his charters, taking precedence over his wife. Mabel of Gloucester was given responsibility for running her son's Norman lands while he concentrated on running those in England.[72] This age difference may have helped to develop an important role for the noblewoman in this feudal society. It is ironic that the desire for young brides, controlled women, may have created the strong older woman who was in control.

There appears to be a striking difference between the heir and others in the family in both general behavior and relations with his parents. Others in the family were reared to work, to serve and seek patronage from the king in order to obtain their lands. This is seen, for example, in another family known for curial service, the Bigods. Roger (I) was the second generation from the Conquest but not of magnate status in 1086, and continued to serve the king until his death in 1107. His heir William, however, though he served as steward in title, shows little actual service and very few attestations before his death in the White Ship—a typical second generation pattern. However, when his younger brother Hugh inherited the patrimony, he served in the pattern of his father. Hugh had not been reared with the expectation of inheritance. His adult behavior had been developed during his youth and did not change even when the circumstances did.[73]

In addition, when these young men are compared to illegitimate males at the court, there is another interesting contrast. There was a significant group of recognized natural sons of nobles in this generation.[74] Most of those who have been identified were reared by Henry I. Some may have been educated differently from the legitimates. Certainly all served in royal offices and as *curiales,* becoming *familiares* of Henry I. Their rewards were substantial, but usually in smaller "parcels" or by marriages to heiresses with less land or from families with less prestige. Their loyalty to Henry and to his designated heir Matilda was strong. No matter what the status of their father, and like younger sons, they did not behave as magnates, even after gaining their rewards. Of course, they were not reared to expect status and patronage because they were not legitimate and could not inherit the patrimony. But furthermore, in most cases, the bastards were premarital products and their fathers often had not achieved their own status yet, so why would they be reared to expect it? In addition, there was a smaller age gap between father (or surrogate father) and this son. As with the mother and heir, a smaller age gap might have helped to create a more equal relationship between father and son, with less chance of spoiling the son.

In other words, legitimacy and its inheritance rights were not the only variables determining the behavior or expectations in life of an illegitimate son. The father's achievements and age at his birth played a role in his relationships that would have made it different from that of father and heir, though in outcome, similar to that of father and younger son. Unfortunately, there is no example of a family with both older illegitimates and younger sons with which to see the full range of relations.

Nobles' generational status was another factor operating in their lives, but should not be seen in a deterministic fashion. There were families that varied from the pattern I have just described. Baldwin de Redvers, for example, partially fits the pattern as a late-in-life heir and ward of Henry who became a noncurial adult. He was, however, uniquely loyal to Matilda, precisely because she was the designated heir of Henry (that is, he was being loyal to Henry).[75] Other exceptions to the "second generation" pattern include the Mohuns, Tancarvilles, and Gloucester/Herefords, all of whom continued the patterns of service and loyalty well beyond the second generation of wealth.

The role of the daughter within the family is more obscure unless she was an heiress or a member of Henry I's family. We know that daughters could and did inherit land if no sons survived.[76] Most evidence we have of the relation between parent and daughter concerns the daughter's marriage. One Anglo-Norman woman, however, has left a glimpse of a mother-daughter relationship. Aelina de Rullos had been an heiress in the gift of Henry I and her price had been high. When she was dying, a widow, in the 1160s, she gave part of her patrimony to her younger daughter. The daughter appears to have been unmarried and relatively old for such a state, perhaps as old as thirty. Even more unusual is that none of Aelina's sons witnessed the document, though they were her principal heirs.[77] In this mother's final attempt to increase her daughter's portion, we see a personal concern. Aelina could have left her daughter's fate to her sons and their alliance concerns. Alternatively, she could have used the daughter's current dowry as an entrance gift to monastic life. Something, however, made her decide to allow her daughter a better chance at a "good" marriage. If it had been pressure from her sons, why were they not witnesses? No, I think the conclusion must be concern for this daughter as an individual.

The relationships among siblings are more evident than parent-child relationships. Brothers, like the St. Johns, especially worked together to help the family fortunes.[78] Fraternal relations could create a political alliance. One group of Duke Robert's supporters in 1101 was lead by three brothers—Robert de Bellême, Roger le Poitevin, and Arnulf Montgomery.[79] Certainly the Anglo-Norman nobles seemed to have believed that family *should* fulfill this function. However, the ideal of "brotherhood" by blood or marriage, while certainly understood by medieval nobles, did not *guarantee* the sharing of labor or consumption.[80] The ducal family's story is the classic example; for at least two generations the ducal competition for lands and titles was too intense even for fraternal ties. Far more examples, however, show siblings, like the St. Johns, working to help each other and enfeoffing each other.

We find another indication of sibling relationship in the way legitimate and illegitimate children were designated in the records. One of the reasons we have trouble identifying illegitimates is because there was no differentiation made between them and their siblings unless the chroniclers

saw a reason (such as the lack of consideration of Robert of Gloucester
as heir to the throne).[81] The same is true for step-siblings. Orderic tells
us that William Moulins-la-Marche had two sons (William and Robert)
by his first wife (the marriage later annulled on the grounds of consan-
guinity), then two more (Simon and Hugh) by his second wife who was
a daughter of Waleran of Meulan (Beaumont). Robert was disinherited
because of rebellion and his half-brother Simon was given his land.[82]
Furthermore, in an 1130 private charter, the designation is simply William
and Simon "his brother." In other words, there was no indication that
this was a half-brother.[83] While the heir's experience may have differed
from his siblings', Anglo-Normans saw each other and acted as sibs. This
practice differs from some contemporary continental practice, where certain names were repeatedly used within families for legitimate males
only—that is, the first name was clearly tied to the inheritance claim.[84]

The relationship between brother and sister was often strong. Henry I's
relationship to Adela, described below, was constant. Also from the royal
family comes the poignant example of William the Aethling. When the
White Ship went down, William initially was saved, However, he went
back into the Channel to try to save his illegitimate half-sister. Both died.[85]
It has been suggested recently that Elizabeth Beaumont's affair with
Henry I was initiated by her in order to gain the king's favor and pardon
for her rebellious brother Waleran.[86]

Family ties continued past the church door. Most noble families had at
least one child in the clergy. The fact that the relationship between cler-
gymen and laymen continued to be noted may imply that contact between
them continued. Such contact is known for the families who held political
power and whose stories were expanded in the chronicles. From his se-
curing the treasury through his reign, Stephen of Blois relied on his
brother Henry, bishop of Winchester. Through this political support, they
continued to act as brothers. The patronage between clergy and laity could
go both ways. A grant made to Walter "camerario et cognato meo," that
is, my relative, was witnessed by other relatives within the clergy, "William nepote episcopi et alio nepote episcopi."[87] A colleague of Orderic
Vitalis sought contributions for his abbey from his kin in southern Italy.[88]

In addition to contact between clerical and lay branches of families,
family relations remained strong within primarily clerical families. Patterns clearly established as family behavior for lay nobles were followed
by clerical families. Brothers helped each other, sons followed their father's
pattern of career, uncles helped nephews. The family of Samson of Worcester provides an example. Samson and Thomas, bishop of York, designated
themselves as brothers in documents throughout their clerical careers.

Furthermore, their career patterns were parallel. Each worked in the royal *scriptoria* and each served specifically at Bayeux. They were similar in interests as well. Each showed a precocious tendency to use surveys to administer their lands.[89] Like Samson's family, the Bohun family clergy "shuffled . . . back and forth" between Coutances and Salisbury using these as centers for their career moves. Furthermore, the nephews continued to use the family toponymic.[90] Henry of Huntingdon succeeded his father as archdeacon and, in spite of Gregorian reforms, had descendants making careers in the cathedral clergy.[91] The clergy were Anglo-Norman nobles in many ways. What is clearest, perhaps, is that in spite of the church view that clergy left their family, the Anglo-Norman clergy remained part of their lay family. Furthermore, clerical families show a definition of family shared with lay nobles.

As for lay nobles, the familial and feudal relationships of clergy overlapped. Seffrid I of Chichester became the abbot of the wealthy monastery of Glastonbury after Henry of Blois moved to Winchester. Seffrid's father was a tenant of Roger of Montgomery, who was the half-brother of the archbishop of Canterbury, Ralph d'Escures.[92] Could Seffrid's father have appealed to his lord to intercede with *his* brother to gain Seffrid's appointment? Certainly, familial patronage verging on nepotism was an accepted practice among the Anglo-Normans. John, archdeacon of Canterbury (*ca.* 1108/1115), became bishop of Rochester in 1125. He was the nephew of Archbishop Ralph d'Escures, who controlled the appointment of Rochester. Walter, archdeacon and clerk of Canterbury in 1139, also was elevated to the bishopric of Rochester in 1148 by his brother, Theobald, archbishop of Canterbury.[93] The archbishop would have understood an appeal from Seffrid's father. Obviously, the Anglo-Norman families shared a view of family without regard to the clerical view; that is, family ties crossed the cloister and the altar.

Within the family, the maternal uncle continued to play a special role. We know of clear examples of the avunculate relationships among the most powerful nobles (such as David of Scotland's support of the Empress Matilda), because of the nature of our sources—their politics was the subject of the chronicles. However, beyond the chronicles and notable political actions, we have further evidence in votive clauses. William d'Albini, earl of Sussex, included his uncle in his donation to Reading,[94] while his uncle Jocelin included William and William's mother (dowager Queen Adeliza) as his sister in his own bequest.[95] The avunculate relationship has been widely studied, in part because of its common appearance in important contemporary literature such as *The Song of Roland*,[96] it was a real social factor, not just a literary device.

A particularly interesting example in this generation occurred during the Anarchy. Whether people believed that the feudal and royal case was debatable or was unassailable, sometimes they stressed family loyalty as a strategy for swaying allegiance. Brian fitz Count equated the avunculate link with that of a brother when he tried to convince Henry of Blois to abandon his brother Stephen for his cousin Matilda. Brian stressed the family obligation that Henry *should* have had to his uncle, the late king.[97] The argument did not persuade Henry. Certainly, the maternal uncle was used for patronage if he offered a good opportunity, even if the family relied on the paternal line for land or identity. If a maternal uncle offered a better opportunity for education, patronage through enfeoffment, or marriage than a paternal uncle did, he was included in the family network, even if the agnatic line was emphasized for land.

In addition to blood relations, I would argue that we have evidence of friendship bonds, strong enough to appear to have created a surrogate family. Barlow provides an example of such a relationship in the story of Simon of Crépy, heir of Ralf IV of Amiens-Valois-Vexin. Simon was educated with the eldest sons of William I and Matilda. The author of his *vita* used the terms *nutrio* and *rutricus* when describing William and Matilda's treatment of him, and indeed, he seems to have acted as and been treated like a son. He left the cloister in 1079 in part to serve as an intermediary between William and his rebellious son Robert, and Matilda paid for his tomb when he died the following year in Rome. Barlow argues convincingly that he should be included as part of the family defined by William and Matilda.[98] It will also be argued that Henry I established a surrogate family, especially to replace his lack of a fraternal companion. These bonds were based upon sentiment but functioned as family ties. It is interesting to note also that one of the few variations in the formula for prayer requests is the occasional insertion of *amicorum meorum*.[99] This type of substitution has been found in other cultures, especially where families both have geographic mobility preventing continuity of residence patterns, and face economic problems creating need for mutual support. Additionally, it is found in conjunction with an adaptable cognatic, bilateral family structure.[100] We know that noble families were scattered through Normandy and England, and younger sons and lesser nobles were in need of provision. We know that a cognatic family pattern is indicated. This was the ideal situation for surrogate families.

Of course, Henry I's own family provides a prototype of the Anglo-Norman family. Here we have the most complete evidence of a family, allowing for the most personalized description of family relationships. Additionally, our evidence encompasses all the facets of family relationships found in bits and pieces elsewhere, enabling the description to be the most complete.

Like that of many other nobles, Henry's definition of his family varied with the situation. The narrowest interpretation, the legitimate, nuclear family, is found in the votive clauses of his charters. In these, Henry included only himself, his wife, his legitimate children, and occasionally Rufus, though not as his brother but as his royal predecessor.[101] However, the behavioral evidence is that he treated many other people as family members as well. The full range of his relatives, including affinal ones, witnessed his charters, and he served as the economic and educational provider for the cognatic and affinal family. Which members of the family participated in or gained from these activities varied with the situation. He kept active ties with relatives who entered the clergy. Finally, he brought into his family his illegitimate offspring and his friends.

Henry was in many ways a typical younger son. He was born "in the purple," probably in 1068, the youngest son of William the Conqueror and Matilda of Flanders. His early life is obscure. He was given a different education (a clerical one) from that of his inheriting brothers. William of Malmesbury makes one of the few extant references to Henry's education in his panegyric, likening Henry to Plato's philosopher-king.[102] We get a very different picture of the boy from Orderic Vitalis. Orderic tells of ten-year-old Henry joining his twenty-year-old brother William Rufus in pouring water on the head of their elder brother, Robert Curthose, in order to deflate the heir in front of his friends.[103] His relative youth also accounted for some differences between his upbringing and that of his siblings. While his brothers were of an age to fight with their father (or against him) in order to learn their role in combat, Henry was not. While still a boy, Henry appears to have been brought by his father on a punitary expedition, but probably was sent back to Matilda when fighting unexpectedly began.[104] Even though he probably had a less personal relation with his parents than did his brothers, Henry's relationships with his own wife and the next generation mirror the way his parents acted in a way neither brother's actions did.

His relations to his brothers were colored by the stakes of their rivalry—the Anglo-Norman realm. Here Henry's history is distinct from that of his nobles, even that of noninheriting younger sons. When the Conqueror died in 1087, Robert became duke of Normandy and William became king of England, while Henry's patrimony consisted of 3000*m*. The money was substantial but not so substantial as land, and Henry spent it trying to gain a land base.[105] In 1088, William II ceded to Henry their mother's lands,[106] but later disseised him of them.[107] Furthermore, since neither William nor Robert was satisfied with his inheritance, Henry's position was tenuous. William of Malmesbury states that Henry had a good relationship with Robert until the duke listened to "tale-bearers."[108] Suspecting Henry of favoring William, Robert imprisoned Henry for six months, releasing him only at the urging of the Norman lords.[109] Following this episode, Henry attempted to remain neutral as his elder brothers continued to try to gain each other's land. Once, he aided Robert against an uprising on William's behalf in Normandy, but this was proper behavior for a feudal vassal. However, when Robert and William signed a treaty in 1091 in which each made the other his heir, they also divided Henry's land between them, and proceeded to besiege him.[110] Luckily for Henry, the treaty did not last. Most of Henry's adult years before 1100, while he was trying to obtain a landed base, were spent generally out of favor alternately with one brother or the other. The six years following Rufus' death were spent in war with Robert, with each trying to gain the other's land. After Henry won in 1106, he would keep his surviving brother, Robert, in prison for twenty-eight years (1106–34).

However harsh this account reads, it hardly means that Henry had no family feelings. Indeed, he became the center of the family network. Henry and Adela of Blois were close in age and probably knew each other as children.[111] Adela ruled Blois successfully in the absence of her husband and during her son's minority, and she and Henry can be said to have had similar attitudes toward the details of government. Adela chose future courses for her four sons' careers, including making and enforcing the decision to pass over the eldest William and name Theobald successor to the county.[112] Henry was her choice to provide for two of her younger sons (Stephen and the oblate Henry) and two daughters (Matilda who married the heir of the earl of Chester but died with him on the White Ship, and Agnes who married Hugh de Puiset). Thus Henry's relation to his siblings was not as negative as it first seemed.

Henry generally had good relationships with strong women in the family. His marriage to Edith/Maud was arranged for obvious political reasons, actually sealing a political and military truce. It became, however, a partnership. Paralleling his parents' relationship, Henry left Edith/Maud in charge of England when he was in Normandy.[113] Both Edith/Maud and Adela can be said to have acted as Henry's "spiritual conscience." They were used as the avenues of appeal in the Investiture Controversy—Pope Paschal wrote to Edith/Maud while Anselm applied to Adela. Paschal and Anselm assumed that Henry would listen to these women. They were right. It was probably Adela who arranged the 1105 meeting between Henry and Anselm that led to the final compromise.[114]

The metaphor of a network is most useful to describe Henry's relationship to the next generation. With the exception of his nephew William Clito (Robert's son), who was a potential enemy,[115] Henry was the focus, the provider, for his children, his sister's children, his younger brother-in-law, David of Scotland, and even his brother-in-law Stephen's illegitimate daughter. Henry went further than providing for them; he seemed to enjoy many of them. Certainly Henry doted on his heir, William the Aethling. William of Malmesbury says that William "with the fondest hope and surpassing care was educated and destined for the succession." Henry of Huntingdon, in an elaborate description in his didactic treatise, has William wearing gold and silk robes, getting whatever he wanted from his father.[116] Henry was thirty-six when his first legitimate child was born. William was the heir Henry achieved after a long, unstable youth—he was the symbol of Henry's triumph. In addition, Henry also served as surrogate parent for the heirs of some of his most trusted *curiales* who had died and left minor sons. Many of these heirs were with William on the White Ship, returning from his homage ceremony in France. They died with him after having given the crew free access to the kegs. It is difficult to picture the image of this "glittering" but irresponsible court without thinking of its members as "spoiled."

Stephen of Blois can be included in this group of spoiled heirs, though his case is somewhat different. He was not the heir, but he had gained his status from his uncle's patronage, and he had been treated like an heir. Whether or not he was reared at court, he received his patronage without performing service.[117] He therefore developed the expectations of a magnate. Like the others, he fit into the noncurial pattern of witnessing described earlier. Though perhaps not reared as an Anglo-Norman, in attitude and behavior he was very much like those magnate sons who supported his bid for the crown in 1135.

Illegitimacy was common in Henry's family. Indeed, Henry grew up with the knowledge of his father's life as a recognized bastard. Obviously, William I was allowed to inherit the duchy in spite of his birth, but his status was not fully respected. Chronicles related that his relatives taunted him with the term bastard.[118] The next generation either changed its attitude towards illegitimates inheriting or, more likely, recognized the problems involved in inheritance and decided to avoid them. In the treaty of 1091, Robert and Rufus made each other coheir unless survived by a *legitimate* child.[119] The Treaty of Alton in 1101 apparently duplicated this agreement, but now between Robert and Henry and with the added significance that both men were now married and Henry's wife Edith/Maud was four months pregnant.[120] When Henry's only legitimate son died in

1120, he went to great lengths to ensure that his legitimate daughter, rather than one of his nephews, would inherit, although there was no precedent for a woman's inheriting the throne and this woman was not personally liked. No mention was ever made of the possibility that one of Henry's illegitimate sons might inherit. Yet fifteen years earlier, in a similar situation, Henry had made a different decision. When the lord of Breteuil died without a legitimate son, Henry had supported the illegitimate claimant to Breteuil over legitimate nephews, sealing his support with his own illegitimate daughter, Juliana.[121]

Though he apparently rejected any idea of his natural children inheriting the throne, Henry recognized and provided for at least twenty-one of them.[122] One, perhaps the eldest, Robert of Gloucester, was highly respected by both Henry and the nobility. Henry seemed to have treated his illegitimate sons, especially Robert of Gloucester, the way he treated his *familiares*—they served him in a variety of administrative, military, and judicial jobs, large and small, witnessed regularly, and received their rewards, their livings, accordingly, usually in smaller favors and exemptions but often adding up.[123] After the Aethling's death, Henry broke this pattern by giving Robert a sudden windfall, which has been interpreted as raising him to a status to rival Stephen's.[124] Herlihy's observations about age gaps may apply here. Robert was closer in age to Henry and was born before Henry's achievement of his crown and marriage. He was reared with the experience that he had to work in order to gain rewards and a career. He had a good working relationship with his father. On the other hand, William was the symbol to Henry of his hard-won achievements, and was doted on.

In contrast, Henry's relations with his daughters were good, but show no evidence of spoiling or of any difference in treatment between his legitimate and illegitimate daughters. His legitimate daughter did indeed have a personality problem, but it is usually attributed to her formative years being spent as Empress of the Holy Roman Empire, not to Henry's indulgence. Indeed, when her wishes—such as her desire to annul her marriage to Geoffrey of Anjou—conflicted with his political plans, the political concerns won over the personal. Though there is no parallel experience with the Aethling, it is hard to imagine Henry denying William. When we compare the Empress's experiences with those of her sisters, we do not find a pattern of different treatment on Henry's part. There was some difference in the status of the husbands provided by Henry for his daughters and nieces. One of his sister's legitimate daughters was married to the heir of an earl, the other to a landed noble. His brother-in-law's illegitimate daughter was given to the illegitimate son of the count of

Maine, who was serving as and being rewarded for being the king's chamberlain. As noted above, Henry's natural daughter, Juliana, was married to a natural son, though one whom Henry successfully supported in his succession battle. From these examples, Henry appears to have seen legitimacy as a status important in choosing spouses. However, it was not overwhelmingly important. Three other natural daughters were married to legitimate heirs of high status, the count of Brittany, the count of Perche and the king of Scotland. Daughters and nieces were equally part of the family, regardless of legitimacy. Furthermore, personal relationships seem to have been established among all of Henry's children, including relationships between the court and the daughters who had been married early in the reign and at a distance. The story of Juliana of Breteuil indicates that father and daughter knew each other well before the assassination attempt. Several of the half-brothers were "generals" for the Empress, and of course, William the Aethling drowned while trying to rescue his sister who was a member of his court.

Henry took the notion of "family" a step farther, including friends, and especially their children, within his perceived family. Men such as Alan Fergant of Brittany, the Beaumonts, Hugh of Chester, whom he trusted from his early days before they became his vassals, became part of his family network. He took care of their children and educated them like his own (even to different treatment of legitimate and illegitimate sons), arranged marriages for them, and forgave those who rebelled against him in a way he did not forgive other vassals.

When Robert Beaumont died after a long curial career, his twin sons were moved to Henry's court. The twins were supervised by a council of four men with ties to both the Beaumonts and Henry. Henry, however, kept the boys' land as a single unit until they came of age. Like William the Aethling, they came of age early, on their sixteenth birthday (1120). Following Clito's defeat, Waleran Beaumont was left in Normandy with his newly formed household. Again, as for William the Aethling, a new household was formed for the young heirs.[125] Waleran, impatient with the curial world where advancement took years, rebelled. The situation echoes Curthose's rebellion against William I. Henry allowed for Waleran's reinstatement.[126] Waleran's biographer gives several possible reasons for this unusual generosity: (1) the death of Clito defused the Norman situation, making it less dangerous to have a rebel holding the Beaumont lands; (2) the split in the royal court over the succession may have led to a Waleran party; (3) the twins' sister, Elizabeth, the only curial ward who had an illegitimate child by Henry I, may have intentionally seduced the king in order to help Waleran, or Henry may have felt guilty over seducing her.[127] Oddly, Crouch does not propose that Henry's decision could have been influenced by his feelings for the boys whom he watched grow up and took pleasure in. Crouch only sees the political motivations for Henry's good treatment of the twins (their Norman land would be very important during Clito's life) although he also writes that Henry obviously enjoyed "young, handsome and lively ornaments in his court."[128] Crouch even omits the possibility that Waleran's twin, Robert, although trusted and in high favor,[129] could have acted as intercessor. The twins had a younger brother, Hugh le Poer, born after the division of 1107. He was given some rents from Paris but probably no English or Norman lands. Oddly, given Henry's involvement with the family, the king did not give Hugh an heiress.[130]

Another of Henry's early supporters was Richard de Redvers. Richard may have been a tenant in the Cotentin, but definitely was with Henry by 1100 and gained much of his land from him. He died prematurely in 1107, leaving his son and heir Baldwin undoubtedly a minor. Baldwin is not heard from until 1121, but was apparently the king's ward, and probably was provided with a wife chosen by Henry I. His adult behavior was noncurial,[131] but he followed a pattern of loyalty that differed from other noncurial heirs by refusing to accept Stephen because to do so would go against Henry's wishes.[132]

Even within this surrogate family there is a difference between the way Henry treated the legitimate sons, especially the heirs, and the illegitimate ones. Many of these friends had illegitimate older children. Hugh of Chester, who died in 1101, was an early supporter of Henry. Hugh had at least two illegitimate sons. Robert, probably the eldest, had entered St. Evroul (Normandy) in the 1080s, but in the coronation elevations Henry called him to England to take Bury St. Edmunds.[133] Another son, Outher fitz Earl, tutored the Aethling, served as king's messenger and witnessed at the court, and had not been given a marriage before his premature death. However, his legitimate half-brother Richard, the designated earl of Chester, was a friend of the Aethling's and married Henry's legitimate niece (Adela's daughter Matilda). There is no record of service for Richard. Outher, Richard, and Matilda all died in the White Ship.[134]

Alan Fergant, duke of Brittany, had been married to Henry's sister Constance who had died young. Except for a short allegiance with Robert, Alan was a constant supporter of Henry. Henry gave one of his eldest illegitimate daughters to Conan, Alan's son by his second marriage and heir to Brittany, thus reestablishing the familial ties between the families. Although Conan was given royal patronage (exemptions in the Pipe Roll), he lived an "aristocratic" life when in the Anglo-Norman territories.[135]

Meanwhile, Alan's elder illegitimate son, Brian fitz Count, probably inherited no land, but his relationship with the king established him as a noble. Brian was a major *familiaris* of Henry and later of Matilda, rivaled only by Robert of Gloucester in the support he gave the crown, in his curial behavior, and in the patronage he received from the king.[136] It was Brian who in the remarkable letter cited earlier asserted the importance of family loyalty to Henry of Blois, bishop of Winchester.

Not only careers but education differed for the legitimate and illegitimate. Several bastard sons, who were not intended to enter the clergy, are known to have been educated at church as Henry had been, while the legitimates in Henry's care were educated at court with tutors. The Beaumont twins even appear to have been removed from the monastic school preferred by their father to the court when Henry assumed charge.[137]

The Anglo-Norman kings of England were still in many ways just nobles "writ large." Henry I's family relations do indeed mirror those of the nobles, though perhaps with an element of a fun house mirror which reflects the whole room but distorts and exaggerates parts of it. Henry's ducal-royal situation distorted his sibling relationship and allowed him to provide for an enormous number of natural children. His perceptions of and behavior toward his family were, however, like those of his nobility.

Notes

1. The kin who are recognized as kin and with whom a person has contacts are his "effective kin." Those closest to him in contact and aid are his "intimate kin." R. A. Houlbrooke (*The English Family, 1450—1700*, p. 40), believes that throughout medieval and modern history the "composition" of these categories was determined by "individual circumstances and preferences, not by any clear set of rules."

2. Mitterauer and Sieder, *The European Family*, pp. 71–92. Mitterauer and Sieder list a seventh function (pp. 93–94), the family as cultural consumers. However, this function is based upon shared residency patterns allowing shared leisure time. Anglo-Norman nobles often did not live together, though they regularly gathered, along with their feudal lord and vassals and neighbors, for holiday courts.

3. For the descent of patronage through the family see Painter, "The Family and the Feudal System," p. 11; Chandler, "Politics and Piety," p. 69; and Holt, "Presidential Address, III. Patronage and Politics," pp. 6–7.

4. D. Walker, ed., "Charters of the Earldom of Hereford" charter no. 3, p. 14. The narrow definition of family in prayer requests would continue at least into the fifteenth century. Rosenthal (*Purchase of Paradise*, p. 17) found in his study of the fourteenth- and fifteenth-century English aristocratic benefactions that "spiritually, if not politically, the family was a nucleated one."

5. Oddly, this charter had no witnesses, but his wife later confirmed it with the approval of her second husband, and his son later confirmed it with additions (Timson, ed., *Cartulary of Blyth Abbey*, vol. 28, #333–336, pp. 214–17). Many examples of votive clauses can be added. A very broad example of "fam-

ily" found in a votive clause is in the 1080 foundation of St. Peter atte Sele by
William I de Braouse: father and mother, Philip his only son, the souls of his
relations (*parentum*), the King, Queen, their fathers and mothers, sons and daughters (Salzman, ed., *The Chartulary of the Priory of St. Peter at Sele*, #1, pp. 1–
3).

William of Warenne included prayers for souls of his brother Rainald le Brun
and father and mother and *parentum* (B.L. Harley Ms. 2110, fol. 2v). The inclusion of the brother is unusual, but the circumstances explain this exception. Rainald had died in 1118, the year William married. William also confirmed a grant
(possibly at the same time) made by Rainald for their parents' souls (ibid., fols. 2v–
3r). In other words, Rainald was included in William's bequest to Castle Acre
Priory because of the simultaneous confirmation.

6. D. Walker, ed., "Charters of the Earldom of Hereford," no. 17; also see
charter no. 3. A charter to Kenilworth by Margaret, countess of Warwick, was
witnessed by her sons and heirs (Robert of Novoburgo and his brothers Geoffrey
and Henry) but also by her relatives-in-law, Waleran of Meulan, Robert of Leicester, and the magnate William Giffard. (B.L. Harley 3650 fol. 11r).

By the reign of Henry I, charters alienating feudal land by free alms included
(either within or as witnesses) the heir of the donor and some relatives in case
the son did not inherit (Thorne, "English Feudalism and Estates in Land").

7. Holt, "Presidential Address. III. Patronage and Politics," pp. 16–17.

8. For examples, see sections below on marriage and the maternal uncle.

9. This will be discussed below in chapter 3.

10. Holt, "Presidential Address. I. Revolution of 1066," pp. 196–98; "Presidential Address. II. Notions of Patrimony," pp. 215–16. Bloch, *Feudal Society*,
1:199–208.

11. Pollock and Maitland, *The History of English Law*, 2:387–88.

12. Ibid., 2:387–89, and 307; Lynch, "Sponsorship Among the Anglo-Saxons."

13. Pollock and Maitland, *History of English Law*, 2:387–88.

14. David Herlihy summarized the evolutionary arguments, especially Duby's
support of them, in "The Making of the Medieval Family: Symmetry, Structure,
and Sentiment," p. 122. More recently, however, Herlihy revised his opinion; see
Medieval Households, pp. 82–88.

Any good and current sociology or anthropology textbook provides an introduction to the theory of the family. Of special interest to the historian: Reiss,
"Universality of the Family: A Conceptual Analysis"; Freeman, "On the Concept
of Kindred"; Clayton, *The Family, Marriage and Social Change*; the many works
written or edited by Jack Goody especially *The Character of Kinship*, *Comparative
Studies in Kinship*, and *The Development of the Family and Marriage in Europe*.
For historical sociology see Laslett, *Family Life and Illicit Love in Earlier Generations*; Wall, et al., *Family Forms in Historic Europe*. Mitterauer and Sieder
(*European Family*) also have an especially good bibliography.

15. Murray, *Germanic Kinship Structure*. For the Anglo-Saxons, also see Lancaster, "Kinship in Anglo-Saxon Society."

16. Bilateral kin remained important into early modern times. Houlbrooke
(*English Family*, pp. 44–53) has argued that kinship ties remained alternatives for
support, especially for the top levels of the class structure. This fluid, bilateral
family, although patrilineal in inheritance, was used effectively for hospitality,
economic help, advice, and legal matters such as the execution of wills. In his
study of late medieval benefactions, Rosenthal (*Purchase of Paradise*, pp. 11–30,
93–95) finds that prayers were requested for both sets of parents. In addition,

some women's burial sites, and sometimes their husbands', were churches associated with her ancestors. Both activities show bilateral choices being made.

17. Smith, ed., *English Episcopal Acta. I: Lincoln, 1067–1185*, #10, pp. 8–9.

18. Goody, *The Development of the Family and Marriage in Europe*, pp. 266–69. Goody also points out the problem of using terminology as evidence of family structure, since the general terminology for English kinship has hardly changed in 900 years while the structure has changed profoundly (Goody, "Under the Lineage's Shadow," p. 197).

19. Holt, "Politics and Property in Early Medieval England," pp. 7–8.

20. This is exactly what J. C. Holt has tried to do. Holt has argued that the Normans introduced toponymic "hereditary surnames" through the agnatic lines. Furthermore, although the majority of the nobles did not begin to "inherit" toponymics until the mid-twelfth century, he argued that this was part of a growing concern by the nobles to define their family (Holt, "Presidential Address. I. Revolution of 1066," p. 200).

21. The Basset family included brothers Geoffrey (II) Ridel (matronymic), and William Basset (patronymic). Richard de Redvers had four sons associated with "surnames." The heir was called "de Redvers," two (seemingly the second and fourth sons) "de Vernon," and one "de St. Mère Eglise." This pattern continued in the next generation. Baldwin de Redvers had two sons who used de Redvers but a third, William, who used de Vernon, as did his cousin, son of William de Vernon. This third son, William de Vernon, however, inherited the Redvers earldom through lateral inheritance late in life, and his son in the thirteenth century took the name Redvers. Obviously, by this time, the name was associated with the title, though not exclusively so (Bearman, "Charters of the Redvers Family," p. 16).

22. Robert, earl of Gloucester, continued to be known as Robert filius regis even after acquiring the title. In *Reg.* II, #1347 and 1372, he witnessed as the earl but in #1373 he witnessed as the king's son. The men known to us as the Beaumont twins were known by many names. Waleran most often used de Meulan, and Robert used de Breteuil but neither used Beaumont (Crouch, *Beaumont Twins*, p. xii).

23. Eustace fitz John's son took the name of William de Vesci from his mother's toponymic (not the *caput*). Robert de Mowbray used the toponymic of his father's (Nigel d'Albini's) first wife's first husband's *caput*. Jocelin of Louvain (brother of Adeliza) married a Percy and his son was called Henry Percy (B.L. Harley Ms. 1708, fols. 109v–1103. This manuscript was recently edited by Kemp (*Reading Cartularies*, vol. 1, pp. 417–18, #553).

24. The name Alice of Essex is an interesting example. The toponymic "Essex" was probably from her first husband, Robert fitz Swain of Essex, not her second husband or father (Round, "Who was Alice of Essex?"). Also Cecily continued to be noted as the daughter of Payn fitz John in spite of three marriages.

25. Freed, *The Counts of Falkenstein*, p. 51.

26. Bouchard, "Structure of a Twelfth-Century French Family," pp. 44–47.

27. Ibid., p. 49.

28. See chapter 1 for the patterns of changes in names at this time.

29. Duby has made a great contribution to the history of the medieval family in his many works, especially: *Medieval Marriage; The Knight, the Lady and the Priest: The Making of the Modern Marriage in Medieval France*; "The Youth in Aristocratic Society"; with Jacques LeGoff, eds., *Famille et parenté dans l'occident médiéval*. However, his work is very much rooted in the sources he uses, whether

those of the Maconnais or the French royal house, and as such must not be too quickly generalized to apply to the Anglo-Norman world.

30. Holt ("Presidential Address. IV. The Heiress and the Alien," p. 2) bluntly states that "women were subordinate" but the only source of a legitimate heir.

31. Newman, "Family and Royal Favor," p. 300; White, "Career of Waleran," p. 24.

32. *FE,* p. 195.

33. OVC 4:160; 6:34.

34. Cronne, *Reign of Stephen,* p. 175.

35. This will be discussed below, especially in chapter 6.

36. Eleanor Searle ("Women and the Legitimisation of Succession," p. 163) reminds us that we must balance wealth women brought to a marriage with the family situation and with their own importance. See also DeAragon, "In Pursuit of Aristocratic Women," pp. 259–60.

37. OVC 4:300.

38. Henry disseised Richard fitz Guy de Raimbeaucourt of a manor, ostensibly in payment for a gambling debt. He demanded the money (25m.) before Richard left the dice table. Then, in spite of taking rents from the manor of Burton which paid most of the debt, he proceeded to disseise it (Fowler, ed., *Cartulary of the Abbey of Old Wardon,* p. 325, n.109b).

39. OVC 4:50, 282–84.

40. For another use of this definition, see Hanawalt, *Ties that Bound,* p. 219. There it is applied to late medieval peasant families.

41. Margaret de Bohun and Cecily, countess of Hereford (D. Walker, ed., "Charters of the Earldom of Hereford," pp. 59–73, 39–41), Alice de Gant (Greenway, ed., *Charters of the Honour of Mowbray,* pp. 75–79).

42. OVC 6:42–44, 156–158.

43. *HN,* pp. 66–67, Patterson, ed., *Earldom of Gloucester Charters,* pp. 95–97.

44. OVC 6:212–14.

45. Rousset, pp. 58–66.

46. OVC 6:402–05.

47. OVC 6:210–14, 278.

48. OVC 6:38; 3:166, 343.

49. *Gesta Stephani* (hereafter cited as *GS*), pp. 150–52.

50. *HN,* p. 56.

51. OVC 6:520.

52. *Reg.* III.

53. OVC 3:242–44.

54. B.L. Harley Ms. 3650, fol. 11r.

55. B.L. Harley Ms. 1708, fol. 20v (Kemp, ed., *Reading Abbey Cartularies,* vol. 1, pp. 404–05, #535).

56. D. Walker, ed., "Charters of the Earldom of Hereford," p. 37. While Walker says that this statement indicates only that her husband was sheriff, I believe it indicates that she had at some point functioned in this office. I know of only one other twelfth-century example of the word used in this way: Ela, countess of Salisbury, who is known to have accounted as sheriff (Great Britain, Public Record Office, *Lists and Indexes,* vol. 9, *List of Sheriffs*).

57. The amounts recorded in the Pipe Roll varied from 2m. (Ingenolda, PR p. 147) to 645m. (Lucy). See below, chapter 5.

58. Lucy was married to Ivo Taillebois, Roger fitz Gerold de Roumare, and Ranulf Meschin, later count of Chester. She had children by her second and third marriages only.

59. *PR*, p. 110; *Ingulph's Chronicle of the Abbey of Croyland*, pp. 259–60 is the only other source for Lucy's life. She is the subject of an appendix ("The Countess Lucy") by Brownbill in *Complete Peerage*, and is discussed in Chandler, "Intimations of Authority."

60. Chandler says that the lack of children by Lucy's first husband perhaps indicates that it was an unhappy marriage (pp. 8–9). I would argue that it is more likely that the marriage occurred closer to Ivo's death in 1094 than in the time of the next most recent record of him, 1071. Taking twenty years off her age makes it more plausible that Henry I could expect her to renegotiate marriage in 1135. I would propose that she was just pubescent at the marriage, which could explain her lack of children. I suggest a birthdate of 1076, first marriage in 1090 at fourteen (a typical age) which would have made her fifty-nine in 1130, still "marketable."

61. Crouch, *Beaumont Twins*, p. 4.

62. Herlihy, "The Generation in Medieval History," p. 364.

63. *Leges*, 59,9; 59,9a; 59,9b.

64. Crouch, *Beaumont Twins*, p. 8.

65. See below, chapter 3.

66. An interesting parallel is seen in the Anglo-Norman romances of the early thirteenth century. Crane (*Insular Romance*, pp. 17–24) argues that the Anglo-Norman hero reflects his noble counterpart's concerns with heritage and status. The literary crises are disseisins, the need to find a noble wife, and the need to continue a family line going back to the early twelfth century. Crane attributes this situation to Henry II's legal changes' eroding the noble's role. However, the noble's fantasy is that he was disseised nobly in battle (as in the literature) rather than with fines and court procedures.

67. Vaughn, "Robert of Meulan and Raison d'Etat," p. 372.

68. Crouch, *Beaumont Twins*, p. 8.

69. Herlihy, "Generation," pp. 360–61.

70. For Matilda of Flanders see specifically OVC 3:103–05. There was no change in William and Matilda's relationship after she argued in favor of her rebellious son, as demonstrated by her continued role in court (*Reg.* I) and the various descriptions of William's reaction to her death (Douglas, *William the Conqueror*, pp. 243–46).

71. Adela of Blois continued to advise Theobald during his majority even after she retired to the convent. Other examples include Agnes Giffard, whom Orderic credits with honorably running lands and educating her son until she lost reason to her passion (OVC 6:38–39).

72. Greenway, ed., *Charters of the Honour of Mowbray*, nos. 37, 200, 289; Patterson, ed., *Earldom of Gloucester Charters*, p. 157.

73. Atkin, "The Bigod Family," p. 138. Roger (1100–07) witnessed 69 times, William (1108–20) only six times, Hugh (1121–35) 44 times (*Reg.* II).

74. For details, see both the section on Henry I's family (below) and Appendix II.

75. Bearman, "Charters of the Redvers Family," pp. 29–40; R. H. C. Davis, *King Stephen, 1135–1154*, pp. 24–26.

76. Holt says that there is no evidence of a division of land among female heirs at the time of Henry I ("Presidential Address. IV. The Heiress," pp. 8–10). Milsom also argues for single daughter inheritance. ("Inheritance by Women in the Twelfth and Early Thirteenth Century"). However, both accept the noble's preference of a daughter inheriting to lateral male inheritance.

77. *PR*, p. 110; Stenton, *Facsimiles of Early Charters*, pp. 82–83.

78. Round, ed., *Calendar of Documents Preserved in France*, no. 724 (here-

after cited as *CDF*); Round, *Studies in Peerage,* pp. 66–67; *Magni rotuli scaccarii Normanniae,* 1:xcviii; Fleming, *Cartulary of Boxgrove Priory,* pp. 17–20. Holt also discusses fraternal behavior in "Presidential Address. III. Patronage and Politics," p. 23.

79. Hollister, "Anglo-Norman Civil War," pp. 317–18.

80. Holt, "Presidential Address. III. Patronage and Politics," p. 19. See also Chandler, "Family Histories," for examples of three different family patterns of cooperation.

81. Round, *Studies in Peerage,* pp. 125–26 *n.*3; Patterson, ed., *Earldom of Gloucester Charters,* passim; *Reg.* II and *Reg.* III, passim; *PR,* passim. In spite of his illegitimacy, Brian fitz Count was called "a man of distinguished birth (*vir genere clarus*)" in the *Gesta Stephani* (90/91) by an author who did not like him (ibid., 210/211). A problem in counting Henry's recognized natural children arises because of this sort of reference. G. H. White ("Henry I's Illegitimate Children," pp. 110–11, 119) labels Male #9, William, as a child of Henry's because he is listed as a brother of another natural child. White does not believe that maternal half-siblings were styled brother and sister and that it was "obviously more likely" that they were Henry's children (111 *n.*a). Closer examination of Anglo-Norman families casts doubt on these assumptions. While either may be true, neither is obvious. Gundrede is assumed to be Henry's daughter because a legitimate child of Sybil Corbet would have been too young to be holding land in 1130, but we cannot gauge the time of Sybil's liaison with Henry (although it seems to have been close to 1100), or her husband Herbert fitz Herbert's age, or the year in which they were married, so it is impossible to calculate Gundrede's age. White never considered the possibility of Sybil having had another lover or husband between Henry and Herbert. Because of the sporadic nature of the sources and the commonality of the designation, either situation is possible.

82. OVC 3:122.

83. B.L. Cotton Vesp. B. XXIV, fol.31r.

84. Freed, *Counts of Falkenstein,* pp. 51–52.

85. *GR,* pp. 454–55.

86. Crouch, *Beaumont Twins,* p. 25.

87. Mayr-Harting, *Acta of the Bishops of Chichester, 1075–1207,* pp. 95–96, #32.

88. Chibnall, *World of Orderic Vitalis,* pp. 73–76.

89. Russell, "Samson, King's Clerk and Compiler of Domesday Book."

90. Spear, "Une famille ecclésiastique Anglo-Normande," p. 25. The translation is Spear's.

91. Partner, *Serious Entertainments,* pp. 11–47.

92. Mayr-Harting, *Acta of the Bishops of Chichester,* p. 5.

93. Le Neve, *Fasti Ecclesiae Anglicanae, 1066–1300,* vol. 2. *The Monastic Cathedrals.*

94. B.L. Egerton Ms. 3031, fol. 41r (Kemp, *Reading Abbey Cartularies,* vol. 1, p. 369, #482).

95. B.L. Harley Ms. 1708, fol. 108v (Kemp, *Reading Abbey Cartularies,* vol. 1, p. 416, #550).

96. Farnsworth, *Uncle and Nephew in the Old French Chansons de Geste.*

97. H. W. C. Davis, "Henry of Blois and Brian fitz Count," pp. 301–03.

98. Barlow, *William Rufus,* pp. 15, 31–32, 36.

99. Examples are found in B.L. Cotton App. XXI, fol. 19r, and B.L. Cotton Titus C.VIII, fol. 18v. Thorold de Lisures gave land for the souls of himself, his wife, his son, and his friends (Timson, ed., *Cartulary of Blyth Abbey,* #341, p. 219). Cumin had friends included in his request as well as his uncle: "Pro

saluto mea et sponse mee et filiorum meorum et amicorum meorum et pro anima Willellmus Cumin avunculi mei et patris et matris..antecess" (Loyd and Stenton, eds., *Sir Christopher Hatton's Book of Seals*, #509, p. 350). Geoffrey de Clinton founded Kenilworth Priory for "my lord King Henry and wife and children (*filiorum*) and all relatives (*omnium parentum*) and my friends" (B.L. Harley Ms. 3650, fol. 2r). Robert de la Haia donated for his own soul and that of his father and mother and all "parentum" and "amicis meis uiuis & defunctis." The witnesses included his wife and sons who are not included on the prayer list (B.L. Harley Ms. 2110, fol. 70r).

100. For a theoretical discussion of friendship, see Allan, *A Sociology of Friendship and Kinship*, pp. 30–45. Pitt-Rivers ("Kith and Kin," pp. 95–97) describes the variations of "amiable relations" including nonjural ones of Friendship. He uses the term "surrogate" for adopted, that is formalized, kinsmen, but I would argue for a more fluid use for Anglo-Norman society. Another interesting discussion of the relation of friend and kin is found in J. Freeman ("On the Concept of Kindred," p. 210, p. 217 *n*.42), who mentions that words for friends were often interchangeable with those for kindred among "ancient teutonic peoples." Lally ("Secular Patronage, p. 168) adds to twelfth-century definitions of "amicitia," Francis Bacon's seventeenth-century one of a "bond of patronage between men." In addition, late Anglo-Norman (thirteenth century) romance stressed friendship as an "absolute value" (Crane, *Insular Romance*, p. 125).

In "Black Family Life Styles," pp. 191–94, Nancy Boyd-Franklin describes a bilateral, cognatic family with "non-blood friends" fulfilling family functions, similar to African tribal families yet adapting to the necessities of the United States. The situation is similar to those of white U. S. families today where geographic job mobility has caused the creation of surrogate families. My thanks to Mary Brennan for bringing this work to my attention.

101. The foundation charter for Reading Abbey by Henry I, Michaelmas 1125 (26 Henry I) included a prayer for King William, his father; King William, his brother; William, his son; Queen Matilda, his mother; Queen Matilda, his wife; and all his ancestors and successors (Kemp, ed., *Reading Abbey Cartularies*, vol. 1, p. 33, #1).

102. *GR*, pp. 467–68. For modern debates see C. W. David, "The Claim of King Henry I to be Called Learned"; Wootten, "Study of Henry I," pp. 4–9; and Turner, "*Miles Literatus*," pp. 934–35.

103. OVC 2:356–59.

104. Wootten, pp. 2–3.

105. William of Malmesbury says he hired mercenaries to fight in Brittany (*GR*, p. 468), while Orderic says that when Robert asked Henry for a loan to enable him to invade England, Henry demanded the Cotentin as feudal land instead of offering a straight loan (OVC 4:118–20).

106. OVC 4:148. Specifically what lands were involved or whether Henry ever actually held them is unknown.

107. OVC 4:220.

108. *GR*, p. 468.

109. David, *Robert Curthose*, pp. 59–63. Barlow (William Rufus, p. 266 *n*.22) doubts the details of this incident.

110. E. Freeman, *Reign of William Rufus*, 1:283–95, 319–21; David, *Robert Curthose*, pp. 78–79; Barlow, *William Rufus*, pp. 281–86.

111. The other surviving sister, Cecily, abbess of Caen presents different problems. She was an oblate in 1066, before Henry's birth, and took her vows nine years later. As such she probably did not have time to establish childhood ties with her older brothers and sisters. Wace, who was connected with Caen, wrote that

Robert presented a Saracen banner to Cecily when he returned from crusade, thirteen years before she became the abbess. Most recently, Marjorie Chibnall characterizes Cecily's administration as abbess as showing the "vigour and practical ability" of the Conqueror and Henry I. Chibnall also links the land surveys made by the abbey during Cecily's tenure to the *Leges Henrici Primi* and infers a "close personal link with the king" (Chibnall, ed., *Charters and Custumnals of the Abbey of Holy Trinity, Caen*, pp. xxi, xxxi. See also David, *Robert Curthose*, p. 124, p. 124 *n*.4.

112. OVC 3:116; Ivo of Chartres, *Epistolae*, #134, *PL*, 162:144.

Sharon Farmer includes descriptions of Adela in her article, "Persuasive Voices." However, she casts doubts on their reliability as descriptions of the real woman. Farmer credits part of the praise of Adela by the monks of Marmoutier to their use of another countess as a model (p. 526). However, both Adela's strong rule and her patronage of the monasteries could have been learned from her parents, with whom she was said to have strongly identified. Farmer also sees an implied criticism in the monk's description of Adela's role as conscience for her husband, Stephen, whom she convinced to return to the crusade which he had fled. Farmer argues that the monk crediting Adela with guiding her husband's decision supports Orderic's "assertion that the society had been feminized" (p. 523). However, the criticism of feminization had been levied against Rufus' England, not against Blois. Stephen certainly is accused of cowardice by most contemporary chroniclers, and rightly so, but I fail to see any implied criticism of his regaining his courage thanks to Adela's bedchamber exhortation.

113. *Reg.* II, p. xvii.

114. Cantor, *Church, Kingship and Lay Investiture*, pp. 217–27. In addition, Edith/Maud appealed to Anselm arguing the royal side (Vaughn, *Anselm of Bec and Robert of Meulan*, pp. 276–77).

115. Henry's treatment of his nephew is fascinating. William Clito was not yet five when he was captured at Tinchebrai. In a critical mistake, Henry not only did not keep him in custody but gave him to Robert's son-in-law (by a natural daughter) and follower, Helias of St. Saens (Hicks, "Impact of William Clito," and David, *Robert Curthose*, pp. 175–87). Clito of course became the focal point for rebellions. Such a mistake in judgment from the usually shrewd Henry has been explained by saying that he felt secure since he had a son of his own, but William the Aethling was slightly younger than Clito. At that age, neither boy could be counted upon to live to maturity. It seems plausible to add Henry's familial feelings to his decision. Henry continually would help the younger generation—his nephews and the sons of close friends—and he would dote on his own heir much as his father had. One would like to believe that Henry felt for his young nephew and allowed the frightened little boy to stay with a familiar relative.

116. *GR*, pp. 454–55 (the translation is from the Giles translation of *GR*, p. 425); Henry of Huntingdon, *Historia Anglorum et Epistola de Contemptu Mundi*, pp. 304–05.

117. Davis (*King Stephen*, pp. 7–8) doubts if Stephen was sent to Henry's court before Tinchebrai as Orderic implies, but says he was there by 1113 when he probably was 17 years old. At that time, he already had received the lands and title of the count of Mortain, and was receiving Malet's land in Suffolk. Whether he arrived at age 10 or at 16 or 17, there is no evidence of service performed for his patronage, nor for the additional lands received during the next five years.

118. OVC 4:83–85.

119. Barlow, *William Rufus*, pp. 280–84.

120. Le Patourel, *Norman Empire*, p. 186.

121. Hyams ("The Common Law and the French Connection," p. 89) argues that Glanville used a combination of French and Northern laws in eliminating a bastard as heir (Norman) but eliminating the concept of bastard through the mother (Northern). The procedure to prove bastardy was Norman, but the common law acceptance of mantle children was not.

122. G. H. White, "Henry I's Illegitimate Children," pp. 105–21; and Newman, "Review Essay of Royal Bastards," pp. 90–93.

123. Hollister, "Henry I and the Anglo-Norman Magnates."

124. Southern, "Place," p. 135 *n*.1. Also see Newman, "Review Essay," pp. 90–93.

125. Crouch, *Beaumont Twins*, pp. 4–8.

126. Reinstating the rebels was an unusual act for Henry. William (II) Warenne and Eustace count of Boulogne fought for Curthose in 1101, were forgiven, and at least in part reinstated. Each established good curial records and support of the king. Henry went on to patronize Eustace's family. The situation with the Beaumonts has a different quality however. W. L. Warren (*Henry II*, p. 211) argues that Henry II had a different attitude towards rebels such as Becket with whom he had had emotional bonds, since rebellion in such a case would be betrayal.

127. Crouch, *Beaumont Twins*, pp. 24–25.

128. Ibid., p. 7.

129. Ibid., p. 27. The nature of the reinstatement is disputed. Crouch says Waleran was high in favor with the court but not given all of his land; Hollister ("The Anglo-Norman Succession Debate of 1126," pp. 25–35) says he was held on a tight rein.

130. Crouch, *Beaumont Twins*, p. 9.

131. Between 1121 and 1136, Baldwin de Redvers left only six attestations— three for Henry I, two for the Bishop of Exeter, and one for the Exeter chapter (Bearman, "Charters of the Redvers Family," pp. 24–29).

132. Ibid., pp. 31–32.

133. Robert lost Bury in 1107.

134. *Reg.* II, #828, 875, 887, 893, 972, 1062, 1175, 1176, 1196, 1204, 1230, 1231; *GR* 2:496–97.

135. *PR*, p. 114.

136. Southern, "Place," pp. 142–43.

137. *Chronicon Monasterii de Abingdon*, 2:123, 137; Crosby, "Origins of the English Episcopate," p. 55; White, "Career," p. 27; Crouch, *Beaumont Twins*, p. 7.

CHAPTER 3

The Life of the Nobility

In many ways, the Anglo-Norman nobility were not unique. As for nobles elsewhere in Europe or like their own English descendants, the economic parameters of their world were set by their relationship to their land. The income derived from the land and the expenses necessary to feudal nobility limited what they could achieve. There are not even many differences through the categories of twelfth-century nobles, only different degrees. However, though much of the nobles' way of life had not changed, some aspects were affected by the governmental and cultural changes. In keeping with the intent of this work—to examine a social group within the context of its time and society—it is worth going through the details of their economic and cultural life.

From his land a noble derived both status and income,[1] his "orgueil et profit."[2] The lord received income from direct farming of his demesne and from the feudal profits of subinfeudating parts of his holding: that is, land produced profits from agriculture and from the obligations of the tenants. A variety of necessary services, such as milling, were the lord's from which either to profit directly or to lease. The right to offer and be paid for many of these services had to be obtained through royal grant, since the king held ultimate rights on feudal land; but, as will be seen, such franchises were quite profitable and much sought after. Judicial power over this land or over other royal land gave an individual status and authority; and the income from collecting fines made such power valuable from a financial standpoint as well. In addition, during Henry's reign, income from land could still be supplemented by rewards for successful military service.

For the Anglo-Norman noble, the land that provided his regular income generally lay both in Normandy and in England, with the English lands usually scattered through several shires. For example, Robert de la Haia, one of Henry's justiciars for Normandy[3] and a baron of the Norman Exchequer,[4] held inherited land in La Huie du Puits in the Cotentin,[5] and additional lands in Lincolnshire[6] and in Monmouthshire,[7] some in chief and some as a rear tenant.[8] Two members of the Ferrers family both held land during Henry's reign in central England, but Robert's were scattered through six counties and Henry's through seven.[9] This pattern of course stems from that established by William I. Scattered lands gave an income but were not easy to use to defy the king. By this generation, we see the nobles' attempts to consolidate these holdings by becoming, as Robert de la Haia was, subtenants for neighboring land. Although in this period all but the richest nobles were concentrating on either English or Norman land,[10] their land within England remained scattered.

A large part of the income from these lands came from direct farming, just as it did in the later Middle Ages. Painter has estimated that the average annual income from a knight's fee for the period 1180–1220 was between £10 and £20 with the value of most fees closer to the lower figure and the greatest of nobles averaging £115.[11] We cannot find equivalents before inflation for 1100–35, but no matter what the absolute amounts, the range between high and low was about the same. If a yearly income was even as high as £50, within the pre-modern world a fine or exemption of 35s. was high. One way to increase income was to expand the area under cultivation. There is some evidence that the nobles were engaged in assarting, though it was not yet as popular a means of expanding holdings as it would become later in the century. In 1130, Walter de Riparia was pardoned 35s. for one assart in Berkshire and owed two horses for a second. The importance of assarting as a source of income is seen in the fact that the horses were specified to be a palfrey and a hunting horse, two valuable types.[12] Possession of cultivated land was central to the nobles' lives and they were willing to pay for adding to it.

Direct agriculture was not the only resource of the manor. Rights over mills, fish ponds, and the like were profitable and highly desirable, since charges were levied on their use and the lord held a monopoly on the rights. Our sources give us many examples of these types of benefits as well as the king's control over them. Peter de Valognes, for example, was granted by Henry the use of two mills, multure, and the labor services of the Hertford burgesses.[13] A similar grant to Eustace fitz John indicated that the mill of Waren Mill in Spindleston "which used to render 60s. annually." This mill actually was worth 20s. more than the annual worth of the holding that went with it.[14] Henry not only gave Walter de Beauchamp the right to keep pheasants on his Worcestershire manors, but added the right to fine anyone 15s. for taking the birds without permission.[15] Walter added to both his table and his treasury with this grant. William d'Albini, Pincerna, received the right of wreck on his coastal land. A more dependable source of income came from a grant of the gilds in King's Lynn (Norfolk) with the right of market, tolls, and ferry.[16] Everything available was controlled. Robert de Lacy held half a fish pond in Cleve.[17] Both Hugh fitz Osbern[18] and Richard de Redvers[19] had saltworks, the only source of food preservation. Eudo Dapifer collected tithes on cow walks, swine walks and sheep walks in his honour of Preaux.[20] In addition to direct grants, the right to have custody of land was valuable. William fitz Baderon had custody of the royal forest and the royal castle of Hereford, a shire where he was a major landholder.[21] This sort of custody of a royal forest or castle was both an obligation and a potential resource. The forest was a mass of arbitrary royal rights, and fines were levied for infringing on these rights which the custodians often were able to usurp. In addition, the power to grant exemption from certain restrictions gave a person power over those dependent on the forest. A royal castle similarly dominated the area in which it lay and was a stronghold from which to defy weaker lords—including the king, as Stephen was to learn. Such rights and a variety of others, each with its customary fine for transgressions, could greatly supplement the ordinary dues from land.

Judicial rights—and especially the right to hold a seigneurial court— were a source of income to those who could hold such courts and such rights were explicitly guaranteed to "omni domino" in the *Leges Henrici Primi*.[22] Judicial rights given by royal grant were also profitable and prestigious. Sac and soc, toll and team and infangtheof—terms so often seen in royal land grants—gave the nobles judicial rights over certain types of cases and the profits derived from such cases. The greater nobility possessed these rights as a privilege of office; and the power and profit conveyed by such rights caused the rest of the upper class as well to seek them.[23] In addition some nobles held palatinates, and marcher earldoms had still other quasi-royal rights besides the more usual franchises. The palatine earldoms—Durham, Cheshire, and the lordships in the Welsh marches—were formed during the Conqueror's reign on the borders of the kingdom. Besides being highly consolidated holdings, they appear to have conferred jurisdictional (judicial and police) powers over justice and sheriffs—more than other counts and earls possessed.[24]

During Henry's reign, advancement and financial reward could still be obtained by military prowess. Southern has written that this continued to be the case in Normandy, more than in England where (as we will see) the emphasis shifted to other means of advancement.[25] Also, it tended to be especially true in the early years of Henry's reign when more land was forfeited in wars and available to give as reward to those who had fought for him. Rualon d'Avranches, a minor Norman noble, was rewarded for leading royal forces in Normandy in 1119—first with marriage to Maud, the heiress of Domesday lord Nigel de Monville, and eventually with the shrievalty of Kent.[26] So the traditional role of the noble, that which originally had justified his privilege, continued to be more than symbolic at this time, but in Henry's peaceful reign it represented a smaller part of his life.

While an Anglo-Norman noble had various sources of income, his expenses were also high. Not only were there expenses necessary to functioning as a noble, but this generation also faced increasing expenses for symbols of status and for cultural patronage.

The first of the necessary expenses, military service, could be a burden rather than an opportunity for gain. The cost of training and outfitting a knight was high: indeed, the need to meet this expense had been one of the original justifications for giving land in military tenure. Later in the twelfth century military obligation was often commuted to a cash payment. While the first reference to scutage occurs in the records of Henry's reign,[27] the evidence does not indicate whether it was a fixed rate or a regular assessment, and it does not appear to have become a burdensome expense until the end of the century. However, simply maintaining military "equipment" was expensive. For example, Robert of Bellême, earl of Shrewsbury, imported Spanish stallions. Going to Spain for horses had long been read as conspicuous consumption, but now is recognized as an attempt to improve his warhorses by breeding in more Arabian stock.[28]

Other feudal obligations could be expensive too. The dower aid collected in 1110 for the Empress Matilda was a feudal aid requiring a cash payment. Reliefs were heavy and sometimes required years to pay. Though the *Dialogus* stated that reliefs were based at £5 per knight's fee, the Master also emphasized the prerogative of the king in setting the rate.[29] Humphrey (III) de Bohun was charged £22 10s. relief for his father's Wiltshire land and an additional 400m. for the office of dapifer. The first year he paid 100m.[30] Alfred de Mayenne's relief for his father's large holdings in Devon was £110, £10 higher than the limit on reliefs set later in Magna Carta, after the beginning of the High Medieval inflation.[31] In 1130, William (II) Mauduit owed 40m. for his father's Norman lands and his mother's English lands,[32] and this sum had been due for nine years.[33] Richard fitz Herbert de Aunay owed 150m. for his father's land in Cornwall but only paid a fraction of it (10m.).[34] While these expenses were high, one of the benefits of subinfeudation was that it enabled a

noble to pass some of them on to his tenants. Most of the feudal expenses—gracious aids, relief, the cost of military service, rights of marriage and wardship, and costs of suit at court—were resources for him
as a lord of others owing him the same obligations.[35]

Besides feudal expenses, the Anglo-Norman nobles had the nonfeudal
obligation of danegeld. Henry apparently levied this Anglo-Saxon tax of
two shillings per hide fairly regularly, as both new and old danegeld
payments are listed in the surviving Pipe Roll.[36] Also assessed at two
shillings per hide was the sheriff's aid, which (though not itemized separately) was collected by the sheriff as part of his farm.[37] Avoidance of
common assizes through royal pardon, especially of the danegeld, was a
much-sought-after privilege and will be discussed when we look at the
relations between the king and the nobles.

Taxes were not the only royal imposts that became an expense for the
nobles. The increased activity of Henry's courts, both feudal and royal,
led to the levying of fines that increased the noble's expenditures. Almost
every shire of the 1130 Pipe Roll lists court payments for pleas of the
forest,[38] *murdrum*,[39] and for *pace fracta*.[40] Some records are general ci-
tations for the pleas before the newer itinerant justices.[41] The courts were
not just royal impositions, however, as the nobles used Henry's courts
increasingly to settle land disputes. A court case between Rualon d'Avranches and Hasculf de Tani over Essex lands ended with a royal fine of
60*m*. and a warhorse levied on Rualon, of which 10*m*. was paid into the
royal treasury in 1130.[42] If all fines had been paid (and from the evidence
this is doubtful), a noble's income could have been lost for several years.
Debt was a noble way of life.

Another major source of expense for the noble class was travel, necessitated by the scattered holdings of the nobility, by war, and by attendance
at the royal court. Humphrey de Bohun's holdings provide an example of
this pattern. His Pipe Roll holdings in 1130 included land in Dorset,
Wiltshire, Surrey, Essex, and Buckinghamshire. Both the *Red Book of
Worcester* (*ca.* 1125)[43] and the *Cartae Baronum* of 1166[44] show that this
line of the family held lands in Worcester as well. The Bohuns' Domesday
holding was a small fief in Norfolk;[45] and they held in addition patrimonial
lands in Normandy.[46] Besides the travel that such scattered lands necessitated, the Bohuns traveled with the court; Humphrey (II) de Bohun witnessed to royal charters from 1103 to his death in 1129 in places including
Salisbury, Norfolk, Nottingham, Winchester, Avranches, and Rouen.[47]
The *Liber Winton* shows that some nobles kept the equivalent of town
houses in the exclusive section of Winchester away from the areas of
commerce.[48] This was the seat of the Treasury and the site of many holiday

courts, which were attended by the nobles both because it was part of the feudal obligation (suit at court) and because they found it useful to help gain some privilege or decision from the king.

It does, however, seem unusual for the Anglo-Norman noble to have had a major residence in a town other than Winchester. Robert of Gloucester was a rare exception, with an establishment in Bristol. It may even have been part of royal policy to ban or discourage town residence, because walled towns could become positions of defiance or nobles might usurp royal town income. Henry would have given Robert the right to have a residence in Bristol because he posed no threat to the king.[49] In no case, however, did a town residence preclude constant travel.

Expenses for the average noble were increased by the necessity to maintain his own residence and court at the level of his status. Indeed, when he built, he did so not only for shelter but for this status as well. Orderic implies that this was the first act of men raised to noble rank, those "who have heaped up riches and built lavishly, on a scale far beyond the means of their fathers."[50] Later he wrote of Richard Basset, son of a "new man," who continued himself to serve the king, that he built a tower at Montreuil to magnify his own worth.[51]

The need to manage his estate as well as to enhance status led members of this generation to build households similar to the royal one.[52] Nobles' writs were addressed to "omnibus justiciis et ministris suis,"[53] "senescallo suo,"[54] or to "constabular' dapifer' baronibus castellan' iustic' vicecomitibus ministris et baliuis."[55] Some of the officers appear in royal witness lists,[56] making it evident that they sometimes traveled at least to court with the noble. Dapifers were common. Geoffrey de Clinton's confirmation of his tenants' gifts to his foundation at Kenilworth was witnessed by William fitz Radulf, "dapifer meo," as well as by the dapifer's brother, while another charter included William, dapifer of Hugh de Clinton.[57] William Peverel of Dover gave land to his dapifer Thurstan.[58] Chaplains, of course, are the most common officials. Margaret, countess of Warwick, had two of her own listed as witnesses in her charter to Kenilworth.[59] The late eleventh- and early twelfth-century counts of Brittany had stewards, chamberlains, and butlers for their honour of Richmond. These officers were given a great amount of responsibility for administration. By Henry II's reign, the count of Brittany, Conan (II), had nine officers in evidence as well as local stewards in Brittany and an hereditary moneyer.[60] The servants of the highest ranking nobles, like the servants of the king, were of the noble class themselves, and keeping these men as befitted their status would have been a major expenditure. Some officials held quite a bit of land in their own right. William fitz Nigel, constable of Ranulf, earl of Chester, was sufficiently wealthy to found the Augustinian priory of Runcorn.[61] Others were given exceptional responsibilities. The count of Meulan's steward, Morin du Pin, and the count's butler, Ralph, were given custody of the twin heirs.[62] Most of the early twelfth-century examples of large households come from the titled ranks, that is, from the richest of the class. By the 1140s there is evidence of at least four noblewomen having *scriptoria*.[63] By Henry II's reign, there is evidence of great but untitled tenants having large households.[64] Again, the long-term change, here the growth of a noble retinue, is seen to have begun during the reign of Henry I.

One way of safeguarding family interests as well as reducing expenses was to have a relative help to run the lands, even if the relative was a woman. There are many contemporary examples of a noblewoman running lands in her husband's stead, though again, they come from the top of the class and were usually recorded during wars (and as such, increase by mid-century during the Anarchy). We have already seen examples of women serving in various capacities—holding the *caput* against siege, negotiating her husband's release, running lands, supervising education and careers. This was especially true of widows who had developed good relationships with their sons. The practice has already been noted as evidence of the accepted behavior of noble women outside their prescribed role, the relationship between mother and heir or husband and wife, and the enlarged freedom of the widow within society, but it also reflects practical economic needs. As such, it raises an unanswerable historiographic question—is the *primary* motive for roles and actions economic or personal?

Another strain on income came from paying for the various means to salvation. Some twelfth-century nobles took part in crusades, and (though England was less affected by the crusading fever) English nobles like Payn Peverel did leave their lands for the east.[65] Roger, nephew of Hubert, sheriff of London, left for Jerusalem between 1128 and 1130. Higher on the social scale, Waleran, count of Meulan, went on crusade (in 1147–49) and returned to found the Cistercian abbey of La Valasse. Though the cost of the crusade may have been high, while he was gone his lands were granted immunity. We see this was beneficial since Waleran's lands were attacked by Stephen on his return.[66]

A major reason for crusading, especially for the older nobles, was to obtain grace needed for salvation. The same motive led to the vast number of donations of free alms to churches and the founding of religious houses. Since one of the purposes of alms and foundations was to obtain prayers for the donor's and/or his relatives' souls, the newer, "holier" orders (mainly Augustinian canons, Clunaics, and Cistercians) were heavily patronized, though Benedictine and secular houses continued to receive alms. Common types of donations were a church with its tithe on the donor's land, a church with its manor, or a manor with its income given to an established house. As Painter has noted, this type of alienation could be "a very serious drain on the demesne."[67] It eliminated income from the land in question not only for the donor but also for his heirs. When Ingelram d'Abernon gave his Surrey estate of Molesey to the Augustinian priory of Merton, the gift was confirmed by his nephew and heir Ingelram, and his overlord, Gilbert, count of Clare,[68] since in effect, this gift took income from these individuals as well. The dangers here are shown by the Braouse grant to St. Peter at Sele (f. 1080). His son witnessed the grant and "freely" gave his consent but later confiscated the land.[69] The Buillis offer a touching example of the opposite behavior. In about 1130, Jordan de Builli (a lesser noble) entered the house his uncle had founded. He was his uncle's heir because his cousin had died earlier, and he gave additional land with the consent of "filiis suis et amicis." The day he died, his eldest son placed the deed on the altar.[70] Motives are not always clear. When Countess Lucy founded Stixwould, a Cistercian women's house, in about 1135, her grant was confirmed by both sons, stepbrothers Ranulf, earl of Chester and William Roumare.[71] Since she founded this house at about the time that her five-year grace period was running out, the act may have indicated either her intent to enter it if Henry were to decide that she should remarry or a donation prayer that she should not have to marry. If it was the latter, the prayer worked. Henry died.

Almsgiving was varied and continuous. Robert de Lacy not only founded Pontefract (*ca.* 1090) but continued to make grants for its upkeep.[72] A glance at the Kenilworth Priory cartulary shows the wealth "which Geoffrey de Clinton endowed his new Augustinian foundation, making it one of the richest in England."[73] Variations in alms given might include practical extras. Adeliza gave Reading candles to light the crucifix and tomb of "nobillissimi" Henry I.[74] Even more practical was Alan de Percy's grant to St. Peter's hospital, York, which included two bovates of land for a vaccary with pannage for the swine bred there and a license for the monks to grind their own corn.[75] Other gifts to religious orders included sources of continuous income, such as Roger de Nonant's gift to Totnes of the tithe on the local fair.[76] Ralph Passelewe gave St. Mary's York two measures of wheat annually and sixty sheaves at his death.[77] Miles Crispin gave one-half of a hide to Abingdon in 1107 along with "hospitium in via Lundonia" at his manor of Colnbrook.[78] Giving hospitality like this could be an expensive drain on the noble's resources, but left the donor with the source of further income. In such ways as these nobles with less land could give alms without damaging their source of income. Men fairly far down on the social scale gave alms. One extraordinary case was the foundation by Rahere, the royal minstrel, of a priory and hospital of Augustinian canons with a stone church in London, both still bearing the name of St. Bartholomew.[79]

While Rahere, who was relatively low in status, gave to the Augustinian canons, so did high ranking nobles. No one section of the nobility seems to have given religious patronage in any unique way or to one particular order. For example, of the forty-three Augustinian houses founded during Henry I's reign, thirty-three were aided by members of the royal entourage.[80] However, these same houses were also aided by noncurial magnates, while curial families aided other orders as well. Southern makes an interesting point about the Augustinians. He argues that they appeal to the curial group because they represent a compromise between holiness and worldliness and have an independence—a description applied to curial nobles.[81] Among the Anglo-Normans, families and feudal tenants often patronized each other's foundations.[82] Reading, founded by Henry I, was patronized by his brothers-in-law David of Scotland and Jocelin of Louvain.[83] Patronage continued in both families. Henry's second wife Adeliza's family became special patrons—both her son by her second marriage (William, count of Sussex) and her brother's son made donations,[84] and another Reading calendar especially noting the patrons' deaths includes Adeliza and David.[85] Not only familial descendants gave alms to an ancestor's religious house. Nigel d'Albini gave alms to the foundation of de la Wirce[86] and to Selby, each of which had been patronized by the Domesday lords of de la Wirce and Tison.[87] Since Nigel had received the land of both of these lords, it would appear that a tradition of charity went along with the land. Such traditions passed to in-laws as well. Robert de la Haia founded Boxgrove Priory on his honour of Halnaker in Sussex when he acquired the land.[88] This honour was the dowry of his daughter Cecily when she married Roger St. John,[89] and the St. Johns became major patrons of Boxgrove.[90]

Very few nobles gave to one order only. Eustace fitz John, for example, patronized at least three orders with a variety of large and small gifts. He gave two churches and one bovate of land to the Augustinian priory at Bridlington,[91] land to the Cistercian abbey at Fountains,[92] land with a mill to the Benedictine priory at Whitby,[93] and land, perhaps in the city of York, to the hospital of St. Peter's York.[94] He also witnessed the foundation charter of Rievaulx (Cistercian) for his cojusticiar Walter Espec.[95] This pattern was usual. Robert Ferrers gave a church to the Augustinian priory at Nostell,[96] another free-alms church to an individual clergyman, Bernard the Scribe,[97] and land to the Templars.[98] He endowed Cistercians on both sides of the Channel: he gave 40s. worth of land in Northampton to the Norman Cistercian abbey, Savigny,[99] and one knight's service from his Oxfordshire manor of Skipton Lea to the nearby English Cistercian abbey of Thame.[100] And finally he gave part of his land and the tithe on it to the Benedictine house at Burton, a house from which he held land as tenant-in-chief as well.[101] Patrick de Chaources gave a mill to the Benedictine St. Peter's Gloucester,[102] land to the Augustinian Dunstaple,[103] and a Bedfordshire church in Toddington to La Mans Abbey[104]—the last being one of many possessions given by various individuals to alien houses during this period. Ernald de Bosco, steward of Robert (II) earl of Leicester, founded the Cistercian abbey of Bittlesden[105] and donated land to the Augustinian priory of Kenilworth, which was heavily endowed by earl's cousins, the Warwick branch of the Beaumonts. At the other end of the noble spectrum, Queen Adeliza gave gifts to both Reading (Cluny) and the Temple at Jerusalem.[106] Patterns changed in this time, reflecting the greater variety of religious expression. Beginning in the early twelfth century, after a long history of giving to Bec-associated houses only, the Clares gave a variety of grants to Benedictine and Cistercian monks, as well as to Augustinian and Arrouaisian canons.[107]

Occasionally the donation of alms for a soul's salvation caused conflicts among the donees. Roger Bigod, a great landholder in Norfolk, gave alms during his lifetime to Norwich Cathedral. In 1103, he founded Thetford, a Cluniac priory.[108] When he died in 1107, Roger was buried by the bishop in the cathedral, but the monks of Thetford claimed the body. The dispute required royal settlement in which the bishop proved that Roger had given himself and his family to the cathedral before 1103.[109]

The St. Johns are among the few Anglo-Norman families whose disputes with monasteries caused a clerk to record the story and thus leave an interesting glimpse of the personalities of the nobles. Thomas, the eldest brother, quarreled with Mont St. Michel because he cut timber in disputed woods to build his castle. According to the author (who, as a monk of Mont St. Michel, undoubtedly exaggerated), the monks prayed for Thomas, an act which caused Thomas "in horror" to rush "like a madman to the Mount" with his brothers to beg forgiveness "at the feet of the abbot." While penitent, he gave the monastery new land and the homage of himself and his men, and restored land over which the abbey claimed to have rights.[110]

In the twelfth century, patronage of the arts became still another expense. While we can and do attribute this to the nobles' interest in the

literary developments of the Twelfth-Century Renaissance, we also recognize that this patronage celebrated the patron's name and thus enhanced
his status. Evidence for this patronage is sparse, though both literature
and art showed major stylistic developments during Henry's reign. In
literature, both vernacular works and secular histories were written. As
was discussed in chapter 1, the first known Norman-French literature
dates to shortly after Henry's accession, with the earliest extant production being a translation by its author of a Latin text of the *Voyage of St.
Brendan*. This work was made at the request of Henry's wife Edith/Maud,
possibly for the benefit of the court ladies who did not know Latin.[111]
Most of the known patrons of both Latin and Norman-French secular
literature were members of the court, as would continue to be the case
in the second half of the century. Edith/Maud may have commissioned
William of Malmesbury's *Gesta Regum*.[112] Henry's second queen, Adeliza,
followed her predecessor's behavior, and Philippe de Thaon's *Bestiaire*
was dedicated to her; after 1135 she commissioned a now lost history of
Henry I from a poet named "David." However, Legge says that Edith/
Maud was the real patron of the arts. Adeliza was beautiful, full of good
works and piety, but not knowledge.[113] Yet, even if we accept this evaluation of Adeliza's intelligence, what we can see is that patronage of literature was now expected, at least of the queen and her court.[114] Custance
fitz Gilbert de Clare, an heiress who lived at Adeliza's court, was a patron
of Gaimar's secular works.[115] Another noblewoman, Alice de Condet,
probably the sister of Ranulf of Chester, commissioned a Norman translation of Proverbs. Again what was changing was both the role of a noble
and that noble's education. Both Alice and Custance would have been
educated during Henry I's reign.[116] Among the men, Henry's son, Robert,
earl of Gloucester, was the best known literary patron, with two of the
greatest twelfth-century writers, William of Malmesbury[117] and Geoffrey
of Monmouth,[118] dedicating their works to him. Two other nobles are
believed to have been direct patrons of literature as well. Either the royal
servant Eudo Dapifer or his chaplain Humpfrey de Thaon influenced Philippe de Thaon to write *Li Cumpoz,* a poetic calculation of moveable feast
days. The work was written perhaps as early as 1102, and not later than
1119, that is, very early in the century and the reign.[119] Walter Espec,
who was curial and active in royal service for a time, seems to have been
particularly interested in newer cultural developments. Walter, founder of
Rievaulx and Old Wardon, had a library which included Geoffrey of Monmouth's work[120] and was the patron of Ailred of Rievaulx' *Relatio de
standardo.*[121] One example of indirect patronage of twelfth-century schol-
arship generally is the earl of Warwick's grant of the right to hold a school

specifically "so that the service of God may be maintained by an abundance of scholars."[122]

Most of the secular interest in literary developments, however, were focused on Anglo-Norman works. This literature reflected the generation itself. The idea of using the language displays pride in the Anglo-Norman heritage but the language already was separating from the continental versions of French and had incorporated some English words. This process mirrors this generation's development of an Anglo-Norman society.[123] Still, literary patronage had not become a necessary part of every noble's life but was rather a growing part of curial life.

Changes in Anglo-Norman art and architecture are evident as well in the first half of the century. As already discussed generally, Anglo-Saxon sculpture and manuscript illumination were emphasized after almost disappearing during the previous generation. The more decorative Romanesque motifs broke the extreme severity of the architecture of the previous generation, and once again smaller stone churches were built. Evidence of lay patronage for art is even rarer than that for literature. Many of the religious foundations established by the nobles built stone churches during the founder's lifetime, probably with his financial aid, but in most cases, we cannot be sure if the founders indicated architectural preferences. Exceptions include Gilbert the Sheriff who founded Merton Priory in 1114, built the church at his own expense, and is believed also to have had it painted.[124] Patronage of more than one art form was evident. Three men who were patrons of literature also appear to have taken some direct interest in their buildings—Robert of Gloucester in the Tewkesbury facade,[125] Walter Espec at Rievaulx,[126] and Eudo Dapifer in Colchester keep.[127] Some variations in architectural preference have been ascribed to this generation of nobles. Earl Simon of Senlis, founder of St. Sepulchre, Northampton, had a round church built,[128] and Herbert the Chamberlain founded the priory of Weaverthorpe, with its many Anglo-Saxon architectural features, including the carved dial stone attributing the church to him.[129] A uniquely documented example of a noble's interest in art is the church of St. John at Shobdon, Herefordshire. Its founder was Oliver de Merlemond, dapifer of the Hereford lord Hugh de Mortimer. Oliver went on pilgrimage to Santiago de Compostela just after building had begun on Shobdon (*ca.* 1131–43) and returned by way of St. Victor in Paris. The decoration of Shobdon is so much a combination of the Anglo-Saxon style and the art of the pilgrimage route that art historians infer that Oliver may have been accompanied by his sculptor.[130] Obviously, many of the nobles in all ranks of nobility not only alienated income by founding churches, but also contributed to the expensive building in stone and were aware of and concerned with architecture. Less evidence exists for interest in illuminated manuscripts, usually restricted to books produced for the church and clerical patrons. However, one of the greatest clerical patrons of the age was the ecclesiastical noble, Henry of Blois, for whom the great manuscripts were produced at Winchester.

Expenditures on household, ecclesiastic, and cultural patronage, added to the necessary and expected costs of noble life, were a great strain on income. Many nobles could not meet their expenses and were often in debt. As an alternative to default, some nobles borrowed from the Jewish community. In 1130, for example, three Jews paid Henry for his help in obtaining payment of the debts owed them by Richard fitz Gilbert de Clare and Ranulf, earl of Chester.[131] Another example is seen in the ninth year of Richard I's reign when a debt of William Fossard held by the Jews was cancelled. It had been incurred by his father, probably during the Anarchy.[132]

Finally, over and above the need to maximize income to cover expenditures was the need to gain income to provide for family. Major concerns for the noble class were retention of their status and increase of their wealth. Of equal importance was the necessity of providing for the entire family.

All of a noble's children had to be provided for. The heir or heirs had to be educated and knighted, and younger children had to have income or professions. A well-documented example of how one might provide for one's children comes from the unusual situation of twin heirs. Robert, count of Meulan, divided his land between his twin sons (probably three years old at the time), naming their sister as heir if both should die and adding a provision for redivision should any of the land be lost.[133] When Robert died in 1118, his fourteen-year-old heirs were moved to the royal court, with tutors, and were knighted there.[134] The expense of supporting a court tutor would vary with the family. Knighting the sons was an expense that in the case of the eldest son (like the knighting of the royal heir) would be shared by the noble's tenants.

Where and how sons were educated is a puzzling question. The Beaumont twins (or at least Robert) originally were sent by their father to be educated at Abingdon. The king preferred that they complete their education at court. The indication is that there was a palace school run by Outher fitz Earl who was tutor to the prince. However they were educated, the twins definitely were "learned." The Gesta Regum reports that they took part in a religious dispute in the pope's presence.[135] Certainly, other young nobles were at court throughout the reign, implying the existence of some kind of on-going school. William of Aumâle was probably one of the last of these young nobles, spending his teen years there after 1127.[136] However, the nobles who are credited with being literate and patrons of literature had, like the Beaumonts and the king and queen, spent some time at a church school. Robert of Gloucester, for example, was sent to Robert Bloet of Lincoln for an education. The monks wrote of nobles generally who knew letters, that is, could read. There is a possibility even that Brian fitz Count may have been able to write as well as read. So far, however, there is very little concrete evidence for where specific nobles were educated.[137]

Younger sons presented more of a problem, and there were different strategies of providing for them. One strategy was to acquire more land to divide among the younger heirs.[138] Some men, like Robert of Meulan, were able to divide their land during their own lifetimes. Alan fitz Flaad, for example, left his English lands to his son William, his Scottish lands to his son Walter, and his Breton lands to his son Jordan.[139] In other cases the younger sons were enfeoffed of the elder, probably during the father's lifetime. In the *Cartae Baronum*, Alexander de Alno's only tenant was his father's brother Hugh de Alno. Most likely Hugh had been his brother's tenant. William (II) d'Albini Brito had subinfeudated almost half of his land to his brother in 1166.[140] Geoffrey de Clinton confirmed, as lord, a donation by his brother Robert to Kenilworth.[141]

Many younger sons and daughters went into the church in positions commensurate with their status. Students of the period know of Henry, bishop of Winchester and abbot of Glastonbury, younger brother of Theobald, count of Blois, and Stephen, later king of England. Adela provided for William, her eldest son, through marriage to an heiress; for Theobald, the second son, through inheritance of the patrimony; for Stephen, by the favor of relatives, that is, through King Henry's patronage; and for Henry, the youngest son, through the church as an oblate, later using the relative's influence for advancement. Henry I's clerical coronation appointments included the elevation to more prestigious and lucrative positions of three sons of noble families—Richard fitz Gilbert de Clare to abbot of Ely; William Giffard, son of the earl of Buckingham, to bishop of Winchester; and Robert, illegitimate son of Hugh, earl of Chester, to abbot of Bury St. Edmunds.[142] All of the appointees either were related to or were themselves loyal followers of Henry. Clerical life was a way of providing for daughters as well. Three of the daughters of Robert fitz Hamon entered religious life; Cecily to Shaftesbury, Hawise to Wilton, and a third to Malling. Shaftesbury was particularly popular for noble daughters.[143]

Another way of providing for younger sons and for daughters was to arrange a marriage to an heir of equal or preferably higher status and wealth. As we will see, the arranged marriage was crucial for the family's success and various strategies are evident. Some tried to join particular families, others to stay within a general region, still others to stay within a certain rank. The fitz Johns made three marriages into the Lacy family.[144] Miles of Gloucester's family ties were concentrated in a region.[145] Robert of Meulan's third son, known as Hugh "the Poor," reestablished his birth status as a great noble by marrying a Bedford heiress, the daughter of Simon de Beauchamp.[146]

Through a unique document, we have a record of an 1123 marriage settlement in which Richard Basset was granted the right to marry Matilda, daughter of the late Geoffrey Ridel. Although her dowry of land was worth only four knights' fees, he also received marriage rights over Geoffrey's other daughters.[147] Richard was also able to become the guardian of Geoffrey's heir, Robert, and to arrange for Robert to marry Richard's niece with the proviso that if the marriage produced no children, Richard was to be Robert's heir. By the terms of this grant, Richard Basset not only received the income from his wife's dowry and provided for his niece, but also received Robert's income while he was a minor and became Richard's potential heir. Obviously, guardianship and rights to marriage could be a very profitable addition to a noble's income. If marriage was to a widow, other profits were possible. For example, Drew de Moncei was granted the wardship of Hugh de Gournai, son of Edith de Warenne, widow of Gerard de Gournai.[148] Taking on the obligation of guardianship could add to the noble's income as well, though not as permanently as marriage did. In 1130, Geoffrey de Clinton owed 80m. for the custody of the minor son of William of Dives with his Northampton land.[149] Lucrative guardianship was not restricted to children, however. John Belet was appointed custodian of Battle Abbey after the abbot died by the regent Roger of Salisbury while Henry was in Normandy, and as the Battle chroniclers noted, John held it "not to his own disadvantage."[150]

All the alternatives which the nobles could use to add to their income could be obtained on their own or with royal favor. However, as we will see, the most profitable increasingly depended on royal favor—often as a function of royal service—as a means of enhancing status and increasing income.

To illustrate the way in which one family provided for itself and the types of expense such a family incurred, let us consider two generations of one family, Nigel d'Albini and his son Roger de Mowbray. While the family had been in England for a generation, Nigel was a younger son who received little, if any, of his father's land, while his brother received the Norman patrimony. Mostly through royal favor, Nigel acquired much land both in England and in Normandy, making him the first generation to attain high noble status.[151] His English holdings lay mostly in the north, but included some lands in Essex[152] and Kent.[153] For his service he received land near his other land in the north, and was thereby helped to consolidate his holdings.[154] The family was tied to several other families by feudal and marital connections. They held land of the counts of Meulan[155] and Mortain,[156] and were lords to Eustace fitz John,[157] another justiciar in the northern counties.[158] Subinfeudation could benefit a noble. This is seen in a case involving the wills of Slenigford, Grantelay, and Cnarrford, which Roger held of the archbishop of York for a quarter of a knight's fee as his father Nigel had held them. Roger granted this holding to Hugh de Cramaville and his heirs for half a knight's fee, though Roger would "not demand more than belongs to half a knight's service according to what is demanded from him for the fourth part of a knight."[159] In other words, they had been making a profit from it.

Both generations used marriage well, and so increased the family's holdings, especially in the northern counties. Nigel's first wife was the heiress Maud Laigle. Maud had been divorced from the imprisoned and dispossessed earl of Northumberland, Robert de Mowbray. The king gave Mowbray's lands to her to take to her new husband whom the king chose for her, a great reward for Nigel. Her life appears to be a textbook case of the controlled heiress. Nigel had the childless marriage annulled but retained Mowbray's land, including the Norman *caput,* and her northern land. He then married another heiress, Gundrede de Gournai, who also held northern land with castles. Their son Roger married Alice de Gant, a widow, also a northern heiress.[160] Obviously, all three marriages were used to build a feudal base in northern England. However, the role of the women in this family varied. Orderic says that Nigel treated Maud with respect only while her brothers lived. Her activity appears strictly limited. No charters of hers survive, although she witnessed Nigel's.[161] She appears to have been the classic pawn. However, as already noted, Gundrede was active in her twenty-five years as a widow. Though she does not appear to have been her son's guardian, she later worked well with him. Her attestations, preceding those of her daughter-in-law, show her role within the family. She also issued charters on her own. Roger's wife, Alice, not only issued and witnessed charters but had a seal. All this makes it apparent that Nigel gave a less active role to women than did his son. We can also see that Nigel maintained ties with his elder brother. To ensure that the inheritance remained in the family, Nigel had made this brother, William d'Albini Pincerna, heir prior to Roger's birth.[162] However, the brothers do not seem to have acted together politically or administratively.

Though Roger was a minor at his father's death, we do not know who his guardian was (though it does not appear to have been his uncle or mother), we only know that a court case having to do with one of his inherited fees was postponed in 1130 until he was knighted.[163]

Nigel would have spent much time traveling among his landholdings, including Normandy, since the Norman land was considered the family's *caput*.[164] In addition, he traveled a great deal both as royal justiciar in the northern counties,[165] and with the court.[166] Nigel maintained his own household, as evidenced by the Pipe Roll reference to his minor son's dapifer.[167] Evidence of numbers of household officials and even entertainers increases in Roger's charters. This would have increased his prestige and free time, but also his expenses. Both men, along with Gundrede and Alice, had their own chaplains.[168] Both Nigel and Roger, as did their wives, gave much patronage to a number of religious orders;[169] and as already noted, Nigel continued donating to the church patronized by the original tenants of the land that he had been granted. As did others of his class, Roger went on crusade. His biographer states that he probably went on three, each after some failure or disappointment—the first in the 1140s after his first adult military experience failed; the second after the collapse of a rebellion in the late 1170s; and the third after his wife's death in 1186–87. During the last crusade, he was captured and ransomed from the Saracens, and then died at age sixty-five.[170]

Nigel had made the family fortune through royal service and marriage, and had established a network of feudal ties through the nobility. His son, born late in Nigel's life, was reared like a great noble. Roger increased living expenses, and lived a noncurial life as seen in his lack of attestations, typical of a second generation noble.

The description of the Albini/Mowbray family shows how social mobility and status could be increased by royal service, royal favor, and family connections, though expenditures also increased with any increase of income and status. The king was often the source of additional income and power, and rewards for serving him included grants of land and rich heiresses. Henry I's growing administrative needs and his preferences for men dependent upon his favor gave many the opportunity to gain such rewards. The description of this family, however, also shows how the second generation could change the family lifestyle and resources.

Notes

1. A full discussion of twelfth- and thirteenth-century nobles' income and expenditure is found in Painter, *Studies in the History of the English Feudal Barony.*

2. Boutruche, *Seigneurié et féodalité*, 2:40.

3. *Reg.* II, p. xii.

4. Haskins, *Norman Institutions*, pp. 89, 99.

5. Loyd, *The Origins of Some Anglo-Norman Families*, p. 51.

6. *PR*, pp. 120, 121; *Reg.* II, #1816; *Lind. Surv.*, pp. 239–59, passim.

7. *Reg.* II, #1307.

8. In the Well wapentake of Lincolnshhire, Robert held three carucates in chief and an additional three carucates and four bovates as a tenant (*Lind. Surv.*, L 6/2 and 6/4).

9. Robert Ferrers held land in Nottinghamshire (*PR*, p. 7), Staffordshire (*PR*, p. 76), Berkshire (*PR*, p. 124), Leicestershire (*Leic. Surv.*, pp. 14, 15, 18–22, 26), Northamptonshire (*Nhants Surv.*, pp. 365, 374, 382), and Lincolnshire (*Lind. Surv.*, L 1/13). Henry Ferrers held land in Oxfordshire (*PR*, p. 6), Nottinghamshire (*PR*, pp. 11–12), Buckinghamshire (*PR*, p. 102), Rutland (*PR*, p. 135), and Herefordshire (*Heref. Dd.*, p. 77).

10. Boston, "Territorial Interests of the Anglo-Norman Aristocracy," pp. 38–49. Boston's table of families deemed "Anglo-Norman" consists mainly of those I term magnate, although a few service families and new men who began in Normandy are on the list. Those deemed "English" have the full range of my classifications *except* the magnates.

11. Painter, *Studies*, pp. 46, 170, 172.

12. *PR*, p. 125 (*bis*).

13. *Reg.* II, #1121.

14. Ibid., #1279.

15. Ibid., #1024. He also received the right of free warren for his land and the land of one of his knights (#1808).

16. Ibid., #911.

17. *Heref.Dd.*, p. 9.

18. *The Cartulary of Worcester Cathedral Priory* [hereafter cited as *Worc. Cart.*], #149, p. 24.

19. Wrottesley, ed., *Burton Chartulary*, p. 51.

20. *CDF*, #97, p. 27.

21. *Herefd. Dd.*, pp. 9, 18, 55, 56. For the forests during this period see Young, *The Royal Forests;* and Cronne, "The Royal Forest in the Reign of Henry I."

22. *Leges*, c.55, 1,1a and 1b (p.173).

23. Ibid., c.9,11; c.20,2; c.20,3. Examples of grants are found in *Reg.* II, #648, 911, 1222, 1224, 1279, 1517, and 1524.

24. Painter, *Studies*, pp. 112–16. For decades, historians believed that marcher lords held almost absolute judicial power in their areas. This view has been seriously undermined by Alexander ("The Alleged Palatinates of Norman England"). However, the marcher lords did have power greater than the average.

25. Southern, "Place," p. 136.

26. Stapleton, "Observations upon the Succession of the Barony of William of Arques," pp. 216–20.

27. Stenton (*First Century*, pp. 177–81) and more recently, Keefe (*Feudal Assessments*, p. 26) present the evidence of scutage in Henry's reign.

28. Giraldus Cambrensis, *Giraldi Cambrensis opera*. vol. 4, p. 143. R. H. C. Davis's recent investigation of medieval horsebreeding ("The Production and Breeding of the Medieval War Horse") has shown this to be more than conspicuous consumption.

29. Richard fitz Nigel, *Dialogus de Scaccario*, p. 96. The Magna Carta (c.2), of course, fixed a reasonable relief for a baron at £100, for a knight at £5 (100s.);

but Painter's studies show that for thirty of forty-one barons, it was at least a year's income (Painter, *Studies,* p. 57).

30. *PR,* p. 18.

31. Ibid., p. 153. He paid £40 the first year.

32. Ibid, p. 38.

33. *Reg.* II, #1255. This presumes that the Norman lands descended to him with his mother's land.

34. *PR,* pp. 158–59.

35. Full discussions of the feudal system and its obligations are found in Stenton, *First Century,* and in Pollock and Maitland, *History of English Law.*

36. Painter, *Studies,* pp. 74–79. Also see Mooers' various works on the dane-geld in the Pipe Roll.

37. Painter, *Studies,* pp. 83–84.

38. For example, *PR,* p. 47.

39. For example, *PR,* pp. 69–70.

40. For example, *PR,* p. 45.

41. For example, *PR,* pp. 34–35.

42. Ibid., p. 58.

43. Hollings, ed., *The Red Book of Worcester,* 2:412, 418.

44. *RB,* 1:299.

45. Painter, "The Family and the Feudal System," pp. 7–8.

46. *RB* 2:628 (a survey of 1172).

47. *Reg.* II, #626, 877, 918, 1160, 1015, 1427, 1598.

48. *Liber Winton.* For example, greater nobles such as the counts of Meulan (p. 56, #158) and Warwick (pp. 66–67, #279) and rising clerks like Bernard the Scribe (*Reg.* II, #1365, 1676) held land or houses at Winchester. Biddle notes that the distribution of property indicates that the richest only held property in Winchester for their visits to the court (*Liber Winton,* p. 387). A glance at the map on p. 388 (fig. 21) shows that the magnates, nobles, and *curiales* held property mainly on less populated streets while the commercial area centered on High Street.

49. Russell, "Demographic Aspects of the Norman Invasion," p. 19.

50. OVC 6:17.

51. OVC 6:468. Using the more complete later twelfth-century records, Painter estimated that a castle would have cost a minimum of three to four years' income (*Studies,* p. 173).

52. Stenton, *First Century,* pp. 69–80.

53. Ibid., Appendix 14, p. 265.

54. Ibid., Appendix 15, p. 266.

55. Ibid., Appendix 24, p. 271.

56. For example, Odard, steward of the count of Meulan (*Reg.* II, #1235); Geoffrey, chancellor of Ranulf, earl of Chester (*Reg.* II, #1389); and Stephen, dapifer of Richard fitz Gilbert, count of Clare (*Reg.* II, #1874).

57. B.L. Harley Ms. 3650, fol. 3r.

58. *Reg.* II, #1295.

59. B.L. Harley Ms. 3650, fol. 11r.

60. Farrer and Clay, eds., *Early Yorkshire Charters* (hereafter cited as *EYC*) 4:102, 105–06. Conan's nine officials were dapifer, constable, chamberlain, lardiner, marshal, butler, sheriff of the honour, bailiff of the lord's court, and chancellor. As Clay points out, chancellors were rare.

61. *Reg.* II, #1838 gave land of Pyrton and Clare (Oxfordshire) to the monks of Harley; #1905 confirms fitz Nigel's son's gift of the manor of Norton to its monks; *Reg.* III, #119 gave the church of Flamborough in the East Riding of

York to Bridlington; Ransome, ed., *Chartulary of Tockwith alias Scokirk,* #64, p. 201 gave one-half carucate of land to Nostell. Tait, ed. (*The Foundation Charter of Runcorn (later Norton) Priory,* pp. 10–11) says fitz Nigel had thirty manors in Cheshire. Tait also believes that he may have been a member of the wealthy Gant family (ibid., p. 7).

62. Crouch, *Beaumont Twins,* pp. 4–8.

63. Examples of women issuing their own charters include Mabel of Glouces-ter (Patterson, *Earldom of Gloucester Charters,* p. 167), Cecily, countess of Here-ford (D. Walker, "Charters of the Earldom of Hereford," pp. 39–41), Margaret de Bohun (ibid., pp. 59–73), and Alice de Gant (ibid., pp. 75–79).

64. For example, William fitz Humphrey's grant of land to Rievaulx was witnessed by Hugh fitz William, dapifer to Everard de Ros (*EYC* 4:#95, p. 126). The Ros family had been dapifers to the counts of Aumâle, although Everard de Ros paid to be released from the service in 1130 (*PR,* p. 32).

65. Edgington, "Pagan Peverel," pp. 90–93.

66. White, "Career," pp. 38–41; Crouch, *Beaumont Twins,* pp. 66–69, 74.

67. Painter, "Family," p. 12. For an examination of the motives involved see Chandler, "Politics and Piety," pp. 63–71; Harper-Bill, "The Piety of the Anglo-Norman Knightly Class"; E. Mason, "Timeo Barones et Donas Ferentes." It is interesting to compare this to the royal benefactions; See E. Mason, "*Pro Statu et Incolumnitate Regni Mei:* Royal Monastic Patronage 1066–1154."

68. Heales, *Records of Merton Priory in the County of Surrey,* Appendix #2, pp. ix-x; translation, pp. 13–14.

69. Salzman, ed., *Chartulary of the Priory of St. Peter at Sele,* #1 pp. 13 and xii.

70. Timson, ed., *Cartulary of Blyth Abbey,* vol. 28, p. 213, #331.

71. B.L. Add. Ms. 46701, fol. 1r–1v.

72. Holmes, ed., *Chartulary of St. John of Pontefract,* 1:23–24, #vi. It was, of course, less of a burden to found a Cistercian house since wasteland or land far from areas of cultivation were sought by the Cistercians (B. Hill, *English Cistercian Monasteries,* pp. 46–50).

73. Southern, "Place," pp. 137–39 for the quotation and evaluation of B.L. Harley Ms. 3650.

74. B.L. Harley Ms. 1708, fol. 20v (Kemp, ed., *Reading Abbey Cartularies,* vol. 1, pp. 404–05, #535).

75. *EYC* 11: #6 and #7, pp. 22–23.

76. Watkin, *History of Totnes Priory,* vol. 1, pp. 27–31.

77. Dugdale, *Monasticon Anglicanum* (hereafter cited as *Mon.Ang.*), vol. 5, pp. 142–43.

78. *Chronicon Monasterii de Abingdon,* vol. 2, p. 97.

79. Dickinson, *The Origins of the Austin Canons,* p. 126.

80. Ibid., p. 128. For a brief analysis of the Anglo-Norman Cluniac houses and their patrons see Golding, "The Coming of the Cluniacs."

81. Southern, "Place," pp. 138–39.

82. Painter ("Family," p. 11) gives the example of the d'Oilli foundation of Oseney, which was patronized by his descendants and by his tenant family of Basset.

83. B.L. Harley Ms. 1708, fol. 19r (Kemp, eds., *Reading Abbey Cartularies,* vol. 2, p. 345, #1276); fol. 108v (Kemp, vol. 1, p. 416, #550).

84. Ibid., fols. 109–10 (Kemp, vol. 1, pp. 417–18, #552, 553; p. 420, #556).

85. B.L. Cotton Vesp. E.V. fols. 12v and 13v.

86. *Mon.Ang.,* 7, p. 996, I, II, III, Monk's Kirby, Warwickshire.

87. Ibid., 3, p. 500, #X.

88. Fleming, *Cartulary of Boxgrove Priory,* pp. 16–17.

89. *Magni rotuli scaccarii Normanniae,* vol. 1, p. xcviii.

90. Fleming, *Cartulary of Boxgrove Priory,* pp. 17–20.

91. *Reg.* III, #119, 120; *EYC* 1, #360, p. 282.

92. *Reg.* III, #335.

93. Ibid., #942.

94. *EYC* 1, #219, pp. 181–182.

95. Atkinson, *Cartularium abbathiae de Rievalle,* #XLII.

96. *Reg.* II, #1320; also Smith, *English Episcopal Acta. I,* #12, p. 10.

97. *Reg.* II, #1677.

98. *Reg.* III, #863.

99. *CDF,* #806. For the Ferrers family relationship to Savigny see M. Jones, "The Charters of Robert II de Ferrers."

100. Salter, ed., *The Thame Cartulary,* vol. 1, p. 78.

101. Bridgeman, ed., "The Burton Abbey Twelfth Century Surveys," pp. 216, 240.

102. *Historia et cartularium monasterii Sancti Petri Gloucestriae,* vol. 1, p. 89.

103. Fowler, ed., *A Digest of the Charters Preserved in the Cartulary of the Priory of Dunstable,* pp. 67–69, 80.

104. *Reg.* II, #960.

105. *Reg.* III, #103.

106. B.L. Harley Ms. 1708, fol. 20v (Kemp, ed., *Reading Abbey Cartularies,* vol. 1, p. 405, #536).

107. Ward, "Fashions in Monastic Endowment," pp. 427–51.

108. *Reg.* II, #682, 834.

109. Ibid., #886. The Bigods are also an example of a family who founded one major house, several minor ones and gave donations to other houses without a discernible policy. See also Atkin, "The Bigod Family."

110. *CDF,* #724, pp. 259–62.

111. Legge, "The Rise and Fall of Anglo-Norman Literature," pp. 1–2; Legge, *Anglo-Norman Literature and Its Background,* p. 10.

112. Thomson, *William of Malmesbury,* pp. 15, 34–35. Thomson uses the dedicatory letter found in the Troyes manuscript as evidence. However, he then misidentifies William's later patron, Robert of Gloucester, as Edith/Maud's son (p. 5).

113. Legge, "Rise and Fall," p. 2; Legge, "L'influence littéraire," p. 683.

114. The women of this generation of the ducal-royal family (whether born to or married into it) appear to have shared this interest. Elisabeth Van Houts cites poetry written for Henry I's sisters, Abbess Cecilia and Adela of Blois ("Latin Poetry as a Source for Anglo-Norman History, 1066–1135").

115. Legge, "Rise and Fall," p. 3.

116. Ibid.

117. *HN,* p. 1.

118. Gransden, *Historical Writing in England,* p. 206.

119. Legge, "Rise and Fall," p. 3; Clanchy, *From Memory,* pp. 168–69.

120. Legge, *Anglo-Norman Literature,* pp. 27–28.

121. Gransden, *Historical Writing in England,* pp. 187–88.

122. Southern, "Place of England in the Twelfth Century Renaissance," p. 163.

123. Short, "Bilingualism in Anglo-Norman England," p. 469.

124. Heales, ed., *Records of Merton Priory,* p. 2.

125. Boase, *English Art 1100–1216,* p. 93.

126. Ibid., pp. 145–46. Besides Walter's foundation and his relationship with

Ailred, he entered the monastery three years before his death (Sanders, *English Baronies,* p. 52).

127. Boase, *English Art,* p. 70.

128. Ibid., pp. 217–18.

129. Ibid., p. 148.

130. Zarnecki, *Later English Romanesque Sculpture,* pp. 9–10, and Boase, *English Art,* pp. 78–81. Thurlby ("Romanesque Sculpture at Tewkesbury Abbey," pp. 93–94) argues that Shobdon was begun in the early part of this period, that is, 1131–34.

131. *PR,* p. 148, 149. Richard fitz Gilbert also owed the king 200*m.* for Henry's help regarding his debt to the Jews in Essex (*PR,* p. 53).

132. *EYC* 2, #1088, p. 391.

133. *Reg.* II, #843.

134. B. Walker, "King Henry I's 'Old Men,' " p. 8; Crouch, *Beaumont Twins,* pp. 4–8

135. Crouch (pp. 7–8) disagrees with the idea of a palace school. *Chronicon Monasterii de Abingdon,* vol. 2, pp. 123, 137; Crosby, "Origins of the English Episcopate," p. 55.

136. English, *Lords of Holderness,* p. 17.

137. Turner, *"Miles Literatus,"* pp. 936–37.

138. With the increased acceptance of primogeniture in the late eleventh century, the custom developed that all land which the father had inherited had to be passed on intact to the eldest son, while anything which the father had acquired could be divided among younger children. Another form of this provision allowed the eldest son a choice of patrimony between the inherited and acquired land (Pollock and Maitland, *History of English Law,* vol. 2, p. 268; Holt, "Politics and Property," pp. 9–19; Oggins, "Population Growth, Inheritance and European Expansion," pp. 32–34). For the variations and contradictions of twelfth-century inheritance, see Holt, "Presidential Address. II. Notions," pp. 193–220. There was no "legal" or absolute system of inheritance—examples of all types are far too common.

139. Round, *Studies in Peerage,* pp. 115–24. Holt ("Presidential Address. II. Notions" p. 112) argues that division of inheritance was far from rare.

140. Holt, "Politics and Property," p. 43; *RB,* 1, pp. 230, 328.

141. B.L. Harley Ms. 3650, fol. 6r.

142. OVC 5:296–98.

143. Cooke, "Kings, Knights, and Abbesses: Shaftesbury Abbey in the Twelfth Century."

144. Wightman, *The Lacy Family,* genealogical tables 1 and 2. Also see below, chapter 6.

145. D. Walker, ed., "Charters of the Earldom of Hereford," pp. 3–5. Also see below, chapter 6.

146. Stenton, *First Century,* pp. 235–36. Hugh was born after his father had made the land division (Crouch, *Beaumont Twins,* p. 9).

147. *Reg.* II, #1389. By 1130, Richard still owed three-quarters of the fine for the wardship (*PR,* p. 81).

148. OVC 6:190–93.

149. *PR,* p. 83.

150. *Chronicle of Battle Abbey,* p. 130.

151. Greenway, ed., *Charters of the Honour of Mowbray,* p. xvii. On pages xvii-xxxii Greenway discusses the family history. She says that Nigel was landless in 1101, but *Reg.* I, #470 is an agreement with the Abbot of Selby concerning Nigel's land of Crowe (Crull) confirmed by William II.

152. Greenway, *Charters,* #11, p. 15.

153. *Reg.* II #743.

154. Greenway, *Charters,* pp. xxii-xxiv.

155. Ibid., #10, p. 14.

156. Heales, ed., *Records of Merton Priory,* p. 10.

157. *Reg.* II, #1722. Greenway (*Charters,* p. xxvii) says Roger was forced to enfeoff Eustace fitz John in 1141, but as can be seen Eustace had held land of Nigel.

158. *PR,* p. 31.

159. Lancaster, ed., *Abstracts of the Charters and Other Documents Contained in the Chartulary of the Cistercian Abbey of Fountains,* 2:646, #1; Greenway, *Charters,* #359, p. 230.

160. Greenway remarks (Charters, pp. xxvii-xxviii) that Roger's marriage was forced on him by his Anarchy enemy, the earl of Chester. Whether this was true or not, the marriage was advantageous in terms of both land gained and status.

161. OVC 4:282–84; Greenway, *Charters,* pp. 11 (#5), 13 (#7), 15 (#10).

162. Ibid., pp. 7–10 (#3).

163. PR, p. 24. Mooers ("Patronage in the Pipe Roll," p. 284) is surprised that Roger was not heavily favored in the Pipe Roll exemptions. This fact could either be typical of a minor or an indication that Henry was aware that he would not be like his father.

164. Greenway, *Charters,* p. xvii.

165. Ibid., p. xxiv.

166. Nigel witnessed 156 times between 1101 and 1129.

167. *PR,* p. 106. Goisbertus paid 1*m.* for pleas of Geoffrey de Clinton in Warwickshire.

168. Greenway, *Charters,* pp. lvi-lxx, details the administration.

169. For example, they gave to the Cistercians (Atkinson, *Cartularium Abbathiae de Rievalle,* #55, pp. 30–31 and Greenway, *Charters,* #95, p. 71), to the Benedictines (*Reg.* II, #1161), and to Durham (*Reg.* II, #1705).

170. Greenway, *Charters,* pp. xxxi-xxxii.

CHAPTER 4

The Nobles and Henry I—
Royal Service

Royal favor always had conferred wealth and influence on nobles, but it had to be earned or at least sought. With fewer opportunities to earn favor through battle and more through administration, the ways of seeking favor changed. Attendance at the royal court gave the nobles an opportunity to be seen, to give advice, and to gain the king's confidence. In addition, court attendance made these nobles available to function as royal representatives when a need for such representation arose. Delegation of authority in the various forms of service showed royal trust and often gave men power and opportunities for gain. Some offices (such as the household offices, shrievalties, and various forest services) existed on a regular basis, while others (itinerant courts and inquests, for instance) were formed as the occasion arose.[1]

Though the service was changing, the major reward remained land, especially land which could be passed on in the family. The service and the land were linked, so offices as well as land had become hereditary throughout the Early Middle Ages. This was to the nobles' advantage. Benefits acquired as rewards for service would provide the family's future status and wealth, but such rewards could also make members of the family financially independent of the king, thus removing the service from royal control. Henry I's attempts to maintain control of authority and revenue were the incentive to great governmental innovations, which included the continued use of clergy in office as well as the employment of new families.

The starting point for our exploration of how the nobles were affected by these changes is an attempt to determine who was at court frequently—perhaps travelling with it. Here the assumption is that those who travelled with the king and were used in various capacities had his trust and perhaps counselled him in important matters of administration. We determine this by examining lists of witnesses to extant charters. Since this is a crucial historiographic point, it is worthwhile to examine the technique of using attestations and its limitations before looking at the conclusions that can be drawn from it.

Many questions have been raised about the pattern of witnessing. Perhaps the witnessing was done by a standard formula rather than by using those who actually were trusted. However, the only formulaic feature apparent is the order of the witnessing[2]. Was the selection of witnesses affected by the type of charter being witnessed?[3] The editors of the *Regesta* suggest that the witnesses were those most likely to contest the documents later. While it is true that heirs to land grants were most likely to witness, it did not exclude the general court from witnessing the same document. However, a real problem is that the extant charters present an unnaturally biased sample consisting of an overabundance of grants and court cases involving the clergy—from a rough count of the grants in the beneficiary index, about ninety percent were clerical. This is due, of course, to their preservation in cathedral and monastic archives. In addition, the small number of charters (*ca.* 1520 for thirty-five years) prevents any controlled statistical analysis. Therefore, it must be remembered that all conclusions based on the charters are tentative. Even dating the documents presents problems and most are dated at best by a range of possible years. For this study, the latest possible date for the charters was used in accordance with the ordering in *Reg.* II. Yet another possible complication is that people may have attended court and have witnessed documents which did not survive. Again, survival rates for kinds of charters may have biased the sample. The possibility has been raised that some people may have attended court and not witnessed all documents,[4] although it seems probable that men of status would, if present, have been called upon to witness in order to give credence to writs or charters. As with all other evidence, then, the charters can yield only tentative conclusions which must be analyzed with other evidence.

There are limitations to what this evidence can tell us. Unless his witnessing is correlated with other evidence, the power of a given individual may be misinterpreted. This is true of several men in this generation, each for his own particular reason. Of these men, the most prominent is Roger of Salisbury, considered by many contemporaries and most modern historians to have been second in power only to the king.[5] Since Roger acted as regent in England while the court was in Normandy and served as a chief justice in eyre, he was often away from the court. His attestations of the documents in the *Regesta* fall off drastically during the years when the court was in Normandy. Even then, his attestations are regular (in most years he witnessed a few documents) but sometimes fairly low in number, and so do not reflect the magnitude of his power. If we were to use the attestation as an absolute gauge of power, we would totally miss Roger of Salisbury's role in the reign.

On the other hand, the chancellor consistently attested a large number of documents. Since during Henry's reign the chancery and chancellor travelled with the court, it may be that the chancellor witnessed more as a matter of form rather than as a result of his personal power. The chancery as an organized department was growing at this time,[6] and an increase in the chancellor's level of involvement might be a reflection of an increase in the department's power, either because of increased business or because the king used the office as a vehicle for his trusted men. Therefore, as in the case of Roger, the evidence of the witness lists must be examined in conjunction with other evidence. Of Henry's chancellors, four became bishops of wealthy sees when they resigned the chancellorship.[7] The fifth, Ranulf, was given desirable land grants including the barony of Berkhampstead (Hertfordshire) which had been forfeited by the count of Mortain.[8] Obviously, these men were rewarded and were presumably trusted by Henry. It may be assumed that he also took their counsel. Still, the extent of their witnessing might be somewhat out of proportion—a reflection, in part, of administrative form.

Witnessing would not always have reflected trust or counsel. Members of the titled nobility attending court would witness by virtue of their status, which would give extra credibility to a document. They might have attended court fairly frequently to pursue law cases or to gain favors. Yet it is hard to imagine these men not attempting to give counsel, whether it was sought or not. Their relative influence with Henry would be seen in favors obtained and in any positions of trust (such as special commissions) given to them.

Robert Bloet, bishop of Lincoln, presents still another problem. From chronicles, from the frequency of his witnessing, and from the various services he rendered, it is evident that he was a highly trusted royal servant through most of his episcopate. However, one chronicler, Henry of Huntingdon, described Bloet's fall from favor shortly before his death in January, 1123.[9] Since Henry was in Bloet's household, this is probably an eyewitness account; yet no change is seen in the frequency of Bloet's attestations for 1122. If a man who was no longer trusted still witnessed so frequently, it might appear to cast doubts on the reliability of witness lists as a reflection of influence. However, the circumstances of Bloet's fall from favor help to show this to be an exceptional case. Bloet was not disseised or disgraced outright, but rather lost lawsuits and was fined by justices of lower rank. Outwardly, Henry praised him. Henry of Huntingdon reports that Bloet recognized that Henry's words did not always reflect his intentions. While this may indicate that some people who fell from favor continued to frequent court, it still affects mainly the evidence of bishops who could afford to attend in the face of subtle disfavor.[10] So the doubt would seem to affect primarily the evidence for the upper clergy. Magnates known to be out of favor did not continue to witness charters. William of Warenne, for example, did not witness between 1101 and 1107, even though he was reseised of his land in 1103. Bishops, however, still retained the status of their office and would lend credibility to documents even if personally out of royal favor. They also had the resources to pursue the court for a prolonged time seeking the resumption of favor as well as new favor. Therefore, while Bloet's case affects the interpretation of witness lists where bishops and abbots are concerned, it does not destroy the basic assumption that in most cases frequent witnessing is probable evidence of royal trust— though the case does strengthen the need for additional evidence.

A pattern other than mere attendance at court which might explain witness selection is the supposed convention that nobles witnessed charters concerning other nobles of similar rank, magnates for magnates, servants for other servants. Upon examination, this supposition does not appear to be the case except for charters of men of the lower noble ranks (which are rare). The charters of grants to Bernard the Scribe are examples of this—when the grants were by men of the lowest rank of noble, they were witnessed by new men; when they were made by others, they were witnessed by a selection of the court.[11] However, grants to any established noble or to churches of land held by older families were witnessed by the donor's retainers, often by his relatives, and by a selection of the court, including new men.[12] It would seem, therefore, that witness lists do in general appear to reflect attendance patterns at court.

In fact, it is when we get to the attestations that we see the need and the opportunity to group the nobles into the seven categories described in the Introduction: retainers, lesser nobles (a general group, untitled and not associated with royal service), service families (identified with royal office in 1100), "new men" (having no noticeable status in England before 1100), magnates (top of the class, most with titles), royal family, and upper clergy. These will allow us to see the nobles' relationship to the court and how they used curial service as a means of gaining favor which could bring upward mobility.

The first of these (Category 1 in Appendix A) is composed of retainers of bishops and nobles, episcopal staff, and a small group of unidentified men who witnessed only a few times during the reign—many only once or twice—and who have not been identified in other sources. Their low incidence of witnessing seems to indicate that these men had come to court to plead, or, as in the case of the retainers, to witness a specific case, or else that the court had come to their neighborhood, thus making them available to witness.

A second category of witnesses is composed of the majority of the upper class, the untitled nobility holding land by military tenure (Category 2). This group ranges from Robert de Ferrers, heir of a Domesday baron who held extensive possessions (especially in Staffordshire and Leicestershire), to Roger de Conyers, evident at court only twice (1101 and 1129/33), who held castle ward and land in Durham but who appears in no other document.[13] Through most of the reign, this group witnessed a much lower percentage of the surviving charters than their numbers would warrant. Most witnessed only a few times. In 1102, for example, men of this group composed 18 percent of the witnesses but witnessed only 9 percent of the time. At the beginning of the reign most of the men in this group who witnessed frequently were nobles with large Domesday holdings—that is, they represent the upper levels of the group. By 1105, however, the category included men of lesser status—reflecting, perhaps, a broader spectrum of people having business at court as Henry established his power. Another possible explanation of this phenomenon, to be considered later, is that the decrease in witnessing by the nobility reflects an actual decrease in attendance at court by men of status after their initial acceptance of Henry's right to rule. This would have allowed Henry to rely upon whomever he chose at court and would have allowed the opportunity for a small group to benefit.

The third category is composed of families identified with royal service (Category 3). The lower ranks of this group include the sheriffs who held a county for only a few years but who were recorded in the role of or with the epithet of sheriff. The elite of this category were the hereditary service families, usually endowed by the Conqueror. By 1100, many of these held much land by military tenure as well, but they continued to perform their serjeanty offices, which sometimes formed the family surname and which were coveted parts of the patrimony. Included in this sub-group are the families of Bigod, Bohun, de Vere, d'Abetot, fitz Hamon and both families of Albini/Cainhoe. The frequency with which these men appeared as witnesses was maintained throughout the reign; and in several years, these men as a group witnessed a significantly higher percentage of the time than their numbers would warrant.[14] As time went on, though the group continued to be heavily relied on, the actual number of people in the group and the percentage they constituted of the total number at court declined, as Henry came to rely on a smaller, more select group within this category. However, it is significant that none of these men "fell from grace," or lost the king's favor. As will be discussed later in this chapter, it is in the treatment of this group's inheritance that Henry I's administrative skill may be seen.

The fourth category consists of the "new men," laymen and royal clerks who had relatively little position in England before Henry I. With respect to these men a clear case can be argued that their family wealth was established in England through royal favor and service (Category 4). The phrase "new men" comes from Orderic's famous description of men raised from the dust which was quoted in chapter 1. Orderic mentioned nine men by name, but three of them— Guillegrip, Guiganan Algaso, and Robert de Bostare—are not identified with any certainty in any records of Henry I's reign.[15] The fourth, Hamo de Falaise, witnessed five times for Henry I and once for Duke Henry. He was pardoned 13s. (6½ hides of land) for the danegeld of Warwickshire in 1130.[16] There is little other evidence for him, however, including his descent, which makes it impossible to trace his family. A fifth, Hugh de Bocland, is included in the new men in Orderic's description, but since he was a sheriff under Rufus, I include him with the service families. Like Hamo de Falaise, it is difficult to term Bocland a *familiaris* since only eight attestations have survived a fifteen year period. That leaves four of Orderic's new men, Geoffrey de Clinton, Ralph Basset, William de Trussebut, and Rainer of Bath (sheriff of Lincoln). I have included in this group Brian fitz Count (the illegitimate son of Alan, count of Brittany), who gained land, marriage, and power through service and not through family connections, although his original access to the king seems to have come from the latter. In the beginning of the reign, this group of men was composed of Normans who served Henry before his accession—royal clerks or chaplains like Roger, later bishop of Salisbury, or Norman nobles such as Richard de Redvers. This group grew steadily during the reign, both in numbers and power, usually witnessing between 20 percent and 30 percent of the time. From the late 1120s to 1135, the new men evidently became the core of the administration, and their witnessing grew to above 30 percent. The Bassets, Geoffrey de Clinton, Brian fitz Count, the fitz Johns, Geoffrey fitz Payn, William Maltravers, William Mauduit, William de Pont de l'Arche, Robert de Sigillo, and the chancellors Ranulf and Geoffrey Rufus all appear repeatedly in charters applying to England; Robert de Courcy, Robert de la Haia, and Henry de la Pomeroy appear in those applying to Normandy.

There is no break, no particular time when Henry seems to have switched to new men in place of the old. Rather, there is what appears to be a steady trend towards using new men. The size of the group grew as Henry found—as a result of the increased business of the monarchy and through personal experience—more men he could rely on.

The "magnates," here defined as titled nobility (Category 5) were members of important landed families who relied on status, family connection and military service to increase their power. As a group, the magnates present a surprisingly low incidence of witnessing throughout the reign.[17] Generally, their witnessing declined while the court was in Normandy, but it was also very low during the busy English years of 1121–22, so their witnessing was not dependent on court locale. Several individuals were prominent even when the group as a whole was not. The Beaumonts, Robert, count of Meulan, and Henry, earl of Warwick, were particularly frequent witnesses, but this was not true of their sons. Robert's son Waleran was out of favor from his rebellion in 1123 until the 1130s, and though he was restored to his lands, he rarely witnessed. Robert's other heir, Robert, earl of Leicester, and Henry's sons, Roger, earl of Warwick, and Robert Neufbourg, though major landholders with traditions of court attendance, figure little in the witness lists of the 1120s and 1130s.[18] In other words, as the "old men" died they were not replaced as trusted advisors or *curiales* by their sons. William (II) Warenne, earl of Surrey, played a major role against Henry in the 1101 civil war. After Henry forgave him (1103), Warenne supposedly became one of "the closest of his [Henry's] friends and counselors."[19] The witness lists do attest to his being a fairly regular member of court from 1107, but rarely did he witness more than three times per year, hardly significant when compared to the service families, the new men, the bishops or the Beaumonts. Warenne held no office to have kept him from court. He did prove himself in battle against Clito's forces in 1119, and Henry granted him large danegeld exemptions in 1130. At Henry's death in 1135, the council gave William control of Rouen and the district of Caux to secure for the crown.[20] However, the judgment of his intimacy with Henry is not borne out by the witness lists. This may be because the witness lists are not, after all, a good index of intimacy with the king, but it just as likely may reflect the fact that the king, while trusting Warenne as a warrior, would not rely on him for his administration or nonmilitary advice. It might have been a choice of Warenne's. Even within the top of the nobility, there were different roles and lifestyles.

The only other magnate who attested to any extent was Ranulf Meschin, heir of the vicomte of Bayeux, who gained the earldom of Chester through lateral inheritance. Like Warenne, Ranulf appeared infrequently and does not seem to have been trusted as the Beaumonts.

The magnates as a group continued to attend court on state occasions—the holiday courts for example.[21] This appears to have been an aristocratic or baronial pattern. Since a large number of charters were issued on state occasions, an individual magnate's number of attestations does not reflect the amount of time spent at court.[22] Indeed, after their initial approval of Henry's rule in 1101, they did not frequent the court to make their counsel known.[23] They do not seem to have been formally displaced; rather their absence seems to be a manifestation of the usual baronial apathy toward everyday royal government. At the beginning of the reign, Henry wanted them present to give his reign legitimacy, and they wanted to be at court to safeguard their rights with the new king. Had they been present after 1101, it seems likely that Henry would have used them as witnesses, since their status would have been an asset to his charters. In general, the initiative to give counsel had to come from the nobles, except when they were present at traditional state occasions. Few besides the older Beaumonts had the desire to put in the work necessary to gain royal trust. In addition, the younger men of the next generation, those born to their status, "fiercely independent, accustomed to wealth and power,"[24] were likely to expect favor without having earned it, and to rebel when it was not received. These were the men inheriting the greater estates during Henry's reign, the men of the second generation of magnate status.

A small group of witnesses who became important late in the reign is composed of members of the royal family (Category 6), whose claim to power rested on kinship. William, the king's son, suddenly began to appear as a witness in 1115 at the age of twelve,[25] a reasonable age for the heir to begin assuming some position at court. Henry's eldest illegitimate son, Robert, and his nephew Stephen both figured prominently in events and grants in the later years of the reign. There is a difference, as noted in chapter 2, between Henry's treatment of his legitimate and illegitimate kin. This is reflected in the attestations of Robert of Gloucester and Stephen of Blois. Stephen had been heavily favored with grants of land by his uncle until William's death, at which time Henry began to fear his power. To counterbalance Stephen's influence, Henry raised Robert's status to match Stephen's.[26] Stephen, while a favorite, was not in royal service; but Robert, one of the main witnesses from 1121 to the end of the reign, was often used and trusted by Henry.[27] Stephen's attestations show the magnate pattern: he witnessed regularly but infrequently.

Throughout the Middle Ages, the upper clergy (Category 7) were of great importance to government. These bishops and abbots controlled a large portion of England's landed wealth, were competent administrators, and continued, in essence, appointed by the king. Unlike the service families, Henry did not have to deal with the problem of hereditary office which might produce a disloyal heir. As a group, the upper clergy comprised a high percentage both of the men used and of the attestations in the witness lists, averaging about a quarter of the court. Undoubtedly, this is due in part to the fact that a very high proportion of the surviving grants was made to the churches represented by the upper clergy. In addition, as noted above, the bishops had the resources and interest to follow the court in order to pursue lawsuits and royal favor. As bishops, their attestations also would add particular credibility to the charters. Quite aside from these qualifications, the trust which Henry placed in some of these men can be seen in the frequency with which they acted as witnesses. An examination of the attestations of Bernard, bishop of St. David's from 1115–48 demonstrates this. During the years between 1115 and 1135 the charters show he was with the court in southern England[28] and Normandy[29] at times other than the holiday courts. The subject matters of the charters he witnessed seemingly have no connection either to each other or to the lands relating to St. David's: the charters involve such varied concerns as William de Beauchamp's lands[30] and a claim by the monks of Marmoutier against the bishop of Sées.[31] Since St. David's was a minor frontier see, the witnessing by its bishop must be due to something other than the importance of the see. We are therefore led to the conclusion that Bernard, a new man and a former royal chaplain, was often at court and was trusted by Henry. Within the group of greater clergy, in fact, Henry most often used new men as witnesses: Roger of Salisbury and his family; Thurstan of York and his brother Audin of Evreux; and Robert Bloet of Lincoln. Most of these men were entrusted with royal service as well. From the witness lists, Henry's reliance on new men, even in these nonhereditary offices, is evident, as is the willingness of new men as opposed to magnate sons to serve. William Giffard, for example, was a younger son of a major noble, though he served as chancellor under Rufus and in the first two years of Henry's reign. Yet after 1103, though he was bishop of Winchester, the only year in which he witnessed any significant number of charters was 1121, a busy year for everyone. Giffard, a man with divided loyalties to service and family, was overshadowed as a witness by new men. Witnessing as a reflection of trust is probably least reliable for the clerical group, for reasons already cited; but in most cases evidence from the witness lists agrees with evidence based on service and on the chronicles.

Little can be determined about the court in Normandy, as the number of extant documents decreases sharply for the periods when the court was there, especially early in the reign. Some observations, however, can be made from the charters of the 1120s and 1130s. The "English" men travelling with the king tended to be the same men who witnessed heavily in England—that is, mainly new men and service families. The exception, of course, is Roger of Salisbury, absent because he was regent of England. Certain names which do appear regularly in connection with Normandy correspond with what is known of the Norman administrators—these include Robert de la Haia, the Courcys, the Tancarvilles, the Pomeroys, and the bishop of Lisieux. It would seem that Henry spent the years after 1120 building his administration, both in England and in Normandy, basing it on the willing new men and service families.

Certain conclusions about court attendance seem plausible on the basis of observations drawn from the witness lists. From his accession, Henry seems to have been aware that a loyal administration would have to be based on men dependent upon him. Though witnessing is an uncertain index, it provides a picture of the court. In the first few years of the reign, the court was composed of the wealthier nobles—the magnates and the top of the group of lesser nobles. After 1105, however, the court "opened" to the whole range of lesser nobility. Yet witnessing also supports the idea that from early in his reign Henry relied heavily upon the service families and upon the new men. Within this group, by late in the reign there may have been an increasing emphasis (though not consistently) on the new men or at least on a smaller number of members of service families. Some of the attrition is accounted for by nature not favor. Some of the the older servants (especially among the sheriffs) died and were not replaced, or left minor or female heirs, or left aristocratic heirs. Whatever the reason, the picture is one of a larger variety attending court but a smaller, though never closed, central group of *familiares*. The king's ability to rely on the service families and new men rather then on baronial councils, was in part due to the greater nobles' lack of initiative in attending court rather than to actual displacement. The magnates continued to be present on state occasions, but they do not appear to have attended court frequently and so were thereby not available to counsel Henry on actual administration.

If, as in fact seems to be the case, a loyal administration was one of Henry I's chief goals, then various forms of royal service must have played a large role in the lives of many nobles who hoped to gain royal patronage; and they should be examined in this light. Personal services in the royal household are particularly open to this kind of examination, since we have the record of the "Constitutio Domus Regis" which indicated the relative status of the household officials at the end of Henry's reign. According to the "Constitutio," the chancellor was most important; the steward, master chamberlain, and constable were all slightly lower in importance. The names of some of the officials are also known from this work— William Mauduit, treasurer; William fitz Odo, Henry de la Pomeroy and Roger d'Oilli, constables; John the Marshal.[32] One office in particular reflects Henry's use of patronage, that of keeper of the seal, which was held by Robert de Sigillo from 1131–35. The "Constitutio" records that the king had just about doubled the pay for this office, the *magister scriptorii*.[33] As a chaplain at court, and then as keeper, Robert witnessed occasionally from 1121–25 and frequently from 1126–35.[34] The only land he is known to have held was a small fee in Gloucester,[35] and he was not rewarded by promotion after 1131 until Matilda's reign in 1141. His appearance in the witness lists, then, seems to indicate that Robert had succeeded in gaining royal favor before receiving the office. Having become keeper, however, he continued to be a loyal servant, and the rewards of his office were increased to compensate him personally rather than as a decision by Henry to increase the importance of the office.

The "Constitutio" describes the household frozen at one point in time, but it has been shown that beginning probably in Henry I's[36] reign there seems to have been a multiplication of offices within the household without the displacement of personnel. The new offices were usually held by new men, thus opening a further opportunity for favor.[37]

While household officials handled the daily court tasks, the sheriffs were the major local representatives during Henry's reign. A study of royal shrievalty holders also shows a definite increase in new men at the expense of the hereditary sheriffs. In 1100, twelve sheriffs either had inherited their shrievalty or had held it for a considerable time. In 1123, only three hereditary sheriffs held office—Richard fitz Baldwin de Clare, Walter of Gloucester, and Walter de Beauchamp.[38] By 1128, Richard fitz Baldwin no longer held Devon. One of the others, Walter de Beauchamp, was a new man who gained the shrievalty through marriage with the d'Abetots. The third, Walter of Gloucester, though his family had held the sheriff's farm since Domesday times, actually made his family's fortune during Henry's reign through personal service. How other shrievalties changed hands is not known. In some cases the change occurred at a death: Hugh of Bocland, for example, held eight shrievalties during Henry's first decade as king, but after his death his son William was granted only one.[39] In other cases, such as the Grantmesnil shrievalty in Leicester, Henry regained control through forfeiture.[40] If not all shrievalties were considered hereditary at the time, then Henry had ended any chance of their becoming so. Whatever the method, once control was regained, Henry used his trusted men to fill the sheriffs' offices. By 1130, only seven men accounting for approximately thirty-five counties were noncurial men. Of these seven, two, Rainer of Bath (sheriff of Lincoln) and Odard of Northumberland, were mentioned by Orderic as advisors close to the king and were clearly new men.[41] Interestingly, both of these men disappear from history, not having been able to use this opportunity to establish a family with status. The sheriffs in the surviving Pipe Roll show what appears to have been an experiment in office holding. Henry appointed two of his servants, Richard Basset, a new man, and Aubrey de Vere, a member of a rising service family, to hold jointly seven counties. Unfortunately, it is not known whether Henry continued the experiment, but it shows both the great amount of trust placed in these men and an attempt to control the offices through a few trusted men. In general, Henry's treatment of the office of the sheriff shows an actual displacement of hereditary shrievalties; and it was as a result of a study of this office that the phrase "administrative revolution" came to be applied to Henry's reign.[42]

Other out-of-court representatives, the officers of the forests, were subject to periodic accounting. The kings had a number of prerogative rights in the royal forests which Henry retained in chapter 10 of his coronation charter. The keepers of the various forests, like the sheriffs, controlled powerful neighborhood favors and received various kinds of income. The Engaines, keepers of the forest of Northampton, are the best documented of Henry I's foresters. Richard (I) Engaine held lands in Pytchley, Northampton for the royal serjeanty of wolf-hunting, presumably in the forest.[43] His son Vitalis (I) continued to hold these lands and was acting as keeper in 1121.[44] In the same neighborhood, Richard (I) held tenure of the Abbot of Peterborough,[45] and the Northamptonshire Survey shows the family to have had other large holdings in the county.[46] In 1130, a damaged entry in the Pipe Roll records a marriage fee of $300m.$ for the land and daughter of Richard Engaine with the ministry of the forest;[47] obviously royal service had been profitable to the family. There is no evidence that Henry attempted a major reorganization of the foresters as he had of the sheriffs in 1130. However, efforts were made to keep control over the individuals. Of the extant references to six forest families, only one concerns forfeiture: in the 1120s, the king granted to Eustace de Barenton in serjeanty the forest of Essex, previously held in part by "Adam who incurred forfeiture of the forest."[48] Unfortunately, no mention is made of the reason for Adam's forfeiture of a forest which covered most of the county. While Henry retained control, this service did not open any new opportunities for the nobles.

Royal rights over forests were enforced by special justices who heard forest pleas, that is, pleas concerning crimes and claims peculiar to the king's special territories. These were recorded in the Pipe Roll and show that the king occasionally used military tenants in chief to hold these pleas; for example, Robert de Arundel, a Domesday tenant in Dorset, Somerset and Cornwall, accounted for forest pleas in Dorset in 1130.[49]

Henry I made much use of royal representatives as justices, either locally or in eyre as he expanded royal judicial power. In the early years of the reign, lesser nobles acted as justices in areas where they held land.[50] Some sheriffs, such as Hugh of Bocland and William fitz Ansger, held pleas in their shrievalties.[51] Fitz Ansger was also a justice in Normandy, where Orderic identified him as the richest citizen of Rouen.[52] Roger Marmion, whose family were the hereditary champions of the Dukes of Normandy, was also used as a Norman justice.[53] Justices and specially designated royal servants sometimes were used to check the sheriffs' efficiency, especially in the cases of the older sheriffs.[54] The major evidence for Henry's policies in this area comes from the Pipe Roll. The majority of the justices listed there were new men (Ralph and Richard Basset, William d'Albini Brito, William de Houghton, Geoffrey Ridel, Eustace and Payn fitz John, and Geoffrey de Clinton) or were from service families (Nigel d'Albini and Aubrey de Vere). Two bishops, Robert Bloet of Lincoln and Roger of Salisbury, were also among the prominent justices. Some members of lesser baronial families, for example, Alfred of Lincoln, Walter Espec, and Henry de Port, are mentioned as having held *placita*. Reedy has shown a high correlation between the areas where the justices held land and those where they held pleas. Local landholders were likely to have more force behind their decision.[55] The author of the *Gesta* Stephani wrote that Miles of Gloucester and Payn fitz John dominated justice in western England, where they were major landholders.[56] Tout has noticed a pattern established between grants of land and office in relation to the Winchester justices. These men, who were probably not itinerant, tended to hold much Hampshire land. This was especially true of Geoffrey de Clinton and William de Pont de l'Arche.[57] Therefore, it seems that Henry used his *familiares* as justices and that the lands which they held, and some which they received in patronage, were in some way connected with this service. If one received land in this way, an additional service—which could be either an additional opportunity or a burdensome duty—went with it.

As local justices and justices in eyre were increasingly used by Henry I, so were the special commissioners whom he sent out to make specific inquiries. This use of the inquest is generally associated with Domesday Book and with Henry II, but several surveys exist for Henry I's reign

which were the result of such inquests. When a dispute over land between
the sheriff and the church of Worcester was brought to royal attention,
the Worcestershire Survey (1108–18) was ordered.[58] However, the exact
procedure used to obtain this hidage is not known. Three surveys are
extant with lists of commissioners: the *Liber Winton* (1103–15) to determine the royal holdings within the city of Winchester; the York Inquest
(1106) to determine the minster's customs; and the Bayeux Inquest (1133)
to determine the extent of the cathedral's subinfeudation. The Winchester
survey named five commissioners: William, bishop of Winchester, the
major tenant in the area and a man appointed by Henry; William de Pont
de l'Arche, sheriff of Hampshire and tenant in the city; Herbert the Chamberlain, royal servant and local tenant; and two *curiales,* Ralph Basset and
Geoffrey Ridel.[59] Only the bishop came from a great family; the rest were
curiales of the new order. Three of the five men were locally known. The
roughly contemporaneous York Inquest (1106) also mentions five justices—Robert Bloet, bishop of Lincoln; Ranulf Meschin, a northern landholder and lateral cousin of the earl of Chester, later to be the earl himself;
Peter de Valognes, a noble with mainly eastern holdings; and, again, Ralph
Basset and Geoffrey Ridel. At York, the reeve, Anschetill de Bulmer, later
sheriff of York, served as translator.[60] The Bayeux Inquest at the end of
the reign was held before one justice only—Robert of Gloucester, the
king's son. Twelve jurors were chosen, most likely from among local men.
Of these Roger de Suhard and Hugh de Crevecoeur were tenants of the
bishop; five jurors were possibly Norman members of English families,[61]
and two of these, Courcelle and Port, may have been related to tenants in
the survey; a constable, Helto, served as a juror, but since he appears in
no English records, it may be assumed that he was a local constable. Only
one juror's name—Ralph de Roffa or Rochester—bears any connection
to England; but once again, he left no evidence other than his surname.
The other three appear only as jurors for this inquest. Obviously, there
are not enough examples to draw definite conclusions about Henry's inquests or their impact on noble life and opportunities. The Winchester
and York surveys appear to have been conducted in very similar ways—
with five justices, of whom three were *curiales,* one a bishop of the area,
and at least one local man who was also a *curialis.* Whether they served
as jurors or sat before a group similar in composition to the Bayeux jury
is not recorded. The Bayeux jury sat before only one justice, but he was
of royal blood, was a *curialis,* and was known in the region. In all cases,
however, Henry used trusted officials, not always of high rank.

Most of the services discussed were formal offices, but some involved
tasks requiring immediate services of a very general nature. Occasionally

writs were carried by confidential messengers named in the text. Most of these cases occurred early in the reign, suggesting either that a different system was later adopted or that the name of the messenger stopped being recorded. A list of the messengers shows two things. First, few people were used more than once. Only six of the thirty-six are recorded more than once, and half of these may have carried more than one writ at one time. Secondly, no one type of person was used. The messengers range from Queen Edith/Maud and two sons of titled nobility to clerks of the chapel and chancery, with the majority consisting of members of service and lesser noble families. Some messengers possibly were concerned with the grant they carried, but most seem rather to have exercised royal authority in the area concerned, such as Robert de la Haia carrying a writ to the nobles of Cotentin.[62] Perhaps in such cases Henry depended on the messenger to guarantee that the order was carried out by those to whom the writ was addressed. Another possibility is that the person was returning to the area, was trusted enough to be used to carry the order, and simply took it with him. Whatever the case, it is evident that Henry used an assortment of people attending his court to perform a variety of services.[63] Again, merely being present at court provided the opportunity to perform services which might be rewarded or at least become known to the king.

One of Henry I's aims was to secure loyal officials, that is, to know the men who actually performed a service and to have proof of their loyal service. Therefore he had often to deal with the second generation of nobles and its expectations. The system of inheritance of service might lead not only to possible disloyalty on the part of sons of such families, but to lack of incentive to perform their duties. As described throughout the previous chapters, many of this generation expected rewards by virtue of their birth status, not their service. These young, wealthy men were evident among Duke Robert's supporters in 1101–06[64] and in the rebellion of Waleran of Meulan in 1123.[65] The same problems of service and loyalty are seen later with the Gloucester/Hereford family. Walter of Gloucester served as sheriff, constable, and castellan through most of Henry's reign. He was able and loyal, and appeared at court regularly. His son Miles, who inherited his father's offices separately between 1127 and 1130, appeared at court only four times before inheriting but became one of the great *curiales* in the active later years of the reign. By the time of the Anarchy, Miles was rich, powerful and well-connected enough to be sought after by both sides; he was made earl of Hereford two years before his death in 1143. His son Roger, reared as a great noble, was at court only on great occasions and was "less experienced in war and administration."[66] Roger's national power decreased, he rebelled, and his heir (his sister's son) was not allowed to inherit the earldom.

Apparently aware of the possibility of lack of incentive to serve and even of disloyalty among the second generation, Henry I seems to have made an effort to keep control of delegated authority in order to avoid its use by independently wealthy nobles. Where possible, Henry detached the inheritance of land from particular offices or divided large holdings that included multiple offices. The holdings detached in this way were given to men of proven loyalty. Eudo Dapifer, for example, inherited the office of dapifer from his father, Hubert de Ria. Eudo's estate was already large when he inherited it, with lands in ten counties,[67] and, through royal favor, he added to it.[68] Yet his lands and office escheated to Henry at Eudo's death in 1120, and most of it was still in royal hands in 1130.[69] Hamo Dapifer, hereditary steward and sheriff of Kent, was also a regular witness and loyal servant of Henry. Yet during his lifetime, his shrievalty was given to William of Eynesford, a new man,[70] and after his death, his stewardship was given to a service family of lesser status, the Bohuns. Neither dapifer was survived by a direct male heir, and it is uncertain whether the Anglo-Normans would have accepted inheritance of an office by a member of the female line.[71] However, neither of the new families seem to have had any familial claim to the offices.

Where male heirs existed, Henry allowed inheritance of the office. Urse d'Abetot's son Roger inherited both the shrievalty of Worcester and the constableship in 1108, though he soon forfeited both for murdering another member of the royal household.[72] His brother Osbert held the offices and land for approximately four years, at which time land and shrievalty were regranted to his brother-in-law, Walter de Beauchamp, a new man.[73] It is doubtful, however, that Walter ever served as constable. In effect, the offices were split, and the king retained control of some of the delegated power and land attached to it. Where the next generation proved loyal and able, their strength continued and grew. This was the case of the Bigods. Roger's eldest son William died on the White Ship, and his younger son inherited. Ironically, William, who was noncurial, may not have succeeded whereas, his younger brother, not expecting to inherit, was curial in his behavior.[74]

Inheritance of office depended therefore on various factors. Where families were of lesser status and wealth in 1100 (for instance, the Tancarvilles), their growth in strength did not make them independently wealthy of the king, and they continued to be favored. Robert de Neufbourg, younger son of the earl of Warwick, became chamberlain under Henry I, and his family held the office at least until 1212.[75] Some offices were fought over: at some time in Henry's reign, for instance, the right to the marshalsea was proven in court by Gilbert the Marshal against Robert de Venoiz and William de Hastings.[76] The circumstances of the dispute are unknown, but John fitz Gilbert was allowed to succeed and became a *curialis* in the last years of the reign.[77] In Normandy there is an example of a woman, Adela de Montfort, inheriting the Norman constableship, which was performed by her husband Simon de Moulins-la-Marche in her right. Simon was a younger son who had been allowed to inherit his brother's forfeited patrimony, indicating that Henry believed him to be loyal.[78] In these cases, too, Henry continued to rely on individual members of noble families, usually men who were also frequently at court; but where the occasion arose he transferred great offices to less wealthy, dependent men.

Another answer to the problem of hereditary service was to avoid the problem altogether by using clergy, and Henry relied heavily on clerks as his advisors. As mentioned, Henry's earliest clerical patronage, the coronation appointments, were given to members of three baronial families. However, one of these appointees, Richard de Clare of Ely, was deprived of the abbacy from 1102–05, and a second, Robert of Chester, was deposed by the monks of Bury St. Edmund in 1107. Giffard of Winchester had been a *curialis* of Rufus', but continued to witness heavily only in the early years of Henry's reign.[79] Only the fourth appointee, Gerard, who had risen through Rufus' chancery, continued to rise, being translated to York in 1102. Henry's next appointment was that of Faritius, the royal physician, to the abbey of Abingdon. During Faritius' abbacy Abingdon was heavily favored in patronage;[80] in 1114 the king tried to translate him to Canterbury, but met with opposition from the monks.

Henry's promotion of lesser men within his household was paralleled in his clerical appointments. Through Henry's reign, men from families of low status were favored within the clergy. These were often men known to have served in the chancery or in the royal chapel; they were thereby personally known to Henry.[81] Of the thirty-one bishops whom Henry appointed in England, Wales and Scotland, seven are of unknown family origin.[82] Only two are from identifiable magnate families—Giffard of Winchester and Everard of Norwich, son of Earl Roger. One other bishop, Henry of Blois of Winchester, was Henry's nephew. Twenty-one appointments were new men from either Henry's or Queen Matilda's household.[83] Less is known of Henry's continental appointments. John was appointed to Lisieux after a "long apprenticeship" as justice and royal chaplain.[84] Geoffrey was appointed to Rouen for his "eloquence and learning."[85] Audin of Evreux was a royal chaplain. It appears that Henry generally elevated men to the episcopacy who had already shown their capacity for service to him.

The churchmen, of course, figure prominently in the extant charters, partly due to church care in preserving documents, but also due to royal favor to churches. Aside from favor in the form of giving land or allowing it to be given to their churches, once Henry found certain people to be reliable servants, he often employed members of their families as well. This may been seen as royal favor or influence by the men in question in obtaining the initial appointments for their relatives. In most cases of which we have any record, however, the relative's first position was in a minor household capacity where he served an apprenticeship and proved his loyalty and ability. Once he had proved himself, he was promoted. Roger of Salisbury's two nephews were elevated by Henry "out of love for the bishop,"[86] but both Nigel of Ely and Alexander of Lincoln had been in the royal chancery. Both men proved themselves and were favored by danegeld exemptions in 1130.[87] Richard of Belmeis, Bishop of London, who had been a sheriff and steward,[88] got clerical appointments for two sons and two nephews, but none was given a high position by Henry. Samson of Worcester's two sons were elevated to bishoprics, Thomas (II) promoted from royal chaplain to York, Richard (II) to Bayeux.[89] Thurstan of York and Audin of Evreux, sons of one of Rufus' chaplains, had served royal apprenticeships, and are seen as frequent witnesses after their elevations. The same pattern holds true for Normandy. John, bishop of Sées, nephew of the bishop of Lisieux, had served as keeper of the great seal. Some appointments were clearly not gifts. Geoffrey de Clinton bought the bishopric of Chester for his nephew Roger for £2000.[90] Generally, though, Henry appointed new men to bishoprics, may have rewarded them by grants of land and favors, and often used their relatives, but did not promote the latter to high office until they had served apprenticeships.

This study of court attendance and service demonstrates Henry's growing reliance on new men and members of service families. Older families were not displaced, but were relied on only if the individual noble made the effort to serve and prove himself trustworthy. While giving advice, performing royal service, or just being associated with the king conferred a certain status and honor, it also put one in a position to receive various royal favors. It is clear, however, that to some extent the older families regarded some of the more important forms of patronage (such as granting of land or the marriage of heirs) as theirs by right—a situation that could easily lead to resentment if these families felt they were not getting their proper share of these favors.

Notes

1. E. Mason, "Magnates, Curiales, and the Wheel of Fortune," presents a case study using the Beaumonts' and the Tosnys' luck with the "wheel of fortune."

2. For a discussion of witnessing in Henry I's reign see Wootten, "A Study of Henry I," pp. 235–41; Hollister, "Magnates and *Curiales*," pp. 63–81. For a discussion of status and witnessing (though dealing with a later period of administrative development) see Russell, "Social Status at the Court of King John." Hodson ("Medieval Charters") argues that the last clerical witness was usually the scribe of the charter but does not specifically use the *Regesta* collections.

3. *Reg.* II, p. xxviii.

4. For example, the biographer of Herbert of Norwich questions the low frequency of Herbert's attestations, believing him to have been at court far more often (Alexander, "Herbert of Norwich," p. 148, *n.*168).

5. For a modern biography of Roger of Salisbury, see Kealey, *Roger of Salisbury.* West (*The Justiciarship in England,* pp. 16–23) analyzes Roger's role as justiciar, as does Green (*Government,* pp. 38–50).

6. Tout, *Chapters in the Administrative History of Mediaeval England,* vol. 1, p. 14; Green, *Government,* pp. 28–30.

7. William Giffard became bishop of Winchester, Roger of Salisbury, Waldric of Laon, and Geoffrey of Durham.

8. Sanders, *English Baronies,* p. 14.

9. Henry of Huntingdon, *Historia Anglorum,* pp. 299–300.

10. Ibid. See also Partner, *Serious Entertainments,* for a discussion of Henry of Huntingdon, especially pp. 11–48 and 183–230.

11. *Reg.* II, #1363–1366 are all witnessed by new men. *Reg.* II, #1676 is a grant by Stephen to Bernard and its witnesses include the vicomte of Rouen.

12. For example, see *Reg.* II, #1015a.

13. *Reg.* II, #546, 1825; Clay and Greenway, *Early Yorkshire Families,* p. 22.

14. See Appendix I, Table B. In 1102, they comprised 21% of the witnesses yet witnessed 32% of the time; in 1105, they comprised 23% of the witnesses and witnessed 36% of the time. This pattern continues late in the reign. In 1129, they made up only 15% of the witnesses but witnessed 25% of the time.

15. Chibnall (OVC 6:17 *n.*9) says that Guigan Algason was vicomte of Exmes under Stephen, but there is no evidence of him during Henry's reign beyond Orderic's statement.

16. *Reg.* II, #1338, 1441, 1442, 1764, 1982; *Reg.* III, #81; *PR,* p. 108

17. An examination of the patterns of witnessing shows all groups witnessing in approximately the same proportions throughout the reign except in 1107–09 and 1125. During these years, witnessing of the baronial groups increased at the expense of the service groups. The data, however, are not conclusive and it cannot be determined whether the apparent pattern reflects the actual occurrence.

18. Robert, count of Meulan died in 1118; Henry of Warwick in 1119.

19. OVC 6:14–15. "et inter precipuos ac familiares amicos habitus effloruit."

20. OVC 6:450.

21. Crown-wearing and holiday courts are discussed by Green, *Government,* pp. 20–23.

22. For example. *Reg.* II, #1243–45. The magnates were present at the Christmas court in 1120–21, a year of otherwise little attendance by them.

23. Hollister ("The Taming of a Turbulent Earl," p. 84, 84 *n.*8) substantially agrees with this conclusion, though his statement that "in 1135, the greater barons tended to be *curiales* and frequent attestors" is misleading unless read carefully

with the footnote. In the note he states that direct lines of great noble families "attested less frequently than their fathers had done" and that Stephen witnessed relatively few times. The Bigods, whom Hollister classifies as an established great family, continued to perform their curial services; their inclusion with the magnates is due to the differences between Hollister's and my classification systems. Those remaining from his classification as both magnates and *curiales* are Robert, earl of Gloucester and the greater clergy, including Roger of Salisbury, a new man but in the clerical category. In addition, while the numbers of total attestations seem high, they include those of many members of the family. The strength of the statement does not appear to be justified by the evidence, especially with the differences in classifications. In an article published the following year, Hollister directly examines the question of magnates' witnessing. By Rufus' reign, magnates were noncurial. Hollister considers Rufus the cause of this change, but mentions that the sons of the *curiales* seldom witnessed—an observation that supports a generational rather than a political analysis.

24. Hollister, "The Anglo-Norman Civil War," p. 318

25. William was seventeen when he died in 1120.

26. Southern, "Place," p. 135, *n*.1.

27. Robert of Gloucester was one of the three men to be trusted with the foreknowledge of Matilda's marriage to Geoffrey of Anjou. The others were Brian fitz Count and the bishop of Lisieux (*HN*, p. 530).

28. *Reg.* II, passim, for example #1483, 1642, 1757.

29. Ibid., #1204–1205, 1439, 1547, 1896.

30. Ibid., #1710.

31. Ibid., #1439.

32. "Constitutio Domus Regis," pp. 133–34. Green discusses the household at this time (*Government*, pp. 29–37).

33. "Constitutio Domus Regis," p. 129. G. H. White ("The Royal Household Under Henry I," p. 400) attributes this increase to an increased importance of the office, but this is the only case in which the author of the "Constitutio" mentioned a pay raise in direct connection with an individual. The *Regesta* (II, p. x) editors raise the possibility that Robert filled the role of chancellor after Geoffrey Rufus' election to Durham in 1133, and that the raise was an indication of this rather than an increase in the role of the office or the prestige of Robert.

34. *Reg.* II, passim. Robert de Sigillo witnessed 12 times from 1121–25 and 83 times from 1126–35.

35. He was granted exemption for 5*s*. 6*d*. of danegeld for this land (*PR*, p. 80).

36. Chrimes, *Introduction to the Administrative History of Mediaeval England*, pp. 18–32.

37. There are only two mentions of problems with the loyalty of these household men. Suger (*Vie de Louis le Gros*, p. 190) wrote that a certain "H" rebelled. Malmesbury (*GR*, p. 488) described a rebellion by an unnamed, base-born chamberlain.

38. Morris, "The Sheriffs and the Administrative System," pp. 162, 165. For another analysis of the shrievalties under Henry I see Green, *Government*, pp. 194–214.

39. Morris, "Sheriffs," pp. 164, 167; Green, *Government*, p. 201.

40. Morris, "Sheriffs," p. 162.

41. Ibid., p. 170; Green, *Government*, pp. 200, 233.

42. Morris, "Sheriffs," p. 172. Green credits the reorganization to a short-term financial need (*Government*, pp. 205–06) although she recognizes that Henry's move to control the shrievalties through separation of the office from the

inherited land and through appointment of trusted men was a long-term policy (ibid., pp. 205–14).

43. *Reg.* II #583n. In Domesday, there are two apparently unrelated foresters in Northampton with the same surname, Richard and William Engaine. However, their family heirs married during Henry's reign. For the Anglo-Norman royal policy on the forests and how it fits into the history of royal forests, see Young, *The Royal Forests*. Green also discusses the forests within Henry I's local government (*Government*, pp. 124–31).

44. *Reg.* II, #1262.

45. *Magni Rotuli Scaccarii Normanniae*, p. 169. King (*Peterborough Abbey, 1086–1310*, p. 24) identifies these lands as the holding of Engaine-Pytchley.

46. *Nhants.Surv.* pp. 365–89. The descendants of William Engaine (Richard I and Vitalis) held 8⅙ hides(h) and 9 virgates(v). This is an increase of 1½h and 4½v from 1086. Also 1½h and 3½v which were held in 1086 of another lord were held by descendants in chief. The Domesday Richard's descendants held 8h and 4v of which 4h were new to the family. At some time after this survey, the lands were united through the marriage of the two heirs. Their holds are, of course, far less than the 81⅓h held by the earl of Leicester but are substantial for a serjeanty family. Robert de Caux, a lesser noble, held only 1h and 1v in chief in the same area.

47. *PR*, p. 85.

48. *Reg.* II, #1518. The other references are the mention of three foresters in #687 and #688, a family's inheritance in #1556, and the references to the Engaines.

49. *PR*, p. 13. In the same year, Robert de Wyville, a vassal of Nigel d'Albini, settled an old account for the census (tax) of the forest of Pickering (Yorks.) (*PR*, p. 26) as well as an old accounting of the farm of Mowbray (*PR*, p. 137).

50. For example, Durand de Mohun and Herbert d'Aunay held pleas in the Devon-Cornwall area (Round, "Bernard the Scribe," p. 421).

51. *Reg.* II, #423.

52. Haskins, *Norman Institutions*, p. 98 and OVC 4:226.

53. Haskins, *Norman Institutions*, p. 95.

54. Wootten, "A Study of Henry I," pp. 251–52. In the case Wootten cites, Henry named a royal crossbowman to guarantee that Osbern of Lincoln carried out the order (*Reg.* II, #642).

55. Reedy, "Origins of the General Eyre." The exceptions are for the Bassets and Geoffrey de Clinton, where only a "rough correlation" exists between the land and the area of jurisdiction (pp. 721–22). It is possible that nonconsolidated land holdings gave a different kind of power, allowing the influence of the king's *familiares* to be felt over a large area, rather than letting any one to become the major influence in one area. Also see Green, *Government*, pp. 108–11.

56. *GS*, p. 24. It should be noted that the author had a strong bias for Stephen, and any condemnation of the Empress' forces must be treated accordingly. But while the description of the injustice of their courts might be biased, the extent of their jurisdiction is borne out by their Pipe Roll accounts.

57. Tout, *Chapters*, vol. 1, p. 80.

58. *FE*, p. 170.

59. *Liber Winton*, p. 33.

60. Leach, *Visitations and Memorials*, p. 192. Peter's son Roger de Valognes held two carucates in Burton by Lincoln in 1115 which were subinfeudated (*Lind. Surv.*, L 3/23); Peter held these in 1086 (ibid., 60/1). Hill (*Medieval Lincoln*, p. 52) infers that, since the previous tenant had been a "lawman," Peter succeeded to the duty as well.

61. *RB* II, p. 647. The possible family names are Crevecoeur, Port, Courcelles, and St. Quentin, but all could indicate place of origin rather than family. The fifth, Hareng, is a name that appears three times in the later *Cartae Baronum* (*RB* I, pp. 210, 205, 326) but not in earlier royal records.

62. *Reg.* II, #1951.

63. *Reg.* II, p. xxvii, *n.*34. For a discussion of the possible reasons for the lack of a formal messenger service see M. Hill, *The King's Messengers,* pp. 8–9. In addition to the thirty-six messengers in the *Regesta,* Osbert the Chaplain carried a writ from Queen Edith/Maud to Worcester (*Worc.Cart.,* #40, p. 25). He does not show up elsewhere as a messenger.

64. Hollister, "Anglo-Norman Civil War," p. 318

65. G. H. White, "Career of Waleran," pp. 23–25. D. Walker, "Charters of the Earldom of Hereford," p. 3.

66. Though Roger was at least third generation in terms of service, he was only the second generation to possess great wealth.

67. Denholm-Young, "Eudo Dapifer's Honour of Walbrook," p. 205.

68. *Reg.* II, #522 (fortification of Colchester), #519 (manor of Witham, possibly royal demesne), #661 (the Mandeville lands, held "in custody" for his son-in-law). These lands (#661) were the subject of disputes by the Mandeville heirs during the Anarchy.

69. *Reg.* II, pp. xi–xii.

70. Morris, "Sheriffs," p. 165.

71. There is only one extant case of an office passing through a female line—Adela de Montfort and the Norman constableship—but it passed directly to her husband.

72. *Reg.* II, p. xvi.

73. Ibid., #1062.

74. Atkin, "Bigod Family," and *Reg.* II, passim.

75. Round, *The King's Serjeants,* p. 121.

76. Painter, *William Marshal,* p. 34.

77. *PR,* p. 18; *Reg.* II, passim. John witnessed six times in 1133.

78. *Reg.* II, p. xv and OVC 3:134.

79. *Reg.* II, passim. In the first three years, Giffard attested 29 times; the next 26 years, 50 times (14 times in 1121). In most years, he witnessed fewer than four times.

80. *Reg.* II, p. xlii.

81. Brett (*English Church Under Henry I,* pp. 111–12) sees a major break in this policy beginning in 1125, after which more ecclesiastically oriented men were appointed. The numbers, however, are not clear evidence of any trend. Three of the eight were royal servants. Of the five others, one was Henry's nephew and another was the half-brother of Archbishop Ralph, a loyal follower of Henry. For a concise description of the bishops, see Barlow, *The English Church,* pp. 54–103; the chart on p. 318 graphically shows Henry's use of men who had served in the administration.

82. The seven are Godfrey of Bath, Seffrid of Chichester, Gilbert of London, Simon of Worcester, David of Bangor, Robert de Bethune of Hereford, and Hervey of Ely. Hervey was translated from Bangor.

83. The bishop of Rochester, a tenant of Canterbury, is not appointed by the king. Of the three bishops elected during the reign, only one, Ralph d'Escures, can be considered a new man, and he came with high clerical credentials as well.

84. Haskins, *Norman Institutions,* p. 88. Brett (*English Church,* pp. 8–10) points out a decrease in the number of positions in England which Henry filled with ecclesiastics from Normandy, as both Williams had done. Normans did

continue to be appointed, but generally only after serving an apprenticeship in England. Again, for individuals, see Barlow, *English Church*, pp. 54–103.

85. OVC 6:172–73. "Eloquentia et eruditione pollens."

86. *The Anglo-Saxon Chronicle,* edited by D. Whitelock, p. 190. "Þis he dyde eall for þes biscopes luuen." (*Anglo-Saxon Chronicle,* edited by Charles Plummer, 1:253).

87. Alexander was twice pardoned (*PR,* pp. 6, 12), while Nigel was heavily favored (*PR,* pp. 22, 23, 41, 49, 56, 126, 152).

88. Morris, "Sheriffs," p. 163.

89. Crosby, "Origins of the English Episcopate," pp. 19–20.

90. Southern, "Place," p. 139.

CHAPTER 5

The Nobles and Henry I—
Royal Patronage

For the nobles, what was important about these adminstrative changes was how they could be used. Could a noble use the changes to raise his status or could the king use them to prevent the noble from gaining favor? To see what really occurred, we must examine all available types of patronage, both major and minor, and see how Henry distributed them. Henry appears to have had a policy based upon three principles: (1) to antagonize as few people as possible; (2) to prevent the accumulation of large blocks of territory in the hands of nobles; and (3) to reward his friends in ways appropriate to their status. To demonstrate this, we will look at the types of favor Henry gave, and then how they were distributed among the various categories of nobles.

The most important types of favor that the king possessed were land and the granting of rights to the marriage of heirs. During the reign, there were four ways in which the king played a part when land changed hands: (1) when land was forfeited or escheated; (2) when the king created a new holding from the royal demesne; (3) when tenants agreed to exchange parcels; (4) by allowing only partial inheritance and reallocating the rest. The role of the king in these exchanges varied. When a noble gained land that had previously been part of the royal demesne, it was a result of the king's initiative and purely due to the king's need or desire to reward someone. When two nobles agreed to exchange land, it was noble initiative, and favor (or influence over the king) was only needed for the king's approval. The situation was different, however, when land reverted to the king due to either forfeiture or escheat. In neither case did the king or the noble recipient take the initiative; however, it was the king who redistributed the land, taking advantage of the situation. The case is the same in a partial inheritance. However, in these situations (forfeiture, escheat, inheritance) we see involved in the redistribution not only favor, but also the expectations of nobles in this feudal world (who felt they "deserved" the land) and the relative strength of noble and king (those the king must pacify as well as those he wished to reward). Could any feudal king have been able to divide an inheritance of a strong, independent noble? Looking at the redistribution of land, then, gives us insights both into how the nobles made use of the royal court to gain land and into the relative strengths in the relationship between Henry I and the Anglo-Norman nobles.

There was much forfeited land available in the early years of Henry's reign, when some of the greatest noble families lost their English estates through their support of Duke Robert.[1] Escheats, of course, occurred throughout the reign.[2] How and to whom forfeits and escheats were regranted is especially important in understanding social mobility for the newer families and the alienation of older families. These were the most "conspicuous" grants the king could make, because when a great noble forfeited his land or died without a male heir, all other great nobles knew of it. The king's grant of such land was watched closely, and was most likely to alienate any noble who felt the land had been unjustly reallocated. On the other hand, grants made from the royal demesne (while possibly envied) would not be viewed by nobles as already their possession, something necessarily to be regranted to a particular group. A third method of gaining land required a less direct form of patronage. Nobles exchanged land among themselves, probably to obtain more consolidated holdings. Since an exchange needed royal consent, it required royal favor. Records of consent are extant, though it is not known whether there were cases where the king refused consent. In the final form of reallocation, a noble might not inherit his father's entire holding. A number of partial inheritances appear in the documents, especially those in which land acquired by the father had not been inherited with the patrimony, and they often were subject to dispute in later generations.

Among the other forms of patronage, royal help in obtaining a "good" marriage was the most important. No noble could afford to view marriage as simply as the union of individuals—it primarily was a means to increase land and status. Since the marriages of heiresses or minor heirs of tenants-in-chief needed royal approval, such approval became as much a means of showing royal favor as the granting of marriages to heiresses "in the king's hand." Like the regranting of large portions of land, potential grants of great marriages were conspicuous: people knew the marriages were available and had opinions as to whom they should be given. Grants of marriage might as easily lead to discord as harmony between the king and nobles.

Finally, there were many smaller ways of showing favor—grants of exemptions from the danegeld, judicial fines, and a variety of other allowances. These gave the king the opportunity to favor large numbers of people—those from different levels of nobility and those with different political behavior.

Ultimately, to understand the relationship of the nobles to the court, we must examine these forms of reward, of royal patronage. We will look at each form of patronage—land, marriage, and the many smaller forms. Then we can combine these findings with those of the last chapter to discover how each category of noble benefited from royal patronage and how it related to their service. From this we can see Henry's subtle and successful policy of rewarding people with rewards commensurate to their status yet without creating great nobles through these rewards.

Of course, the most coveted form of favor was land, the major source of wealth and status. Because of the lack of complete sources, we cannot look at the landholding of the entire nobility and see what was gained from the king. Instead, we are forced to look at parts of the whole. One "part" which is available is a collection by Sanders of material relating to land which later formed baronies, that is, major holdings. This collection includes all of the most "conspicuous" reallocations of the reign. A second "part" of the picture is provided by the individual surveys of particular areas. Here we use an individual source as a case study. Neither approach provides the whole picture but weaknesses in one can be balanced by the strengths in the others. The result is much like a jigsaw puzzle, with some pieces missing but with enough important pieces available for us to recognize the picture.

Sanders has compiled information for 131 fiefs which he identifies as baronies.[3] Of these baronies, 121 existed at least in part in 1135. In addition, Sanders lists 72 more fiefs which he considers to have been probable baronies (early in the century these were usually smaller parcels); of these, 66 existed in 1135.[4] It is not certain that these 187 baronies comprised the largest fiefs in 1135, but they include what we know from the chronicles to have been the major forfeits and escheats, the "conspicuous" land. As a whole the group provides a convenient collection through which to examine how land held in chief changed hands under Henry I. Of these 187 baronies, 81 (about 43 percent) continued in the male line from the time of Rufus to the Anarchy, some changing hands up to three times in this period. The descent of another eighteen (about 10 percent) uncertain. One barony was overrun by the Scots early in Henry's reign and not reconquered until around 1156. Almost half of these baronies, then, were inherited by someone other than the eldest son.

As stated, when land was forfeited, the king was in a position to reallocate a substantial portion of land and everyone knew it. During Henry I's reign, sixteen of these baronies are known to have been forfeited. One, Salwarpe, was forfeited twice, giving a total of seventeen forfeits to study. The largest concentration of baronies[5] forfeited during Henry's reign were in Yorkshire—five out of a total of seventeen forfeits, giving Henry substantial influence in remapping the north. Suffolk and Sussex each had two forfeits. Most of the forfeitures took place early in the reign, and were imposed upon followers of Robert Curthose, thus giving Henry an early chance to redistribute land to followers. However, they also occurred so early that he had not yet achieved independence. Still, Henry showed his strength by keeping two of the seventeen baronies in question in the royal demesne throughout his reign for his own benefit.[6] Three more were held in demesne for a time and then regranted to members of the royal family.[7] Thus, almost one-third were used to reendow the king and provide for his family. One other was granted to a new man shortly after the forfeit, but only for a life tenure, after which it escheated and was given to a royal bastard.[8] This barony was then used to reward a royal servant but all knew that it still could be used again. These six were in effect under royal control, being held directly by the king or by members of his family during Henry's reign (Category 6). In reverse, one fief was held in demesne for awhile, but regranted to a new man[9] (Category 4). Three more were held by members of service families (Category 3)—two by Nigel d'Albini and one by Urse d'Abetot. While land was obviously being used to reward servants, Urse's situation made it less of an obvious reallocation of land and, hence, of power. Urse had been a subtenant on the land, and was regranted the land as tenant-in-chief.[10] Therefore, Henry did appear to be placing a new person on the land. Yet both these men were *curiales,* so even though this land greatly increased their wealth, they would be no more a threat to Henry as great landholders than his family or landless new men would be. Henry, however, by no means limited his distribution of forfeits to types of *curiales.* Three fiefs were granted to lesser nobles (Category 2), one of whom, Fossard, was a subtenant raised to tenant-in-chief.[11] All three of these lesser nobles appear in extant court documents, but only one, Gilbert de Laigle, can even be called a curial man. Furthermore, two of the remaining fiefs were granted to magnates (Category 5)—Beaumont and Clare.[12] Henry did not always alienate the land even though the vassal had forfeited it.

In two cases forfeits stayed in the family through lateral descent to a sister. One was Haughly, given to Alice de Montfort, who was married to Robert of the de Vere service family. The other, the barony of Salwarpe, was forfeited twice, but the second time remained in the family; it was given to the vassal's sister, Emmeline d'Abetot who was married to Walter de Beauchamp, a new man.[13] Thus Henry could be said to be giving favor to the family of the "traitor" Roger d'Abetot by allowing lateral inheritance, but also to Walter Beauchamp, the man to whom he gave the marriage.

Two of the largest forfeited fiefs, those of Robert of Bellême and the Count of Mortain, were divided; that is, Henry did not raise anyone to the status of the previous tenants-in-chief. Bellême had had three "baronies"; one became part of the royal demesne, one was eventually granted to the Queen, and one was granted to the subtenant. However, charters show that smaller pieces of Bellême's land were granted to bishops before Bellême's pardon in 1106.[14] Mortain had held four baronies in chief and the reallocation pattern was essentially the same: one became part of the royal demesne, one was granted to Chancellor Ranulf for life, and the other two were given to the tenant to be held in chief of the king.

At first glance, therefore, we see that the king redistributed the land to all groups, ostensibly not alienating any one. Only two estates of the seventeen were never regranted. Henry could not be accused of extreme greed. Two went to new men, but one of these grants was temporary. Two more went to a single member of an older service family which had no claim on the land. The rest went to lesser nobles and even magnates. However, closer examination reveals that most of the fiefs went to nobles of proven loyalty, whatever their status. Even the two magnates were those most trusted early in the reign. Many of the other fiefs can be considered to have remained under Henry's control within his family.[15] Henry's redistribution of the forfeitures did not reward people who already had major landholdings unless they were already "king's men," but it also did not create new magnates from servants.

The second major type of land reallocation occurred when land escheated. Eight baronies are believed to have escheated during the reign, though none were escheats of greater nobles. In other words, when magnates' lines ran out, the king allowed lateral descent, but with nonmagnate families took advantage (albeit legitimate) of the situation. Henry kept one of these baronies in demesne.[16] Two were granted to his own illegitimate sons, William de Tracey and Reginald of Cornwall.[17] One escheated barony was initially held in demesne, but was later granted to a new man; another was regranted, probably immediately, to a new man.[18] These two were granted to men at a lower social level than that of the previous holders. Two of the eight baronies had been held by a member of a service family and were granted to another service family.[19] The eighth escheat—land previously held by a sheriff—was granted to a lesser noble.[20] Of the eight escheats, then, two were regranted to men of the same status as the former holders, three to a man of higher status, two to new men, and one was kept in demesne. In these eight grants Henry can hardly be said to have brought about any significant social change, though some of the grants were made in a way that might have opened a channel for upward social mobility.

Whenever possible, Henry used partial inheritance to redistribute land. Two baronies appear to have been partially lost by the direct male heirs. Monmouth and Much Marcle (Herefordshire) were held by William fitz Baderon during Rufus' reign. While Monmouth was later held by William's heir Baderon of Monmouth, Much Marcle fell to Hamelin de Ballon early in the reign.[21] The reason for this split and the process by which it occurred are unknown, though it probably happened at William's death. No dispute is recorded, which in itself might indicate acceptance of the loss. The case of the Laigles and Pevensey (Sussex), on the other hand, was recorded. This barony, granted after the forfeiture to Gilbert de Laigle, was not included in the inheritance of Richer de Laigle in 1118, but rather was given to his younger brothers who had served in Henry's army. Richer signed a treaty with King Louis of France; by using this as a threat, he was able to regain the land in 1119 in a settlement with Henry.[22] Henry used this reallocation tactic repeatedly. An example from outside the Sanders collection is that of William de Mandeville, who originally was deprived of his large inheritance for allowing a prisoner to escape from the Tower. Henry modified this penalty and set a high relief, and allowed the marriage of William to the heiress of Eudo Dapifer, who held the land in the meantime. If patient, that is, nonrebellious, William would get his patrimony through his wife, if not through the relief.[23]

Henry's control of the process of inheritance, and of land reallocation generally, is seen in the cases of lateral inheritance. In addition to the two forfeited baronies that were granted to the rebels' sisters, nine had no direct male heirs but were allowed to pass by lateral descent instead of escheating. Six more *could* have passed laterally but did not—some royal choice and favor was involved.[24] The heirs of the baronies allowed lateral inheritance came from all levels of the upper class, although magnates were prominent, and from almost all the counties. In other words, there was no favor to a particular group or area of the country. The count of Clare and the earl of Chester were allowed to transfer land to a cousin or brother, sometimes more than once during the reign.[25] However, after Richard, earl of Chester, was killed in the White Ship (1120), his cousin and successor Ranulf had to relinquish some of his own patrimony before receiving Richard's holding. Still, magnates were not the only beneficiaries. The Balliols, a lesser noble family, passed on their barony to a nephew, while the Lacys twice transferred a Herefordshire estate to lateral heirs.[26] Service families and new men were also allowed to pass on holdings by lateral inheritance.[27] Henry appears to have made these decisions on an individual basis and did not exclude any group from this kind of inheritance. Two baronies that had already had Henry's patronage were allowed to go to lateral heirs. When Bourn (Cambridgeshire) had been forfeited, Henry had granted it to a new man, Payn Peverel. At Payn's death, Henry allowed a nephew to inherit it. Likewise, Bourne (Lincolnshire), which had been created for William Rollos, descended to his brother.[28] In these cases, unlike that of Laigle, Henry allowed the heirs to inherit acquired land and thus pass on the new status.[29]

What of the use of his own land to reward nobles? Twenty-four of the 187 baronies (13 percent) were new creations, carved out of the royal demesne by Henry. This is a substantial increase in new creations over the previous reign—only three baronies of the 187 had been created by Rufus.[30] The greatest concentration of these new baronies was created in the north, with seven in Northumberland, three each in Yorkshire and Cumberland, and two in Lincolnshire. Two possible explanations for this geographical distribution come to mind: either more demesne was available in the north (made up, possibly, of less desirable land), or Henry's creations were a conscious attempt to give local power to loyal men in an area where rebellion had taken place.[31] Only two members of magnate families received baronies created from royal demesne, and neither of these men was in his family's direct line of inheritance.[32] Thus neither creation was used to enrich any already powerful noble. One recipient, William Meschin, was given the barony after he had lost to the Scots the land his brother had given him, so the new land did not add anything to William's existing resources. One barony was given to a lesser noble who was in service to a greater one, possibly adding to the magnate's strength indirectly.[33] Two created baronies were given to service families,[34] and four of the twenty-four to new men.[35] These, of course, rewarded men dependent upon him and raised their status substantially. However, the greatest number, twelve, were created for lesser nobles, only two of whom (Robert de Brus and Adam de Port) spent any great amount of time at court.[36] The remaining three grantees are unidentified.[37] Thus the wealth and power from demesne land was distributed among a variety of people and did not help any one group. Henry occasionally used small pieces of demesne to help friends. Framlingham (Suffolk) was created for Bigod partly out of existing fiefs and partly out of demesne.[38]

In summary, almost half (ninety) of the 187 fiefs discussed by Sanders remained, through direct or lateral male descent, in the hands of the families who held them at the time of the Domesday Inquest. Forfeits and escheats were regranted to men of all ranks of the nobility. Newly created baronies were not given en masse either to new men or to members of service families, but rather were scattered among lesser nobles. However, no magnate's land escheated, even though some of the magnates left no direct male descendants. It appears that such an action may have represented the invisible boundary past which the magnates would have been alienated.

Many holdings smaller than baronies appear to have changed hands. The extant land surveys allow us to examine a particular area and how land was reallocated there. The Worcestershire Survey (*ca.* 1108–18) shows some of the changes that had occurred since Domesday. Many of these changes were involved in the dispute that caused the survey to be made, that is, the dispute over land between the bishop of Worcester and the sheriff, Walter de Beauchamp. Walter had inherited the office and lands of his father-in-law, Urse d'Abetot, and Urse's brother, Robert "Dispenser" d'Abetot, making Walter the largest lay tenant in the section of Worcestershire called the Oswaldslaw Hundred. The bulk of Walter's land was gained through royal patronage when the king "gave" Walter one of the d'Abetot coheiresses in marriage. However, he held more land than this accounted for. The Survey enumerates the hidage per manor,[39] and it is in this way that we see the process of redistribution. In Wike, for example, Walter held 10½ hides, having picked up three-quarters of a hide which the bishop held in Domesday. In Fledebyri, Walter held 22 hides made up of Urse and Robert's land, an archdeacon's land, and four hides which had been the bishop's. The bishop, of course, acquired land in the same way, by small acquisitions. These piecemeal increases appear to have been the usual method of enlarging holdings; as a result, a man often held land of various neighbors or shared even very small holdings with others.[40] How or even whether the king's favor played a role in this process is hard to tell. In other cases, we have evidence of Henry's approval being given (or needed) for very small pieces of land. Here in Worcestershire, though, redistribution may have been due to individual noble's and bishop's initiatives. Whichever the case, it serves to show us that although large fiefs were "conspicuous," small parcels were important and sought by the nobles.

A clear case of Henry's policies concerning the allocation of land may be seen in the Lindsey Survey (Lincolnshire) of 1115. Geoffrey fitz Payn, a new man who was given a created barony in Yorkshire, also acquired the Domesday holding of Erneis de Burun.[41] In addition to Burun's land, Geoffrey probably was given some of Roger le Poitevin's forfeited land, as well as land that appears to have been held by the archbishop of York and the bishop of Lincoln and land from the royal demesne.[42] The greater nobles would have been aware of, and perhaps irritated by, the creation of the barony. They may not have been aware of the land gains in Lincolnshire however, or have been aware only of parts of them, not the total. In this way, Henry could reward a trusted servant without necessarily publicizing the extent of the reward with the risk of alienating others.

Again, the Lindsey Survey provides a case study of land policy. The range of holdings in chief was wide. The earl of Chester, one of the major landholders, held almost 220 carucates, while Geoffrey Murdac held less than two. Substantial tenants such as Nigel d'Albini and Geoffrey fitz Payn each held more than fifty carucates. A little more than half of the lands accounted for in the Lindsey Survey had changed hands between 1086 and 1115.[43] Three major estates had been forfeited—those of the bishop of Bayeux, Ivo Taillebois, and Roger le Poitevin. Three more estates descended through the female line—those of Colswain, Robert d'Abetot, and Countess Judith. Two changed hands through remarriage of a widow—the estates of both Berengar and Robert de Toeni were held by Robert de Lisle, second husband of Berengar's widow Albreda.[44] In addition, fifteen major holdings and an assortment of small holdings escheated. In comparison to all of these, twenty-one descended to sons, though only one of these holdings (the grant to Nigel d'Albini of Geoffrey de Wirce's land) appears to have been passed on intact.

The forfeited land of Ivo Taillebois had been granted to his wife Lucy, and later descended to her third husband, Ranulf Meschin, with an overall loss of less than three carucates. The pattern of the gain and loss is interesting. The land was lost in small pieces—a few bovates lost on several manors, and a few gained on others. For example, in Bradley Wapentake, Ranulf held 4c, 7b less carucates than Ivo held in 1086 while in Gartree, he held 4c, 5b more. This type of change is very like those which occurred in Worcestershire.[45] It could work to the advantage or disadvantage of the noble. Loss of a small amount of land could weaken the holding. A noble could then be gaining a prestigious holding but one not quite as good as his predecessor's, with not enough change to warrant protest but enough to make sure he was less able to defy the king than his predecessor had been. On the other hand, the king might add a small, inconspicuous bit of land to a follower's portion, with just as inconspicuous and just as crucial a result. Furthermore, the net change might not be crucial, but the placement could be. Henry could be allowing (or prohibiting) consolidation of land in an area. The changes are apparent throughout. The bishop of Bayeux's land was forfeited twice: Robert de Lacy, the first tenant after the bishop, forfeited it in 1102, but the next holder, Hugh de Laval, did not hold all of the bishop's land in 1115 and probably had not been granted all of it.[46] Likewise, most of Roger le Poitevin's land was given to Stephen of Blois before 1115, but not every manor of Roger's Domesday holdings can be accounted for, which probably indicates that some were retained by the king.[47] No tenant in the Lindsey Survey held what his predecessor had—especially when his predecessor had been a rebel.

The result of these piecemeal changes was a very different estate map, both as to the composition of estates and with regard to the specific people who held them. The new tenants came from all groups. The upper clergy, titled nobility, and royal family all received large holdings, but most of the new tenants were lesser nobles. Two men—the curial servant Nigel d'Albini and the new man Geoffrey fitz Payn—were of lower status. However, most of the new tenants were from other areas of England than Lincolnshire, and were not members of the family of the previous tenant. Royal favor and disfavor appear to have been active in the reallocation of land in the Lindsey area of Lincolnshire.

The Lincolnshire Survey was not indicative of a special case. The Leicestershire Survey of 1124–29 also shows that there had been a major turnover of land since 1086. The Grantmesnil forfeit of 1102 was given mainly to the count of Meulan, but some of the forfeited land was retained by the king or given by him to religious houses, while small amounts of land were given to lesser nobles. One of these lesser nobles however, Robert de Ferrers, had large holdings in the area, so even small pieces of land were important. One major escheat, the honour of Blyth, was retained by the king in demesne. Robert de Ferrers, who was "the only case of direct succession among the leading families of Leicestershire,"[48] gained small amounts of land near his patrimony—lands formerly belonging to Grantmesnil, to Countess Judith and to various small holders.[49] Who then did this type of turnover benefit? When Slade analyzed the survey, he speculated that "if Orderic's view of men 'raised from the dust' were generally held, Leicestershire society at this period must have been somewhat strained."[50] However, though Slade shows how great the turnover was, it is difficult to see what group would have been alienated by it, even though royal favor was obviously active. Walter de Beauchamp and Robert Marmion split the land of their uncle-in-law (Robert d'Abetot), and William d'Albini Brito inherited land of his grandfather-in-law, although the intervening heiress, his mother-in-law, was still alive.[51] Each of the three men acquired land of his wife's inheritance with no male heir being disinherited. The royal favor operated in the grant of marriage not in direct or indirect alienation of land or denial of land to others who sought it.

The Leicestershire Survey, like the Worcestershire one, shows Henry's skill at redistributing land when it was regranted. Few of the grantees gained an entire holding. Even David, heir of Scotland and Henry's brother-in-law, who spent many years with Henry's court, did not gain all the land of his mother-in-law Countess Judith. Some of her lands went to the earl of Leicester, some to Robert Ferrers, Roger de Mowbray, and Richard Basset; her lands were thus regranted to most of the major lay tenants of the area, who were from all levels of the nobility. Roger de Mowbray, or rather more likely his father, Nigel d'Albini, gained as well a particularly compact holding—most of the estates of Geoffrey de Wirce, which probably had escheated.[52] In general, much of Nigel's acquired land was compact. His two Yorkshire baronies listed in Sanders had their *caputs* only 45 miles apart. However, Henry could have favored Nigel even more: at the time the second barony, Cottingham, was granted in 1107, Henry held a barony adjacent to Thirsk, Nigel's previous grant.[53] The other major change of tenant was directly tied to royal favor. Richard Basset, a new man, was given most of the Domesday land of Robert de Buci. Basset had familial connections to the Ridels, who were in some way related to Buci. It is possible that Buci was married to Geva Ridel, and that his land thereby descended to the Ridel heirs (all of whom were young at the time of the survey), one of whom Basset married, the rest he gained as wards. While Basset was not given all of Buci's 1086 holdings, he was granted other lands belonging to Countess Judith and two others, probably minor tenants.[54] This is a clear case of royal favor to a new man.

Two lesser nobles in the Survey, Robert de Lisle and Nicholas de Verdun, gained honours created for them by Henry from portions of demesne and small pieces of other estates. Other *curiales* or new men also gained land in the area. William Meschin, the earl of Chester's brother, who had received the barony of Egremont in Cumberland, received small pieces of two escheats in Leicestershire as well.[55] Two other men, Peverel of Nottingham and Geoffrey de Clinton, were given small fiefs of unknown descent. Richard de Rollos, a lesser noble, acquired a fair sized holding, but one which is not identifiable from Domesday.[56] The result of all the regranting of holdings seen in the Leicestershire Survey was a great change in the tenantry of the area, but no basic social change, since most of the new tenants had a familial claim on the land. Looking further, however, suggests that this familial claim often was due to a man's marriage to an heiress, which itself required royal favor—an aspect of patronage that will be examined shortly.

When the surveys of Lincolnshire and neighboring Leicestershire, both of which had large turnovers of tenants, are examined together, the redistribution of honours is even more evident. Eight nobles (Guy de Craon, the earl of Chester, Countess Judith, Drogo de Beurere, Roger de Busli, Robert d'Abetot, and Robert and Berengar de Toeni) held Domesday land in both shires. The lands of only two, Guy de Craon and the earl of Chester, descended more or less intact to the heirs.[57] Two more passed almost intact to a new holder—losing manors throughout each county.[58] During Henry's lifetime there was no successor to Roger de Busli on his estate. Much of Busli's land was retained in demesne, while pieces were redistributed. William Meschin received some of it while the Lincolnshire land went in part to William de Lovetot. The lands of both Robert d'Abetot and the Toenis were also broken up, though in these cases the lands were divided among in-laws.[59] These cases may simply represent situations in which a partible inheritance received royal approval, or, on the other hand, may exemplify a deliberate attempt by Henry to divide larger estates. Therefore, most of the land which had been held by seven people in 1086 was held by seven people in 1135. The eighth was replaced by many. However, the king in effect changed the lines (to new holders or chosen husbands of female descendants) and the configuration of the holdings.

Another way of examining the gains made during the reign is by looking at individual families. Many such studies have been done, including one of the Redvers family, Richard de Redvers being an early *familiaris* of Henry's. Much of Richard's direct patronage from Henry came from five different Domesday tenants, most of whom escheated, although two became rear tenants of Redvers instead of tenants-in-chief. Other smaller landholders also had Redvers inserted between themselves and the king.[60] So once again, patronage in land was given in a variety of ways, mostly in small, less conspicuous grants.

The next way land changed hands was through exchange. Though this was initiated privately, royal favor was necessary for transferring any land held in chief; the surviving charters include examples of Henry's approval both of exchanges and of "sales." Early in the reign, Henry granted a multiple exchange of the manor of Duxford (Cambridgeshire). During William II's reign, Hugh Envermou had given it to Westminster Abbey in exchange for Doddington, which apparently was in Lincolnshire near other land which Hugh held. Henry allowed the lands to be re-exchanged, then "restored" Duxford to Eustace, count of Boulogne, giving Hugh another, unnamed manor.[61] Unfortunately, this is the only record of the transaction, so we do not know what prompted the action. It is clear, however, that the original exchange between the abbey and Envermou would have benefited both parties by allowing consolidation of their land. Probably the re-exchanges were permitted by Henry as a favor to the count.

As in the case of other royal favor, however, some men had to pay to exchange land. We especially see this in cases of *curiales,* men trusted by Henry, who were nevertheless dependent upon him. Some favors were gifts, rewards for service. Others, like exchanges, were requested by those involved, so Henry had the upper hand. Robert, a man of Herbert the Chamberlain, a favored royal servant, paid 20*m.* for the right of exchange in 1130.[62] There are two records of sales involving new men. Grimbald the Physician was allowed to sell land in Dorset to be held in fee of Alfred of Lincoln (a lesser noble, although one of status in Lincolnshire, Somerset, and Dorset).[63] Bernard the Scribe was allowed to buy land in Winchester which was also to be held in chief.[64]

Royal favor is also discernible when we look at what land Henry granted, how much, and with what rights. As already mentioned, Nigel d'Albini was given land in the same general area as his other land, but it did not result in a holding which was as compact as possible. His brother William d'Albini Pincerna was granted the barony of Old Buckenham in Norfolk, in the same shire where he held a manor granted by Rufus,[65] and other land previously held by a clerk of Henry I in free alms.[66] Not only were the new lands in an advantageous location, but Henry reconfirmed the lands granted by Rufus with profitable extras—the rights of wreck, the gilds of the town, the market and toll dues, the port's landing dues and the waterway and ferry.[67] Another case indicating royal favor was that of Roger Bigod. The barony granted him was in Suffolk, where he already held land, while much of his patrimony was in Norfolk. Thus, even though his lands did not make up a compact fee, they were in the same general area of England,[68] allowing him to administer his estate more directly and reducing his traveling expenses. Yet certainly not all favorites received such compact grants. Richard Basset, a new man whose family gained greatly under Henry I, held an estimated 176 hides, but they were spread through eleven counties;[69] Geoffrey de Clinton held approximately 570 hides, and though much of his property lay in central England, the total was distributed over fourteen counties.[70] While such extended lands provided wealth, they did not provide power bases from which to defy the king. Land itself could be gained through royal patronage, but it was rarely compact land holdings in an area.

A major way of gaining control of land was through marriage. Examination of the Anglo-Norman marriages in this generation, especially of those of great heiresses, shows that marriages were the most important method of gaining land. In addition, a great many heiresses married "beneath" themselves; in other words, the man and his family gained status through the marriage. This was especially true of the service families and new men. Magnates and members of the royal family consciously intermarried, using marriage to reestablish the birth status of the noninheriting sons. All nobles, male and female, appeared willing to pay the king for various types of marriage rights, and to pay in greater proportion than for other rights.

Thirty-two of Sanders' 187 baronies, that is, 17 percent, descended through an heiress at some time during Henry I's reign. What with multiple marriages and short life spans, thirty-eight marriages of baronial heiresses appear to have been made between 1100 and 1135. In fourteen of these (37 percent), the husbands were of lesser nobility and each married a woman of approximately the same status.[71] Three more appear to involve lesser nobles but are not identified. From what can be determined of the husbands' previous landholdings, only one of these men gained substantial political benefit by marrying an heiress of neighboring lands, uniting two Domesday fiefs into a substantial barony,[72] although some of the husbands were from neighboring counties.[73] Most of these marriages, therefore, united families of similar status, though they had the economic advantage (for the man) of gaining land. Three of the heiresses were married to younger sons of magnates.[74] A fourth was married to the eldest son of a magnate, but his father, the earl of Hereford, had forfeited his land under Rufus.[75] So, like younger sons, he was reestablishing his claim to his birth status when he married "into land." None of these four women were from magnate families, so neither title nor "great" connections were involved. The gain was land. Three of the "best catches" in terms of land and family connections were given to members of the royal family: two daughters of earls to the king's two legitimate relatives and an heiress with large holdings to an illegitimate son,[76] that is, all married men of a wealth and status commensurate with their own.

However, fourteen of the marriages (37 percent) involved noble royal servants; each of these substantially increased his status by the land and the family connections acquired in the marriage. Eight of these marriages were made by men from the more established service families, but six were by new men.[77] Other researchers have studied this question using different samples, and different bases for analysis, yet all have reached the same conclusions.[78] The Anglo-Norman curial men knew the advantage of the "good marriage." As the chroniclers noted, these marriages "increased [the noble's] dignity."[79]

Even a brief examination of Sanders' compilation shows just how advantageous marriage could be, and so how important it was to have the king's favor. The king's approval was necessary for the marriage of the heiress of a deceased tenant-in-chief, and was desired even when the father was alive. The actual extent of royal prerogative while the father lived is unclear. Painter surmises that it probably depended on the relative power of the noble and suitor—that is, the king would not insult a powerful suitor by rejecting the betrothal. Therefore, once again, the king's power was based on individual circumstances and the king's skillful judgment.[80] The powerful but curial count of Meulan's "will" included a provision for his daughter's inheritance should his sons die, but only if she married with the king's consent.[81] While there is no extant case of Henry's preventing a marriage, there are records of his arranging them.[82] Michael de Hanslope designated the king his heir. Henry then arranged the marriage of Michael's daughter to William Mauduit, a new man, along with the transfer of all of Michael's property.[83]

However, with the Norman kings generally, patronage was not always a free gift, and this was the case with marriage. No magnate or member of the royal family appears to have had to pay for a marriage that reestablished his birth status: this appears to have been a favor the magnates expected to obtain because of their status. However, there was a price for "social climbing," and those who could "marry up" were willing to pay for it. The rank of noble (both male and female) varied, as did the amount fined. Fees usually included rights over various lands or family wardships, not just the woman. William Maltravers, a new man, owed £100 to have the widow of Hugh de Laval with Hugh's land and her marriage portion in Yorkshire, and another 50m. for the right to her lands in Leicestershire.[84] The fee was high partially because the king was allowing the first husband's lands to pass to the second husband, as he had done in the case of Maud Laigle. William fitz Richard owed £52 11s. 8d. for the widow of Fulbert of Dover, but no mention was made of her husband's lands.[85] Henry's control of lands transferred through marriage is evident. When the widow involved had a young child, Henry sometimes included the child's wardship in the agreement, in which cases the fines were higher.[86] Wardships made widows highly desirable. The Houghton family, curial servants and justices, had several marriage transactions recorded in

1130, arranging marriages for both William and his son, Payn, to widows. William de Houghton also paid to control his minor stepson's property.[87] While we view the agreements almost as sales of the women, in most cases the payment was technically made in order to hold her land, as when William de Clinton owed 145*m*. for his wife's Norman lands.[88] The types of payments varied as well as the amounts. The Essex heiress of a lesser noble was worth 10*m*. and a warhorse,[89] while the marriage of Humphrey d'Albini's daughter was valued at ½*m*. in gold.[90]

Even nonheiresses commanded high prices. The Pipe Roll of 1130 records much about the family of Herbert the Chamberlain, a loyal servant who had gained much through his own marriage and royal favor, and who had died shortly before 1130. Herbert's heir's relief was 353*m*., yet a new payment for a daughter in marriage with her land was 200*m*. and 2*m*. in gold, nearly two-thirds of the heir's relief. Henry also was able to get yet another payment on Herbert's own marriage—a debt of 20*m*. is recorded by Herbert's widow's brother to regain the land which Herbert had been allowed to hold for his wife.[91]

The noble women also sought royal favor in marital matters, usually for their freedom to act (or not act) without a male. Here the whole range of the nobility was included—even magnate women could not expect this favor. We have seen this in the case of Countess Lucy and her total of 645*m*. fees discussed in chapter 2. Furthermore, the amounts varied greatly, indicating that the need to deal with the king affected women throughout the rest of the nobility. Basilia, the widow of Odo Dammartin, owed 60*m*. to hold her dower lands, in the same year in which her son's relief was 100*m*.[92] Matilda, the widow of Roger de Argenton, owed £8 10s. 8d. for her Suffolk lands and her freedom,[93] while Ingenolda, widow of Roger nephew of Hubert, owed only 2*m*. to hold her London property in her own right.[94] Sometimes wards needed to act in the same way, as when Walter de Canceio owed £15 for the right to take a wife freely, but the examples of women far outnumber those of wards.[95]

The knowledge of the importance of the various benefits gained through marriage is understood by the comparatively high amounts paid for it. Indeed, Mooers' figures show that among the privileges paid for in 1129–30, the amount paid by men and women for marriage privileges far outstripped the other categories (marriage £3,484, office holding £1,902, wardship £387, release from office holding £227). Since the number of offices and marriages entered into were almost equal (36 offices, 33 marriages), the nobles knew the economic benefits of marriage and were more "willing" to be charged for the greater return.[96] Obviously, the king benefited more directly and continually from the grant of an office. The nobles received income, status, and connection, but the king acquired a loyal servant. However, Henry I was aware of the nobles' willingness to pay for marriage rights. This is seen in Henry's charge of an additional 45*m.* made of Countess Lucy to be used to compensate with financial favor the man he would have chosen to give her as marital patronage.[97]

Marriage might have more material advantage than merely that of acquiring land or wardships. Claims to offices were common. It was a prime way in which Henry chose his servants without outright division of family and office. By marrying Robert Mauduit's daughter, William de Pont de l'Arche gained a constableship and a claim to a wardship in the family.[98] Eustace fitz John's second marriage brought him a constableship to add to his first wife's barony.[99] As previously mentioned, Rualon d'Avranches probably became sheriff of Kent because his marriage to the heiress of a Kent barony made him a major landholder in the shire.[100] Brian fitz Count purchased the office of constable and part of the land of Nigel d'Oilli, the uncle of Brian's wife Maud. Brian's marriage to Maud had already brought him a barony that had been her first husband's. Thus Brian gained advantages of several kinds through the familial connections of his wife.[101]

In all, new men and service families benefited greatly by marriages which brought wealth, status and connections. Where there is evidence of royal involvement, these families increased their status through marriage. As will be seen, magnates continued to intermarry and hold their status, but the advantageous marriage seems to have been a common, successful, and, perhaps, the most usual means of showing royal favor to *familiares*. Also, as we will see, the marriage connection had the greatest long term advantage.

The men who appear in the records as having performed royal service are very much in evidence as receiving the smaller or less conspicuous forms of patronage, such as exemptions from certain fines or taxes. Green's figures show a total of £22,864 10*s.* 4*d.* in fines collected; £5251 1*s.* 11*d.* pardoned; £38,894 7*s.* 11*d.* owing.[102] This represents substantial royal income as well as a substantial loss of income due to favor. The amount of danegeld actually collected was about equal to the amount which various individuals were pardoned by Henry's writs.[103] For one type of fine, *murdrum*, almost three times as much was pardoned as was collected.[104] These totals, however, represent a large number of individuals, the majority of whom received smaller exemptions.[105] The range of beneficiaries runs the gamut of my categories of nobles.

One of the most wide ranging grants, and one of the most important to the noble, is the danegeld exemption.[106] Who was given exemption, as well as who was not, is an indication of royal favor. Retainers and clerks (Category 1), while not heavily favored, were listed, several being listed with the epithet "monk" or "clerk."[107] Many of the lesser nobles (Category 2) who appeared at court are mentioned in danegeld exemptions. In Wiltshire, for example, fourteen of the sixty-eight individuals named were clearly of the lesser nobility. In Oxfordshire, eighteen of the sixty-four were nobles; nine additional men, though unidentified, were also minor tenants-in-chief. There are examples, however, of nobles not being given exemptions. Robert de Lisle held land in Lincolnshire, and is mentioned in the Pipe Roll in regard to land and pleas in Yorkshire and in land cases on the Isle of Wight; but he received no exemptions.[108] The largest number of exemptions listed are from Categories 3 and 4, the service families and the new men, although as groups, each represents a smaller number of people than Category 2. In addition to all the familiar names of *curiales,* many epithets such as *ostiarius* and *servientes* indicate relatively less important services. This seems to occur more often in counties such as Wiltshire and Oxfordshire, which have relatively long lists of exemptions. Almost all of the magnates (Category 5) were exempt, but there is some question as to whether all their lands were exempt. In other words, the exemption may not have been worth as much as it could have been. The count of Aumâle, for example, though charged various fines on his land in Yorkshire, was not exempt in that shire,[109] and no titled nobles are listed in the long Oxfordshire roll. Since the exemptions are one of the major sources for determining the amount of land held, the actual proportions of exempt to nonexempt land cannot be shown. The royal family (Category 6), and especially Stephen of Blois and Robert of Gloucester, were given exemptions on land throughout the country. All of the greater clergy (Category 7) in each shire were granted exemptions on their land, as would have been expected. The amounts pardoned to men in each category were, of course, based on the amount of land held, so that the upper levels of society were exempt from more tax. The actual amount of pardon, therefore, was not in itself indicative of favor,[110] while the pardon itself was.

Some of the exemptions may have been indicative of a different type of favor. After the danegeld ceased to be collected, Richard fitz Nigel wrote that all barons of the Exchequer and the sheriffs were exempt from the common assizes as a perquisite of their office.[111] This may have been the case with the danegeld. If so, then the exemptions of Roger of Salisbury, as justiciar, the constables (including Brian fitz Count, Walter de Beauchamp and Roger d'Oilli), Herbert the Chamberlain, and John the Marshal were due to their official role rather than royal favor.[112] The sheriffs, of course, were exempt in their own shires, but in 1130 also seem to have been exempt in others. Possibly other officials—justices such as Walter Espec, Eustace and Payn fitz John, and stewards such as Humphrey de Bohun, all of whom were *curiales*—were exempt due to their offices as well. But not all the evidence points to this explanation. Sheriffs and justices were exempt in counties other than their own,[113] while former servants (for instance, past sheriffs) received exemptions from the danegeld levied in 1130, as did the families of servants.[114] This would seem to indicate that the exemptions were in many cases not perquisites of the office, but favors given to people who had served because they were *familiares*. In addition, the range of men exempted seems to indicate that Henry used this form of patronage for all groups of men but found it a particularly apt way to reward his servants.

Pardoning of fines was sometimes a sign of favor to an individual other than the person actually receiving the writ; for example, the Pipe Roll on several occasions records a grant of exemption *pro amore* of someone else. Two obscure nobles were exempt from the danegeld of Buckinghamshire *pro amore* of Robert of Gloucester, the king's son.[115] William of Warenne interceded for Geoffrey Mauduit and obtained a pardon of the last 2*m.* on Geoffrey's relief payment in Essex.[116] In Yorkshire, an old fine for shire court pleas was pardoned *pro amore* of William Maltravers, a new man.[117] This type of patronage most likely came about through the presence at court of the intercessor and his favor with the king.[118]

Other fines, mostly associated with judicial action, appear in the Pipe Roll with exemptions. Many of the same people exempt from the danegeld were given exemptions for *murdrum*, forest, and shire pleas. In Essex, for example, a list of exemptions for a previously levied *murdrum* lists twenty-five exemptions; of those exempted, sixteen were also listed as pardoned for the 1130 danegeld in the shire. Nine of the fourteen exempt from forest fines in Essex were in the list of danegeld exemptions as well.[119] In both cases, those exempted were of all ranks within the nobility and clergy. The same pattern is seen in the 1130 *murdrum* levy in Wiltshire, when eighteen of the twenty-eight individuals exempted also received danegeld exemptions.[120] In Wiltshire, only £6 11s. 6d. was collected, with another £1 outstanding, while £41 18s. 9d. was exempt. With respect to the danegeld levy as well as the *murdrum* fine, while the amount excused any one individual by reason of patronage might be small, the loss to the treasury was substantial. As a policy, Henry was sacrificing quite a bit of income. Obviously, these exemptions were sought after by the nobles and were used by Henry as a useful form of patronage.

Exemptions were not always complete, however. Some people received pardons only for part of a fine; others had to pay to be released from an expense. When William of Glastonbury owed 308*m*. 2*d*. relief for his uncle's Dorsetshire land and the office of chamberlain of Normandy, a partial exemption was given. In 1130, he paid 20*m*. and was pardoned 20*m*., but the remaining 248*m*. 2*d*. was carried over in debt.[121] Similar entries appear throughout the Pipe Roll. Guy de Laval and Geoffrey Murdac were pardoned their fines for Yorkshire pleas held prior to 1130, each after paying part of his debt.[122] Robert Fossard owed for Yorkshire pleas and for reseisin of his land, as did Walter de Gant in Blyth, and both were pardoned part of the money owed.[123]

Similar examples of royal favor found in the Pipe Roll were payments to avoid greater expense, William fitz Otho, the royal goldsmith, paid 10*m*. on account for a fee of £36 10*d*. in order not the have a master.[124] Ralph fitz Godric owed a horse worth 60s. in order not to plead concerning his land.[125] Everard de Ros was allowed not to be a steward for the count of Aumâle for a fine of 2*m*.[126]

As we have seen, the majority of the favors listed in the Pipe Roll were small. The same holds in other records; for example, Bishop Audin was given a one time favor when his baggage was exempt from tolls crossing the Channel.[127] Other favors could be gotten indirectly. Robert of Gloucester's falconer had gotten a market for Robert and was given the right to enjoy it for doing so.[128]

A major form of indirect patronage that does not show up in documents such as a Pipe Roll is royal support in obtaining good clerical office for a family member. Henry was showing favor to his sister Adela when he got his nephew Henry of Blois the good livings first of Glastonbury and then of Winchester. The Coronation elevations of sons of magnates were forms of patronage to their lay relatives. Henry named Cecily, daughter of Robert fitz Hamon, the abbess of Shaftesbury probably at about the same time he arranged the marriage of his own son Robert of Gloucester to Cecily's eldest sister.[129] Henry also attempted to favor his early supporter, the earl of Chester, by elevating his illegitimate son Robert from a monk at St. Evroul to abbot of Bury St. Edmunds, but lost the battle to the Gregorian Anselm.[130] While in each case, the patronage was not just any position but an important and lucrative one, it can be seen that the favor was not to the recipient but to his or her relative.

Royal Service and Patronage: Conclusions

Having considered the basic types of curial service and royal patronage, let us look now at how each category of the nobility was affected. Was there a relationship between curial behavior or birth and the receipt of royal patronage? If so, was a particular type of favor used for particular categories? Who most benefited from the changes in royal administration?

As we have seen throughout these last two chapters, only some of the evidence (royal witnessing and the evidence from Sanders' collection) lends itself to quantification. Table 1 summarizes these figures by category of noble, and sets them alongside the number of families identified in these categories.

The very definition of the private retainers (Category 1) limits what can be said of their relationship to the court and to royal patronage. Attendance at court appears to have been limited to those times when their lord also attended, and witnessing by this group was usually limited to charters involving their lord or related to their own donation to a church. By definition, this group did not perform royal service. As we have seen, some of the private servants were of fairly high status themselves. Robert fitz Ansketill, a man of the count of Meulan, left land worth 200*m.* in relief, and Maurice of Windsor, the dapifer of Bury St. Edmunds, was exempt from the danegeld for more than 44 hides of land in 1130, each was obviously relatively wealthy.[131] However, in neither of these cases does the land seem to have been acquired through royal patronage. Moreover, no one in this category appears to have made a particularly advantageous marriage during Henry I's reign. Several were given exemptions from the danegeld, but on the whole, the retainers and servants of other lords directly benefited little from royal patronage.

The untitled nobility (Category 2) generally fall into the middle of each category of service and patronage. As a group, they participated in and benefited from all forms of service and favor, but very few individuals or particular families benefited greatly from any one form or from all. The royal court appears to have been open to all, and a great many individuals in this broad category left a record of court attendance, but no one individual attended frequently and consistently enough to be termed a true *curialis* or *familiaris*. As a group, these men witnessed fewer times than their numbers might warrant. During the reign this group averaged 16 percent of those present at court; but they account for (on the average) only 10 percent of the total witnessing. One change can be seen in those who attended the court. Early in the reign, only the wealthier members of the group tended to be at court, while later a broader range of members was present.

Many of the lesser nobles performed royal service at various times in the reign. Some were justices or sheriffs and a few participated in inquests. However, most of the justices and sheriffs of multiple shires were members

TABLE I. Summary of Royal Witnessing and "Baronial" Land Under Henry I

CATEGORY	FAMILIES[1]		WITNESSING		BARONIAL LAND AND MARRIAGE (TOTAL TRANSFERS IN PARENTHESES)[2]					
	# in group	% in total	% of wits.	% of attest.	Forfeits (17)	Escheats (8)	Lateral inherit. (9)	New/from demesne (24)	Partial inherit. (2)	Marriage (38)
1. Retainers	20	6%	12%	5%	0	0	0	4%	0	0
2. Lesser nobles	140	42%	16%	10%	18%	13%	33%	50%	100%	37%
3. Service families	50	15%	17%	21%	24%[5]	25%	11%	8%	0	21%
4. New men	45	13%	20%[3]	25%[3]	18%[5]	25%	33%	17%	0	16%
5. Magnates	17	5%	12%	12%	12%	0	22%	8%	0	11%
6. Royal family	1	*	3%[4]	3%	18%	25%	0	0	0	8%
7. Upper clergy	61	18%	22%	25%	—	—	—	—	—	—
Unidentified holders	—	—	—	—	0	0	0	13%	0	8%
Held in demesne	—	—	—	—	12%	13%	0	0	0	—

*Less than .5%

1. The 334 "families" here include individual clerical offices (bishop, abbot, cardinal legate) for Category 7. The 250 families discussed in the text are Categories 2–6 plus a few identified families from Category 1.
2. I. J. Sanders, *English Baronies: A Study of their Origins and Descent, 1087–1327* (Oxford: Clarendon Press, 1960).,
3. See Appendix I for changes over time in this category's percentage of witnessing.
4. Royal witnessing does not include Henry I.
5. The forfeit totals for Categories 3 and 4 each include one forfeit granted laterally to a sister, then given to a man in this category through marriage.

of service and new families, not members of lesser noble families. In addition, most of the shrievalties held by lesser nobles were of the shires in which they held most of their land, and inquests conducted by them were related to those shires. They exercised power where they had local influence, rather than being entrusted with royal power to exercise throughout the kingdom.

As a group, the untitled nobility profited from royal land patronage. Of Sanders' lists of baronies, the lesser nobles gained three of the seventeen (18 percent) forfeits, one of the eight (13 percent) escheats, three of the nine (33 percent) lateral inheritances, and twelve of the twenty-four (50 percent) newly created baronies. Two of the new creations were given to men—Brus and Port—who appeared at court regularly but not frequently. Both of the baronies that Henry controlled through partial inheritance belonged to lesser nobles. They also gained through marriage. Fourteen of the thirty-eight (37 percent) baronial marriages noted in Sanders definitely were made by lesser nobles. Since the unidentified nobles probably would belong to the lesser nobility, this figure might be as high as 45 percent. In the areas surveyed during Henry's reign, these men as a group benefited when land changed hands. The same is true for exemptions from assessments. Approximately one-quarter of the people in the longer lists were lesser nobles, many of them rather low in status. In general, however, though the group served the king and was given royal favors, very few individuals made a great fortune or gained much power from Henry's favor.

Category 3, that of service families who performed royal service under the Williams and continued to do so under Henry, emerges from this study as the group which benefited most from royal favor, both as a group and as individuals. They attended court frequently and at a fairly consistent rate throughout the reign. They averaged about 17 percent of those present at court, that is, slightly more than the numerically larger Category 2. The service families, however, witnessed more often than their numbers warranted, constituting an average of 21 percent of the witnessing—that is, they were relied on heavily. One change which took place within this group in the course of the reign can be noted: a smaller group within this category came to be relied upon as the reign progressed. This development may have been due in part to Henry's attempts to reduce some of the power that had accrued to the older sheriffs as the next generation came of age. It also was due in part to the deaths of some of the older servants who were replaced because they left minor sons, daughters married to other servants, or aristocratic sons.

By definition, the service families performed royal service, so of course they form a large part of a study of royal service and its rewards. Two points emerge which are of particular interest. First, some of the service families not only continued to perform their old tasks (such as sheriff or *pincerna*), but were also given some of the newer, even experimental jobs. For example, in the 1130 experiment with multiple shrievalties the two principal men, often working as a team, were Aubrey de Vere, a member of a service family, and Richard Basset, a new man. A number of the justices also came from the core group of service families who attended court, served, and received favor, especially Nigel d'Albini, the Bigods and the de Veres.

The service families benefited substantially from royal patronage. Four of the seventeen (24 percent) forfeits were given to servants (including one lateral forfeit given to a servant by marriage and including two to Nigel d'Albini). Two of the eight (25 percent) escheats, and one of the nine (11 percent) lateral inheritances, but only two of the twenty-four (8 percent) newly created baronies were granted to members of service families. The greatest gain for this category was achieved by way of advantageous marriages. Eight of the thirty-eight (21 percent) baronial marriages were made by members of service families, and the land gained by such families in the areas with extant surveys was mostly gained through marital claims. It should be remembered that marriage into a barony carried with it not only land but status: the granting of such a marriage was therefore a higher level of reward than the granting of land alone.

Small favors, such as danegeld exemptions, were frequently given to members of the service families, who, with the new men, benefited the most in these Pipe Roll lists. As was the case with the other groups, servants with very little status and only local power were given exemptions, but the names repeated most often in the lists of exemptions were those of the core group of servants.

Category 4, that of the new men, fared well during Henry's lifetime. This group was never large, but grew steadily through the reign. Members of this group made up a somewhat larger proportion of witnesses than their numbers would suggest (on the average, approximately 20 percent of the court but 25 percent of the witnesses). Their importance in the witness lists is most marked in the latter part of the reign, from 1120–35, when they averaged 22 percent of those attending court but 30 percent of the number of witnessings of court documents.

As royal servants, the new men were employed heavily in the newly created jobs—for instance, as justices. Henry I relied on them in inquests and in other jobs, along with members from older service families. In general, the new men benefited substantially both as a group and as individuals from royal patronage. This is shown by the large number of names of new men which appear as office holders and as recipients of various forms of royal patronage. Such a situation is the direct reverse of that of the lesser nobles. Few of the new men received great and conspicuous rewards, however. Three of the seventeen (18 percent) forfeits (including one lateral forfeit given with a marriage and one for life tenure only), two of the eight (25 percent) escheats, three of the nine (33 percent) lateral descents, and four of the twenty-four (17 percent) newly created baronies went to new men. While they gained more than the service families did in the category of demesne baronies, they were behind in the winning of heiresses. Only six of the thirty-eight (16 percent) great heiresses of the period married new men. They used what they did gain to their advantage, however. As shown in the surveys, several men in this group acquired land through marriage claims, that is, claims on the land of their wives' families. The new men were, indeed, successful gaining exemptions from assessments throughout the shires. It was, however, the benefits gained through marriages which gave the families the staying power within the upper ranks of the nobility.

Category 5, that of the magnates, was not excluded from anything yet overall did not receive a large share of patronage. Early in the reign the group attended court fairly frequently, but their attendance subsequently declined. However, they continued to attend the ceremonial courts regularly, though less often when the court was in Normandy. Their overall average was 12 percent of those attending court, and they also made up an average of 12 percent of the total witnesses; but the figures vary greatly, and the years where large numbers of men from this group attend court and act as witnesses are usually years with a greater number of extant charters from crown-wearing times. This is due in part to a lack of initiative on the part of some of these men after they gave Henry their approval. It is also due, however, to the failure of the sons of the active, loyal magnates to attend court. These second generation young men had grown up with status and felt that they deserved certain benefits by right rather than work. Performance of royal service by magnates was rare, except of course for military service. Sometimes this appears to have been by Henry's choice: for example the loss by the Clares of their shrievalty; sometimes the absence of service was the magnates' choice. The majority of the services required by the king were more menial than a titled noble or his family would be expected to perform; but their absence from inquests is surprising.

The magnates received individual favors commensurate with their status. Two of the seventeen (12 percent) forfeited baronies were regranted to them. None of the eight escheats fell to members of this group; but neither did land held by this group escheat to the king. Two of the nine (22 percent) lateral descents permitted by royal favor occurred in magnate families, along with one of the two lateral forfeits, an indication that Henry I allowed more flexibility in inheritance to this group. Only two of the twenty-four (8 percent) newly created baronies and four of the thirty-eight (11 percent) baronial marriages were regranted to titled families. So, while the group added to their land in the surveyed areas, it was mainly through regrants of early forfeits that they did so. The magnates, then, did obtain royal favors, but not in the same, almost piecemeal way that the lower groups did. Furthermore, while most magnates were exempt from assessments, there is reason to question whether they were exempt for the entirety of their holdings.

The royal family (Category 6) was numerically the smallest of the groups, and there was a wide disparity of behavior within it. The legitimate members of the group—in particular Stephen of Blois and David of Scotland—behaved as magnates did, attending court regularly but infrequently and serving rarely. As might be expected, they were highly favored in all forms of patronage, especially in regranted forfeits (three of the seventeen, 18 percent) and escheats (two of eight, 25 percent). While the figures for baronial marriages (three of thirty-eight, 8 percent) do not seem high, all of the male relatives were married to heiresses. Later in the reign, however, patronage granted to both Stephen and David declined. Stephen probably became too powerful after Prince William died, and David became a king in his own right. The illegitimate members of the family, however, present a different picture. Several of the sons married well and received various forms of patronage. One in particular was favored throughout the reign: Robert, earl of Gloucester was as much a trusted *familiaris* as any of the great servants; he was also a *curialis*, a justice, the justice of the Bayeux Inquest and a military leader with Henry in battle. He was granted an heiress and title.

The upper clergy (Category 7) have been dealt with in less detail, but some conclusions can be drawn with respect to this group. Court attendance was very high, especially among the former royal servants among the upper clergy who were obviously traveling with the court. They averaged about one-quarter of the members of the court and acted as witnesses in slightly higher proportion than warranted by their numbers. Many continued to serve after elevation, the outstanding example of course being Roger, bishop of Salisbury. Some served as justices and held inquests in the areas of their see. Certainly, the churches of Henry's *familiares,* such as Abingdon during Faritius' abbacy, received substantial amounts of land, but whether they gained more than other churches is better left to a study of Henry's patronage generally. The greater clergy all received exemptions from assessments, although this may have been a traditional exemption for the clergy.

This detailed examination of the kinds of royal patronage and the various groups that received it makes it clear that Henry did have a policy as far as patronage was concerned. His policy seems to have been based on the three principles stated at the beginning of this chapter: (1) to antagonize as few people as possible; (2) to prevent the accumulation of large blocks of territory in the hands of nobles; and (3) to reward his friends in ways appropriate to their status. If one looks at the various categories of patronage, one finds that large blocks of territory were re-granted to men in various upper class groups, but very few of the new holders had previously been wealthy men in their own right no matter what group they belonged to. The few cases of major grants to magnates all occurred early in the reign, probably to ensure support or reward those who had helped him gain the throne. Men of all groups picked up smaller portions of land, were allowed to inherit outside the direct line of inheritance, and were allowed to transfer land. All groups were also allowed to marry heiresses, but here new men and especially members of the service families seem to have profited most. The magnates received conspicuous favor—they were granted large estates, married great heiresses, and attended court on state occasions. The new men, and especially members of the service families, obtained substantial fortunes through accumulation of smaller rewards, and were relied upon at court throughout the year. Various exemptions seem to have been the king's most regular form of patronage for his lower-level servants. The types of patronage and service discussed are, of course, only part of the picture. A great part of status is psychological; simply being associated with the king must have been of prime importance for many.[132] Obviously, it paid for a noble to serve the king. The new opportunities which administrative kingship had created indeed could be lucrative ones. They also brought into focus two, not necessarily exclusive, noble patterns of life and social strategies— curial and noncurial.

Notes

1. For example, in 1101 the three Bellême brothers of the Montgomery family (Robert de Bellême, earl of Shrewsbury, Roger le Poitevin, lord of Lancaster, and Arnulf, lord of Pembroke) were allied against the king. Among their allies were Robert Lacy, lord of Pontefract, and Ivo Grantmesnil. All these men forfeited their English holdings for their part in the war. A similar analysis has been done by J. E. Lally for Henry II ("Secular Patronage at the Court of Henry II"). Lally's

comparisons to Henry I use the view that Henry I alienated much land, especially demesne. This is not the view held by all historians of the first Henrician rule; see below, note 30.

2. Among the major escheats was that of Eudo Dapifer in 1120. A fuller discussion of both escheats and forfeitures will follow.

3. Sanders, (*English Baronies,* pp. vi-vii) identifies his baronies as those land holdings on which at some time—mainly in the late twelfth and early thirteenth centuries—a relief of £100 was levied. RaGena DeAragon ("The Growth of a Secure Inheritance," pp. 382–83) succinctly provides the many cautions needed in using Sanders: (1) he includes as single baronies what were multiple, separate holdings in the twelfth century; (2) he misses some digressions in descent, especially during Stephen's reign. Some of the weakness of this source is offset in the present study by also examining forfeits and marriages by individuals not baronies and by comparing it to information from twelfth-century surveys.

4. R. H. C. Davis ("What Happened in Stephen's Reign") has also attempted to analyze Sanders' study, but has derived different figures. He has the same total of 203 baronies, but counts 193 existing in 1135, while I count 187. The ten baronies created later were Ashby (Sanders, p. 3), Biset (p. 5), Berkeley (p. 13), Beverstone (p. 14), Blythborough (p. 16), and Bolam (p. 17), all created by Henry II; Eaton Bray (p. 39, created by John; Flockthorpe in Herdingham (p. 44), thirteenth century; Headinton (p. 51), created in 1142; and Writtle (p. 102), also thirteenth century. The additional six probable baronies were Appleby (p. 103), thirteenth century; Bothal (p. 107), Hepple (p. 122), and Langley (p. 127), created by Henry II; Mitford (p. 131) and Whalton (p. 150), thirteenth century. Other discrepancies between Davis' and my figures are due to his inclusion of Rufus' actions, while I have limited my study to 1100–35 where possible. The Sanders study itself presents problems. Most of the evidence for the size of the various holdings is from later than 1135 and Sanders' analysis assumes that the holdings were all as large during Henry I's reign. The evidence is most shaky for the probable baronies such as Rayleigh (p. 139). The barony of Sotby (p. 79) is traced by Sanders to the Kyme family's holdings. Sanders identified the lands included in this fee as those holdings belonging to Waldin the Engineer in Domesday and Simon fitz William Kyme in the Lindsey Survey (1115). Waldin held a total of 7 carucates, 2 5/6 bovates in 1086. Kyme held only 4 carucates, 3 bovates of this land in 1115, Waldin's other land being held by the king. This hardly qualifies as a barony. (*Lind.Surv.,* no.47; L 2/11, 12; L7/2; L8/11; L11/15; L16/13).

DeAragon ("Growth of a Secure Inheritance," p. 390) also has a different count—185, with two more not in chief—but for various reasons has a few different baronies included in the count. In the end, Sanders' figures provide a convenient sample, not an infallible source of information on the period.

5. For the most part, the baronies were spread throughout England. There was a fairly large concentration in the North, however. Yorkshire had the most—fifteen; Lincolnshire had twelve. Three counties had eleven—Somerset, Northumberland and Essex. Kent was the only county with ten baronies listed, and the rest had fewer than ten each. This distribution seems consistent with the evidence of studies concerning the land holdings of men who rebelled against King John; that is, the northern counties, especially Yorkshire, had more large landholdings than the central ones. For the land concentrations in John's reign, see Holt, *The Northerners.*

6. Sanders, *English Baronies.* Page numbers in the following notes refer to Sanders. Launceston, Cornwall (p. 60); Tickhill, Yorkshire (p. 147).

7. Arundel, Sussex (p. 1) was regranted to Queen Adeliza; Eye, Suffolk (p. 43), and Lancaster (p. 126) to Stephen of Blois.

8. Berkhamstead, Hertfordshire (p. 14) was given to Ranulf the Chancellor, and then to Reginald of Cornwall.

9. Bourn, Cambridgeshire (p. 19) was given to Payn Peverel.

10. Cottingham (p. 37) and Thirsk (p. 146), both in Yorkshire, were given to Nigel d'Albini; Salwarpe, Worcestershire (p. 75) to Urse d'Abetot.

11. Pevensey, Sussex (p. 136) went to Gilbert de Laigle; Pontefract, Yorkshire (p. 138) to Hugh de Laval; Mulgrave, Yorkshire (p. 66) to subtenant Nigel Fossard.

12. Leicester (p. 61) was given to the count of Meulan; Little Dunmow, Essex (p. 129) to the count of Clare.

13. Haughley, Suffolk (p. 120) was given to Alice de Montfort, who later married Robert de Vere, a member of a service family; Salwarpe, Worcestershire (p. 75) to Emmeline d'Abetot and Walter de Beauchamp, a new man.

14. *Reg.* II, #614 and 765.

15. Approaching the question using the same source but in a different way, RaGena DeAragon ("Growth of a Secure Inheritance") has come to the same conclusion.

16. Hatfield Peverel, Essex (Sanders, p. 120).

17. Bradninch, Devon (p. 20) went to William de Tracey; Berkhamstead, Hertfordshire (p. 14) went to Reginald after Ranulf the Chancellor escheated.

18. Great Weldon, Northamptonshire (p. 49) went to Richard Basset; Hunsingore, Yorkshire (p. 56) to Geoffrey fitz Payn.

19. Both Eaton Socon, Bedfordshire (p. 40) and Walkern, Hertfordshire (p. 92) were escheats of Eudo Dapifer granted to Hamo St. Clair.

20. Oswestry, Shropshire (p. 70) was granted to Alan fitz Flaad.

21. Ibid., pp. 64, 66.

22. Ibid., p. 136, and OVC 6:196–200. Henry was at war with Clito and Louis in 1118 and Richer's alliance with them would have allowed the French to control the area around the strategic Laigle castle. Henry apparently settled to avoid this extra battle.

23. Hollister, "The Misfortunes of the Mandevilles."

24. Five tenants whose baronies escheated, or were partially lost—Eudo Dapifer (who held two baronies), William Capra, William fitz Baderon, William Peverel, and Gilbert de Laigle—had possible heirs of lateral descent. Little is known of the other three men—Robert de Buci, Erneis de Burun and the sheriff of Shropshire—other than their Domesday holdings, so no definite statement can be made concerning their possible heirs. Note that two of these men were from service families, the others were lesser nobles.

25. Okehampton, Devon (Sanders, p. 69) was held by three brothers of the Clare family in succession; Chester (p. 32) passed to a cousin after the White Ship disaster.

26. Bywell, Northumberland (p. 25) and Weobley, Herefordshire (p. 95).

27. Framlinham, Suffolk (p. 46) descended to a Bigod brother; Berry Pomeroy, Devon (p. 106) to a Pomeroy brother; Wrinstead, Kent (p. 106) to a nephew of the Peverels of Dover.

28. Ibid., pp. 19, 107.

29. For a discussion of acquired vs. inherited land see above, chapter 2.

30. Rufus created Gloucester (Sanders, p. 6), Kendal (p. 56) and Skipton (p. 142). Southern ("Place," Appendix: "The Problem of the Royal Demesne," pp. 157–69) has analyzed the extent of the alienation of royal demesne under Henry I. He has four major conclusions. First, the treatment of the demesne varied from county to county. Second, where there was considerable alienation (e.g., Northamptonshire), it appears to have been associated with areas of "unsatisfac-

tory state of royal administration." Third, most demesne land grants by royal charter appear to have been conditional, and do not reflect a "continuous or general relaxation of the king's grip." Finally, most evidence points either to high payments or to great amounts of service required for the demesne which was ample compensation for the loss of revenue of the farm. Green ("William Rufus, Henry I and the Royal Demesne") also has closely analyzed the available records; she concludes that Southern understated the amount of demesne land alienated by Rufus and Henry, while agreeing that Henry found other revenues to compensate. Green states this period was crucial in turning royal revenues away from a land base to other sources.

31. The northern counties, like the marcher lordships, still required strong defenses. As shown in William Meschin's loss of land, the Scots were an active threat on the borders, resulting in a special need for loyal tenants in the north. Since many northern nobles had taken part in the early rebellions, Henry must have been conscious of the particular problems involved in the situation. See Kapelle, *The Norman Conquest of the North,* especially pp. 191–230. Kapelle highlights another settlement pattern in which the Normans did not settle in as great numbers in the northwest because of the lack of wheat land.

32. Chepstow, Monmouthshire (Sanders, p. 110) was created for Walter fitz Richard de Clare, and Egremont, Cumberland (p. 115) for William Meschin.

33. Kirklington, Cumberland (p. 58) was created for Boivill who was in service to Meschin.

34. Old Buckenham, Norfolk (p. 70) was created for William d'Albini Pincerna, and Tarrant Keynston, Dorset (p. 146) for Cahaignes.

35. Knaresborough, Yorkshire (p. 59) was created for Eustace fitz John; Christchurch, Hampshire (p. 112) and Plympton, Devon (p. 137) for Richard de Redvers; Warter, Yorkshire (p. 150) for Geoffrey fitz Payn.

36. Bulwick, Northamptonshire (p. 22) was created for Richard fitz Urse; Ellingham, Northumberland (p. 41) for Nicholas de Grainville; Erlestoke, Wiltshire (p. 42) for Roger (I) de Mandeville; Kington, Herefordshire (p. 57) for Adam (I) de Port; Marshwood, Dorset (p. 64) for Geoffrey (I) de Mandeville; Skelton, Yorkshire (p. 77) for Robert de Brus; Styford, Northumberland (p. 84) for Walter de Bolebech; Wooler, Northumberland (p. 100) for Robert Muschamp; Stainton le Vale, Lincolnshire (p. 81) for Ralph de Criol; Bourne, Lincolnshire (p. 107) for William Rollos; Callerton, Northumberland (109) for Hubert Laval; Wark, Northumberland (p. 149) for Walter Espec.

37. Burgh by Sands, Cumberland (p. 23) for Robert de Trevers; Prudhoe, Northumberland (p. 73) for Robert (II) de Umfraville; and Hadstone, Northumberland (p. 119) for Aschantinus de Worcester.

38. Ibid., p. 46.

39. Measures of land found in medieval documents are not always precisely definable, nor is a measure as used in one document always equivalent to the same in other documents. A hide (h) was approximately 120 acres. A carucate (c) was approximately 100 acres, 4 virgates (v) or 8 bovates (b). Wapentakes were local divisions found mainly in the northern counties; they were not always of equal size in 1100, but they were useful measures by which to survey land. For fuller definitions of these land measures see Zupko, *Dictionary of English Weights and Measures,* pp. 22–23, 32, 76–78, 177–78.

40. *FE,* pp. 169–80. Walter de Beauchamp held land which had been held by the bishop and others. Walter's 1½h in Hallhagen cum Bradewasse had been part of Dudo Radmanni's 2h in 1086—a case in which a grantee was able to acquire a small amount of land, though not an entire holding. In this case, it is unknown whether the favor was bestowed on Walter or on Urse by Henry I or by Rufus.

41. This land, which probably had descended to a son before apparently escheating, was disputed later. However, the claim was made not by relatives of Burun, but rather by the Roumare family, who were said to have held it during Rufus' reign, and who either lost the land or were not allowed to inherit during Henry's reign. Stephen eventually returned it to them.

42. *Lind. Surv.*, no. 34; 47/3; 16/1, 2/18; 2/15; L1/7; L4/11; L9/15; L11/15; L16/6; L18/8. The previous tenants and the dispute are discussed in *EYC* vol. 10, pp. 4, 26–27.

43. The following conclusions about the Lincolnshire Domesday and the Lindsey Survey tenants were made by comparing all of the holders of each place name for both surveys and attempting to match holdings. This was possible in most cases, though occasionally the change in amounts held by individuals was too great to determine the exact descent of estates. Given the nature of this method, I have omitted complete footnote information as cumbersome, and shall supply it where specific information is mentioned. All conclusions were drawn from Foster's volume containing both surveys.

44. The evidence does not allow us to follow further the descent of the land and determine who held it after Lisle.

45. *Lind. Surv.*, no.14; L9/3; L13/1.

46. Portions were held by the bishop of Lincoln, Manasser Arsic and others. The bishop of Lincoln received part of Stallingborough, Yarborough wap. (ibid., L11/9; L4/30) Manasser held the bishop's land in Healings, Bradley wap. (L9/10; L4/31–33) and Keelby, Yarborough wap. (L11/20; L4/28–30).

47. Very few of the royal manors were listed in the Lindsey Survey. As I have already noted, a few of Roger's manors were given to a new man, Geoffrey fitz Payn, for example, Swallow, Bradley wap. (*Lind. Surv.*, L9/15; L16/2). Of the escheated estates, several were retained in part by Henry, and others were divided among various people. Two men, Stephen, count of Aumâle, and William Meschin, each received the combined estates of two small Domesday holders. Stephen of Aumâle held the Domesday land of Drogo de Beurere (ibid., no.30) and Martin (no. 45). William Meschin held the land of Durand Malet (no.44) and William Blund (no. 49).

48. *Leic. Surv.*, p. 87.

49. Ibid., p. 88.

50. Ibid., p. 85.

51. Brito's father-in-law, Roger Bigod, a royal servant, also was still alive, but the eventual heir was Brito's wife. This may have been her dowry.

52. *Leic. Surv.*, p. 89. Nigel also received de Wirce's land in Lincolnshire intact—four manors in two wapentakes totalling more than 15c, and the entire wapentake of Axholme consisting of 48c which were de Wirce's in 1086, (*Lind. Surv.*, no. 63; L2/7; L4/1; L11/25; L5/1).

53. Sanders, pp. 146, 37, 52.

54. *Leic. Surv.*, pp. 92–94. Basset was also a subtenant of King David and the earl of Leicester. Part of the land held by Leicester had been held by Buci of Grantmesnil, the relationship between lord and tenant in effect being inherited.

55. Ibid., p. 21. Meschin got 7c in the honour of Blyth and 5c of Lovet's land.

56. Ibid., p. 94.

57. As in the discussion of the Lindsey Survey, the material for this discussion is drawn from my analysis of the surveys in Foster (*Lind. Surv.*) with the addition of Slade's analysis of the Leicestershire landholders (*Leic. Surv.*, pp. 83–95). This section also draws on material discussed and annotated above in this chapter.

58. King David of Scotland received most of Countess Judith's land, though

he lost manors throughout both shires. Drogo de Beurere's lands, far from the largest holdings in either shire, were granted to Stephen, count of Aumâle.

59. Toeni's Lincolnshire land went to the second husband of Berengar's widow—Berengar being Robert's heir—while the Leicestershire estates passed through the female line to Robert's granddaughter's husband, William d'Albini Brito.

60. Bearman, "Charters of the Redvers Family," pp. 56–62.

61. *Reg.* II, #818 (1102–07). Evidence of Envermou's holdings are found in the "Descriptio militum de Abbatia de Burgo," p. 174 and in the *Lind.Surv.*, L6/11.

62. *PR*, p. 32.

63. *Reg.* II, #1369.

64. Ibid., #1850.

65. Ibid., #911.

66. Ibid., #848.

67. Cronne ("Royal Forest," pp. 16–17) has found that forest rights were an exceptional grant during Henry I's reign.

68. Sanders, pp. 46–47; *PR*, pp. 95, 99; OVB 3:270, n.1. For a discussion of the scattered nature of land holding see above, chapter 2.

69. Southern, "Place," p. 140.

70. Ibid., p. 136.

71. Mooers ("Patronage," p. 302) misses this idea. She states that men improved their status by marrying heiresses but does not examine the status of the men before the marriage. They, of course, increased their holdings and eventually their status, but they were relatively equal to their brides before the marriage.

72. Hooten Pagnell, Oxfordshire (Sanders, p. 55) united the Domesday holdings of Surdeval and Pagnell.

73. Hasculf de Tani, for instance, whose lands were in Middlesex and Suffolk and whose wife was heir to an Aveley, Essex barony (p. 4).

74. The younger magnates were Hugh the Poer Beaumont (Bedford, p. 10), Baldwin fitz Gilbert de Clare (Bourne, Lincolnshire, p. 107) and William Meschin (Skipton, Yorkshire, p. 142).

75. Emmeline de Ballon, heiress of Much Marcle, Herefordshire (p. 66) married Reginald.

76. Stephen of Blois married the count of Boulogne's daughter (p. 151); David of Scotland married the earl of Northumberland's daughter who was also the widow of the earl of Huntingdon and Northampton (p. 118); Robert the king's son married the daughter of Robert fitz Hamon of Gloucester (p. 6). Robert fitz Hamon was a member of a prominent and wealthy service family and was "commensurate" with Robert of Gloucester in respect and wealth.

77. The eight marriages of service families were as follows: Miles of Gloucester to Sibyl de Newmarket (Gloucester, p. 6); Roger Bigod to Adeliza de Toeni (Belvoir, Leicestershire, p. 12); Robert de Vere to Alice de Montfort (Haughley, Suffolk, p. 120); Humphrey de Bohun to Maud of Salisbury (Trowbridge, Wiltshire, p. 91); Nigel d'Albini to Maud Mowbray (Thirsk, Yorkshire, p. 146); Rualon d'Avranches to Maud Monville (Folkestone, Kent, p. 45), William de Pecche to Isilia (Great Bealings, Suffolk, p. 48); Hubert de Ria, brother of Eudo Dapifer, to Agnes de Belfou (Hockering, Norfolk, p. 53). The six marriages of new men were: William Mauduit to Maud Hanslope (Hanslope, Buckinghamshire, p. 50); William d'Albini Brito to Cecily de Toeni (Belvoir, Leicestershire, p. 12); Eustace fitz John to Beatrice de Vesci (Alnwick, Northumberland, p. 103); Robert de la Haia to Muriel Picot (Brattleby, Lincolnshire, p. 109); Brian fitz Count to Maud

Wallingford (Wallingford, Berkshire, p. 93); William de Courcy to Emma de Falaise (Stogursey, Somerset, p. 143).

78. DeAragon's study ("In Pursuit," p. 267, Appendix) uses a different starting point—examining "nonmagnate *curiales'* marriages (mainly men of service families and new men)—but gets the same results. Arranged by my categories her figures show that: of nine magnate women one married a lesser noble, four married into service families, and three married new men; of four service family women, two married into other service families and two married new men; of four lesser noble women, two married into service families and two married new men. Three women are from unknown families. Green (*Government*, pp. 176–78) also used a different base—the royal servants of 1130—but comes to the same conclusions. Twelve of the 1130 servants were given important marriages.

79. William of Malmesbury characterized William fitz Osbern's marital plan as an attempt to "increase his dignity" (*GR*, translation by J. A. Giles, p. 289) and Orderic said the same for the Bassets (OVC 6:468).

80. Painter, "Family," p. 8.

81. *Reg.* II, #843. For details of the will, see above, chapter 2.

82. In a court case, ca. 1242–50, recorded in the *Book of Fees* (Great Britain, Public Record Office. *Liber feodorum*, vol. 2, p. 1158), Walter de Gant's descendants claimed that Henry I had alienated part of Walter's patrimony to enlarge his [Walter's] sister's dowry. This allegedly occurred after the king seduced Walter's sister.

83. *Reg.* II, #1719.

84. *PR*, pp. 34, 87.

85. *PR*, p. 158. In the previous year, Henry had consented (without a fine's being mentioned) to Fulbert's son Hugh marrying the daughter of Payn Peverel with a substantial dowry. *Reg.* II, #1609.

86. Turgis of Avranches owed 300*m.*, 1*m.* in gold and one warhorse for the widow and child of Hugh Auberville (*PR*, p. 67); Geoffrey de Trailli owed 300*m.*, 2*m.* in gold and four warhorses for the widow and child of Roger de Capaville (*PR*, p. 88).

87. *PR*, pp. 81, 94.

88. *PR*, p. 101.

89. *PR*, p. 59. Juliana, daughter of Richard of Winchester, married Ralph fitz William, who held 12½ hides in Yorkshire, Cambridgeshire and Leicestershire (*PR*, pp. 34, 46, 89).

90. *PR*, p. 111.

91. *PR*, pp. 37, 125. A payment of 16*s.* 8*d.* was also made for the dowry of one of Herbert's daughters who was married before 1130. S. S. Walker (p. 212) incorrectly cites Herbert's daughter as his heiress. Herbert's family tree often has been confused. To straighten it out, see Hollister, "Origins," pp. 265–68.

92. *PR*, pp. 94, 98.

93. Ibid., p. 95.

94. Ibid., p. 147.

95. Ibid., p. 26.

96. Mooers, "Patronage in the Pipe Roll," p. 301. Green's figures are substantially different: marriage £2506, offices £5882, wardships £456 (*Government*, pp. 223–25).

97. *PR*, p. 110.

98. *Reg.* II, p. xvi, #1255.

99. Sanders, p. 59, n.4.

100. Stapleton, "Observations," pp. 219–20.

101. *PR*, p.139.

102. Green, "Praeclarum," p. 16 Table #3; *Government,* p. 225, Table III.

103. Green, *Government,* p. 225. £2489 5s. 11d. was paid while £2363 15s. 7d. was pardoned.

104. £122 11d. collected, £122 11s. 8d. owing, £318 14s. 2d. pardoned.

105. Mooers ("Patronage in the Pipe Roll," p. 305) has counted 666 recipients, 81.5% of whom received pardons of less than £6.

106. A fine analytic description of the Pipe Roll is found in Green, "Praeclarum," pp. 1–17. For this section, a number of unidentified people who appear only once in the Pipe Roll have been placed in a separate category. It seems probable that they were smaller tenants (Category 2) or lesser clergy (Category 1). These include some landholders with surnames indicating low rank, such as Humphrey Villano and Walter Bordario in Bedfordshire (*PR,* p. 104). The total amounts of danegeld exemptions for individuals may be found in Mooers "Familial Clout and Financial Gain."

107. For example, William the Monk in Essex (*PR,* p. 60) and Theobald *clerico* in Bedfordshire (p. 104).

108. *Lind. Surv.,* L3/8; L4/3; L6/5; L7/5; L10/1.

109. *PR,* pp. 29, 32, 33, 34.

110. Mooers' analysis ("Patronage in the Pipe Roll") shows the problem with ranking individuals by the amount of the actual exemptions. On page 284 she says that *familiares* were "middling recipients" of patronage and on pp. 285–86 that *curiales* were all favored but not necessarily heavily, again based on absolute figures. However, on page 291 she says they held less land. With this being the case, their danegeld exemptions would, of course, be less.

111. *Dialogus,* p. 53.

112. Tout, *Chapters,* vol. 1, p. 82 n.2. Robert of Gloucester and Brian fitz Count may have been in charge of the previous audit of the Treasury and been exempt because of the office.

113. For example, while Walter Espec held pleas in Yorkshire, Northumberland, and Westmoreland, he was also exempt in Bedfordshire (*PR,* pp. 24, 138, 142, 104).

114. Walter of Salisbury was exempt in Wiltshire (*PR,* p. 22) where he was sheriff in 1111–15. Herbert the Chamberlain's sons were exempt in Wiltshire and Leicestershire (pp. 22–23, 89).

115. *PR,* p. 102.

116. Ibid., p. 55.

117. Ibid., p. 28.

118. Mooers ("Patronage in the Pipe Roll," pp. 297–99) argues that *pro amore* was meant literally and is indicative of the "personal side of royal patronage" or of "high regard." There is no evidence of this in law and since some recipients fail to appear in any other record of the time, it would appear to exaggerate the evidence to call them "friends." An alternative reading is that someone interceded with a verbal plea for clemency and the king gave it when no "legal" category existed, that is, "out of the goodness of his heart." The intercessor then was in the king's debt, a situation any king would have liked. This explanation could be applied to *familiares* of the king or to a stranger with an effective argument.

119. *PR,* pp. 56–57.

120. Ibid., p. 22.

121. Ibid., p. 13.

122. Ibid., pp. 28–29. Guy owed 100m., paid £29 13s. 4d. and was pardoned 40m. Geoffrey owed 15m., paid £6, and was pardoned 5m. with 1m. carried over as a debt.

123. Ibid., pp. 25, 30.

124. Ibid., p. 145.
125. Ibid., p. 118.
126. Ibid., p. 32.
127. *Reg.* II, #1555 as pointed out by Spear, "Une famille," p. 23.
128. Coss, ed., *The Langley Cartulary,* #41, p. 11, ca. 1122–35. Robert of Gloucester allowed "that since Benefrei the falconer has acquired a market at Fairfield for him from Henry I, he and his heirs and his men may enjoy the customs of the market."
129. Cooke, "Kings, Knights and Abbesses."
130. OVC 5:298. Orderic's editor Chibnall gives the other sources including Anselm's description of Robert (OVC 5:298 n.1).
131. *PR,* pp. 88, 14, 59, 86, 95, 99, 104, 126, 152.
132. Chibnall ("Mercenaries and the *familia regis*") has found in Orderic evidence of wages for military service given to men of noble families. Prestwich ("The Military Household of the Norman Kings") examines the movement of nobles between the feudal force and the *familia regis*.

CHAPTER 6

Strategies for Success

The successful nobleman sought to extend his influence through marital and feudal alliances. A good marriage, especially, not only brought wealth to a family but formed or strengthened both regional ties and feudal dependencies. The tracing of such feudal interdependencies shows the complexity of relationships in upper class society as it existed in the early twelfth century. We get a far more integrated picture of this segment of society when we look at the marital, feudal, and regional networks together.

This part of the study, therefore, reveals the general interconnections among the various upper class groups. The overall impression is that marriages tended to occur between people of roughly the same levels of society. Where there was a significant upward advantage derived from a marriage (that is, among members of the service and new families), this was generally due to royal favor. Feudal relationships can be seen to be reflections of mutual advantages, and these neighborhood relationships crossed all groups. The relative significance of such relationships in determining political behavior cannot be seen very often for Henry I's reign (with the exception of the alliances among rebels), but some relationships had political significance in later reigns. The social and economic consequences, however, were immediate.

We have already seen some examples of marital connections used to reinforce political causes. Obvious examples were found among the opponents of the king in 1101 and 1123. In 1101, the central core group of rebels were related. In the 1123 rebellion, the marriages of Waleran's sisters were clearly arranged after the political alliance, to seal it, so to speak.[1]

It was far more usual to find family ties reinforced by, rather than creating, feudal or political ties. William Basset, abbot of St. Benet of

Holme, gave the manor of Heigham to Richard Basset for £10 annual rent, though the livestock from the land was to revert to the abbey at Richard's death.[2] As we will see, later evidence shows that land held of relatives was a fairly common practice.[3] Some feudal ties crossed the Channel. Ingelram de Abernon's ancestral lands in Normandy were held in part of Richard fitz Gilbert de Clare, who also was his lord in Surrey.[4]

In any given case, then, individuals could be connected by marriage ties, feudal ties, regional ties, or various combinations of the three. The newer families took advantage of all types of feudal alliances during Henry's reign. By 1135, many new men and service families were feudally connected with one another and with noble overlords. William of Eynsford, for example, held land of the Mauduits, who in turn held it of the tenant-in-chief Robert of Gloucester.[5] Each of the three was also a tenant-in-chief.

The complexity of multiple feudal ties can be seen in the connections among several new and service families. For example, Robert de la Haia was a tenant in chief in Lincolnshire, Sussex and Normandy,[6] as well as a royal and baronial servant. He was also a rear vassal of at least nine others: Robert fitz Hamon (and his successor, Robert, earl of Gloucester), the bishop of Worcester, the abbot of Jumièges, St. Mary's Lincoln, Gilbert fitz Goscelin, William Meschin, Ralph Criol, Gilbert de Gant, and Hugh de Vallo.[7] In turn, de la Haia was overlord to at least seven other nobles: Ranulf (the king's physician), William de Lovetot, William fitz Ansketil, Ansgot of Burwell (a wealthy Lindsey tenant), and two unidentified men, Ernis and Terricus.[8] In other words, de la Haia had feudal connections with men on all levels of the nobility. Similarly, Urse and Robert d'Abetot, brothers from a service family and tenants-in-chief, held Worcester lands of Robert of Bellême and the bishop of Worcester, of the abbeys of Westminster and Pershore, of Coventry Cathedral, and of William fitz Ansketil. In order to consolidate lands, feudal relations could get complicated. Feudal exchanges occurred between Urse and the Lacys, who were his neighbors as well as possibly his lords in Worcester. Feudal ties affected religious patronage. In Normandy, Rabel de Tancarville was Urse's and Robert's lord and Robert was a patron of Rabel's foundation,the Priory of St. Barbe-en-Auge.[9]

In addition to patronizing the church favored by one's lord, witnessing or pledging for one's lord was apparently a common occurrence. Several generations of the families of St. Quentin and Sorus witnessed charters for their lords Robert fitz Hamon and his successors, Robert and William, earls of Gloucester. Odo Sorus was also a guarantor for Robert of Gloucester in his treaty with the earl of Hereford during the Anarchy.[10] Family

members might also witness documents and act as pledges for one another. Alan Belet witnessed for his maternal cousin, Adam de Percy,[11] and
Philip de Braose guaranteed the payment of the fine of 80*m.* levied on
Payn de Braose for the crimes of Payn's men.[12] Geoffrey de Clinton's
confirmation of his tenants' grants to his foundation of Kenilworth was
witnessed by his uncle, William de Clinton.[13] As Holt has pointed out
through thirteenth century examples,[14] the guarantor's function necessitated his ability to support and perhaps to pay. Family alone might not
provide the qualified person, whereas a feudal tie or a neighborhood
might.

The witnessing network also included feudal and regional ties, and what
may be called "social class" or category within the nobility. An 1130
grant to Evesham in Worcester by William and Simon Moulins-la-Marche
was witnessed by Beauchamps (Walter, his two sons, and another possible
relative, Simon) and Payn fitz John, all Worcester landholders. Though
the Moulins are classified in the vague "lesser noble" category (even
though they were of a great family in Normandy), the witnesses are "new
men" and *curiales* who by 1130 had become major landholders in the
neighborhood. The only other identifiable witness is Miles, constable of
neighboring Gloucester, but also a member of a service family who often
worked with Payn fitz John on curial business. No other lesser noble or
magnate witnessed.[15] On the other hand, donations by the earls of Warwick to Kenilworth were witnessed not only by magnate sons (possible
heirs) but cousins (the Beaumont twins) and fellow magnate, William
Giffard.[16] As in other questions, magnates seemed consciously to work as
a group even in witnessing.

While feudal ties were important, it was the marriage connections
among the first three generations after the Conquest that most extended
ties among the nobles./All levels of the nobility used marriages for socio-
economic purposes. When we looked at ways that nobles provided for
children, we saw that magnates used heiresses among them to raise noninheriting sons to their birth status./Beyond this, however, the magnates
intermarried, consciously seeking marriages that would help cement relationships within their own group. The Beaumonts exemplify this. By
the end of the reign, the magnates related to the Beaumonts had created
a network with multiple ties to several major families. Robert Beaumont,
count of Meulan, married Elizabeth, the daughter of the count of Ver-
mandois, establishing a connection between those counties. William (III)
de Warenne, son of Elizabeth's second marriage to the earl of Surrey, thus
became stepbrother to Waleran, count of Meulan, Robert, earl of Leicester
and Hugh the Poer Beaumont. Robert Beaumont's brother Henry, earl of

Warwick, married the daughter of the count of Perche. Through the elder generation, therefore, the Beaumonts were related to two comital houses of France and through the younger generation to the Warennes and the earldom of Surrey. Henry's heir Roger also married a member of the Warenne family, thus creating a double tie between two of the major baronial families. Waleran of Meulan married a daughter of the count of Evreux, who was a member of the important Norman family of de Montfort. The non-inheriting children of Robert Beaumont and Elizabeth were also married advantageously—Hugh to the heiress of Simon de Beauchamp, an important Bedfordshire lord; Adeline to another Montfort; Maud to a Louvel, a member of an important family of Ivry; and Isabel to Clare of Pembroke. By the time of the Anarchy, the magnates related to the Beaumonts represented a substantial bloc of families whose allegiance was sought by both sides. During the period of the Anarchy, the Beaumonts did in fact act as an almost solid bloc most of the time.

/ For other nobles, marriage was even more crucial. This was true especially of the upwardly mobile, the new men and the service families, all of whom were curial servants. | While feudal ties and reward for royal service were important, it was marriage which most extended ties among the first three generations after the Conquest and provided the greatest long-term advantage. Furthermore, different strategies are apparent and with differing degrees of success.

Some sought ties to particular families. The fitz Johns were impressed by the Lacys. Eustace fitz John married two of his children to heirs of the Pontefract branch of the Lacy family. His brother, Payn, had married the heiress of the Hereford branch of the same family.[17]

The d'Albinis tried for the top. By 1135, they were related by marriage to nine major families, among the most important people in the northern counties. Their success included raising both the senior line and that of the noninheriting brother to magnate status. While curial service had brought many nonmarital benefits (jobs and land) which had helped to achieve this status, and the Anarchy politics brought the actual titles, it was the marriage gains which brought the most lands and long-term benefits. Nigel d'Albini married twice, creating ties to the Laigle and Gournai families, both important castle-holding noble families in Normandy.[18] In addition, through Gundrede de Gournai, the family was related to the Warennes, earls of Surrey. Nigel's brother William d'Albini Pincerna married into the Bigods, another (already wealthy) service family, and his son William (II) married the dowager Queen Adeliza, who held a barony and who, of course, had royal connections. Nigel's uncle, Nigel d'Albini Cainhoe, married Amice, daughter of Henry Ferrers (a major landholder through central and northern England); and the heir of Nigel d'Albini Cainhoe, Henry d'Albini, in turn married the daughter of Patrick de Chaources, another tenant-in-chief in the same area. Nigel's son, Roger de Mowbray, married a woman who was a member of one important northern family (Gant) and the widow of another (Lacy). By Roger's generation, in the time of the Anarchy, his cousins and "in-laws" were among the most powerful people and, with a concentration of land in an area, they had the potential of being a politically strong alliance. We have already seen that Roger de Mowbray's life was that of the stereotypical second generation noble. Not only was he reared to inherit the land, but he also was reared with influential and wealthy relatives. The family's pattern of behavior thus changed from curial service to noncurial, aristocratic life. However, unlike the Beaumont case, the family network did not create or even reinforce a political bloc. Roger was not able to count on the others for help in his noncurial politics.

The Gloucester/Hereford family had also made multiple marriage connections by the third generation, but their connections by and large led to alliances in their major territorial area or to other curial families rather than to prominent families. Miles of Gloucester married Sibyl de Newmarket, an heiress with Welsh lands, and their son married an heiress by both her parents of land in neighboring Hereford. None of Miles' and Sibyl's three daughters married a man on the highest levels, but none married men of status beneath her, and all married substantial landholders. By the next generation, they were related to the families of Braose, a major northern family; of Lacy, with substantial holdings in the north and numerous relationships of their own; of Bohun, another established service family; of Herbert the Chamberlain, a rising servant; and of the fitz Johns, prominent new men. That is, they married either into families of lesser nobles with wealth in a certain area or into families of *curiales*. By time of the Anarchy, Miles' son Roger was related to many of the major tenants of Herefordshire, Gloucestershire, Wales, and Yorkshire, as well as to several tenants with southern holdings.[19] He was not related to any major political figures but instead to a substantial number of families in an area or families with similar political strategies, that is, curial. The next generation's behavior is also in contrast to the Albinis, as Roger of Gloucester continued in royal service while Roger de Mowbray did not.

Another rising service family, the de Veres, also established substantial ties through marriage using yet another strategy. They appear to have aimed highest for their sons, who married members of major landed families, while reinforcing their curial alliances through their daughters' marriages. Aubrey (II) de Vere, the *familiaris* so evident in the Pipe Roll, married a daughter of Gilbert de Clare, and their descendants held the land of the important Clare family in 1166.[20] Aubrey's brother Robert married Adela de Montfort, who held the hereditary constablery of Normandy, and who was the widow of Simon de Moulins-la-Marche, a member of an important Norman family, as well as a tenant in Essex. Aubrey (III) de Vere, first earl of Oxford, married Beatrice de Arques, a granddaughter of the Count of Guisnes and heiress of several older Anglo-Norman families. Each of Aubrey's daughters married twice, and though none of their husbands (Robert of Essex, Roger fitz Richard Bigod, Geoffrey de Mandeville, and Payn de Beauchamp) was a great noble, all brought to the de Vere family new alliances with noble curial families.[21]

The Bigod family was another important curial family of the time. Their marital fortunes were slow in coming until there was a magnate marriage. It is hard to tell whether this was a strategy—slow, steady movement until able to gain a great marriage—or simply the failure to gain a great marriage until later. The fortune began with a lesser noble (Robert de Toeni) whose heiress became the second wife of Roger (I) Bigod. The next generation marriages include one to a lesser noble (Robert of Essex), two to members of other service families (William d'Albini, Pincerna, and Juliana de Vere) and one to a new man (William d'Albini Brito)—none providing much mobility. Hugh (II) Bigod, however, began moving up with the annulment of his marriage to Juliana and his subsequent remarriage to Gundrede, daughter of magnate Roger of Warwick.[22] So after two generations of slowly upward-moving marriages and continued curial service, the family status jumped with one spectacular marriage.

While success often depended on marriage networks, a service family might also decline, as did the d'Abetots, in part because of the failure of its members to make profitable alliances. While they had been successful in Normandy,[23] the d'Abetots were not able to continue this marital success in England. During Henry I's reign, Urse and Robert d'Abetot apparently made no new profitable alliances through their own marriages. Nor did they successfully perpetuate their lines. Robert died without heirs. Urse's son and heir Roger killed a member of the Henry I's household and was banished. Urse's daughters, who inherited all of the property but had no strong family connections, were married to royal servants—one to Walter de Beauchamp, a new man who gained greatly by the marriage, and one to Roger Marmion, hereditary champion of the dukes of Normandy, but who had little English land. Though most of the land inherited by the next generation had been d'Abetot land, each line took the father's name, and d'Abetot ceased to be an important curial name after the first years of the reign.

Failure to marry or to have children limited a family's success. The three brothers of the St. John family appeared in England fairly early in Henry I's reign and were loyal and rewarded followers of the king, but only one left children or even a record of a wife. Roger St. John, who held the family land in Normandy, married Cecily de la Haia, daughter of the Norman justiciar. The marriage did create a bond between the families. The St. Johns became patrons of de la Haia's foundation of Boxgrove, and a Robert de la Haia witnessed for Roger's brother John St. John.[24] Some extension of the network continued. Roger's heir William, who was heir to all the land of his uncles as well, married a daughter of the count of Brittany. A daughter, Muriel, seems to have married a man who already was part of the St. John-de la Haia network. Her husband, Rainald d'Orval, has left a charter dated earlier than the marriage which was witnessed by both Roger St. John and de la Haia.[25] In spite of good marriages, however, only one in each of the first two generations produced children to make these affinal connections continue. Still, the family slowly had established a network, a solid though not a spectacular one.

Obviously, marriage strategies were vitally important to the long-term success of a new family. In the new men category, the first or earliest marriages were primarily to curial families. Richard (I) de Redvers had himself married a Peverel, and he married his son who inherited the Norman lands to a member of the Norman curial family of de Tancarville, but he married a daughter to a Roumare (lesser nobles related to magnates). The next generation married into the royal line (children of Reginald of Cornwall and Robert of Gloucester) and the more curial magnates (Beaumonts). One more had been betrothed to a member of the new family of Pont de l'Arche. Redvers' feudal ties also ranged in category, from the Peverels of Dover (new men), to the Avenels (lesser nobles) and Giffards (magnates). Their success in surviving the Anarchy appears to be due to their successful marriage network, the amount of land gained in small pieces as much as the conspicuous rewards, and to Baldwin de Redvers' unique role in the Anarchy itself.[26]

Examination of the magnates and servants has shown some of the ways in which marriage alliances were used to reinforce ties, to strengthen relationships in a certain area, or to make new ties in other areas. Regional ties appear to have been given high priority by the nobles. The most complete record for the period of regional ties is supplied by the extant surveys of Henry I's reign. These surveys only present snapshots of an area at a certain time, rather than show us changes over time. However, they allow us to examine one area in depth, as a sample, and to see the influence of locality in the formation of marital and feudal connections.

The first group of surveys to be examined are feudatories of four churches—Canterbury, Peterborough, Worcester, and Bayeux. These listed both nobles and nonnobles who held of the church. None of the five noble families holding land in Kent of the archbishop or of the bishop of Rochester at the beginning of the reign[27] made brilliant marriages. The Port family's first substantial marriage alliance occurred during Henry II's reign. The heiresses of both the Arches/Arques and Hesdin families married lesser nobles, and their husbands gained the most by the alliance. However, no Kentish family holding of the archbishopric declined in importance. Descendants of three of the families (Ros, Arches, and Maminot) are listed among the Kent tenants-in-chief in 1166[28] and those of Port and Hesdin were prominent in England both politically and economically.

The *Descriptio Militum de Abbatia de Burgo* (1110–20)[29] lists twelve identified military tenants of the abbot of Peterborough. The only magnate listed was Robert fitz Richard de Clare, and the tenants appear to have been unrelated. The feudatories of the bishops of Worcester and Bayeux[30] were of similar composition—they list a few magnates and several members of service families. Some names appear on several lists; the Marmions held land of Peterborough, Worcester, and Bayeux. The Marmions are, in fact, a good example of a family that held land wherever possible. In addition to holding land of the three religious houses mentioned, they held a house in Winchester, the capital, and land in Leicestershire of the king. In Lincolnshire, they held land both of the king (through marriage) and of Walter de Gant. In Northamptonshire, they held of the king and of the abbot of Peterborough. The Cartae *Baronum* (1166) shows that they held in Middlesex of the bishop of London and in Warwick both of the count and of the king.[31] One family (Bolebech) were Marmion's tenants in both Lincolnshire and Warwickshire.[32] Their land holding, feudal connections, and marriages do not show a strategy of concentration (as, for example, the d'Albinis do), but rather gains wherever possible.

The one extant survey of a town, the *Liber Winton,* (1103–15)[33] lists twenty-eight identifiable nobles who held Winchester land of the king. An unusually large number of these tenants were members of service families (seven) and new men (ten), and some of them were connected to each other by marriage. Five tenants were lesser nobles, five were magnates, and one was a member of the royal family. The *Cartae* shows feudal ties among these neighbors as well—descendants of two *Liber Winton* tenants, Port and Pont de l'Arche, were tenants-in-chief; six of the king's tenants were also tenants of the bishop of Winchester; and three held of John de Port.[34] Many of these families were also neighbors elsewhere in

England. However, this is probably because of the unique situation of Winchester, rather than a strategy on the part of the nobles. Since Winchester was the site of the treasury, a town house there would have been useful as a place to stay when attending court. Recent work on Bristol by Robert Patterson shows no real building of marital links among Bristol families either, though they had links throughout England.[35] This evidence supports the hypothesis that towns were seen as useful residences but did not function as centers for networks as shires did.

The four extant major surveys of land—those for Lincolnshire (the Lindsey Survey), for Leicestershire, for Herefordshire, and for Northamptonshire—are far more complex than either the feudatories or the town survey, and each presents a slightly different picture of the interconnections among the nobility.

The earliest of these surveys covered the Lindsey area of Lincolnshire (*ca.* 1115). A study of the connections among the fifty-six noble lay tenants in the Lindsey Survey fails to identify distinct family or feudal groups. Only about a dozen men, however, seem not to have been connected in any way to others in the shire. More characteristic is the case of Herbert de St. Quentin, who held 6 bovates of land in Lindsey of the count of Aumâle, a major tenant in the area. St. Quentin also held land of the earl of Gloucester, another Lindsey tenant, and had land in Winchester on High Street where he was a neighbor of two other Lindsey tenants, Wigot and Percy.[36] Of St. Quentin's lords, Aumâle was the son-in-law of Ralph de Mortimer and the Yorkshire overlord of Ralph and Jordan Paynel, all three of whom held land in Lindsey,[37] while Gloucester was related by marriage to another tenant, Hamo Dapifer, and held his Lincolnshire lands of William Tourniant, son of another Lindsey tenant, Osbert the Sheriff.[38] St. Quentin's Winchester neighbor, Percy, was a Lindsey tenant of Walter de Gant. Walter de Gant, in turn was the son-in-law of Count Stephen of Brittany, and members of the Gant family were to marry into the families of Lacy, Albini/Mowbray, and Percy, all Lindsey neighbors, and Grantmesnil and Courcy, who though not neighbors were related to neighbors.[39] This type of recitation could continue showing various interconnections between most of the tenants. These relationships, of course, do not necessarily mean that St. Quentin, for example, would act with all of the others; but it does demonstrate the complexity of feudal and marital ties within only two generations of the Conquest, and the potential of neighborhood ties, combined with family and feudal ties, for creating power blocs capable of acting with the king or against his interests.

Being someone's neighbor did not necessarily lead to an alliance. Hugh de Lovetot was fined for breaking the peace in an incident involving the men of Roger de Mowbray; and Adam de Tisun was fined on a plea between him and Lovetot's men. The events took place in Nottinghamshire, but all three men were Lindsey neighbors.[40]

There appear to be fewer interrelations among the twenty-four major tenants in the Leicestershire Survey (1124–29). Four tenants were closely related through marriage. Henry d'Albini was an in-law of Edward of Salisbury, as each had married a sister of Patrick de Chaources, as well as being a cousin of Henry de Ferrers and of Roger de Mowbray. Two pairs of brothers-in-law shared Domesday estates.[41] Gant, whose many connections have been described above, was a tenant, along with one of his relatives, Mowbray, and his Lindsey tenant, Marmion. Within the survey area, fewer subinfeudations to neighbors were recorded. In one case, Basset, a new man holding the Ridel fee, was a tenant of two local magnates, the royal in-law David of Scotland and the earl of Leicester, and lord to two other neighbors, Mowbray and Hugh the Sheriff.[42] In Leicestershire the ties were by and large those of family or were feudal connections within the shire rather than through various shires.

The Herefordshire Domesday, approximately contemporary with the Leicestershire Survey, lists thirteen identified nobles, none of whom were either magnates or new men. Six families in the survey had strong ties to one another—Gloucester/Hereford, Newmarket, fitz Pons, Lacy, Braose, and Ballon. As we have seen, Miles of Gloucester married the Newmarket heiress, while Miles' nephew (his sister's son) was heir to the Hereford tenant Drogo fitz Pons. Miles' son married the heiress of the Lacys (Hereford line), and one of his daughters married the heir of the Braose family. Newmarket was married to a cousin of the Ballon tenant in Hereford, and his heir was lord of another Ballon cousin in Gloucester in 1166.[43] This latter Ballon cousin was married to the son of the forfeited earl of Hereford. There were other relationships within the shire. Robert fitz Hugh de Mortimer was lord to his Hereford neighbor, Osbert fitz Richard, in Worcester,[44] and Roger de Lacy was a tenant of both Reginald fitz Count de Ballon and Urse d'Abetot.[45] In Herefordshire in Wales, therefore, there developed strong interconnections, both feudal and familial, which by 1166 had (potentially) united large areas of land.

The Northamptonshire Survey[46] is similar to the Lindsey Survey. Forty-two tenants are identified, representing all ranks of the nobility, and a great many interconnections can be found. Six magnates and two members of the royal family held land in this shire, and all had ties of some sort to more than half of the other tenants. Of the nonmagnates, two were servants of the Beaumonts, one was a servant of the earl of Gloucester, fourteen were lesser nobles, eight were members of service families and nine were new men. Most of the new tenants had multiple ties. The heir of the Engaines, keepers of the forests of Northamptonshire, married the heiress of the neighboring foresters, Lisures, and their descendants were tenants of the Paynels in Staffordshire and Bassets in Northamptonshire,[47] members of all these families being tenants in this survey. While both the Engaines and the Lisures were service families, indeed performing the same service in the same shire, the Paynels were lesser nobles and the Bassets new men. This is typical of the relationships within the shire— none of the groups limited its connections to other members of its own group, nor did any magnate dominate the county with his relatives and vassals.

As one would expect, a comparison of the surveys shows some tenants holding in several counties. In addition to the Marmions (described above), Nigel d'Albini, the Ferrers, and the Gants held land in three of the shires examined, though unlike the Marmions, none held land of the churches surveyed or in Winchester. As might also be expected, seven of the Abbot of Peterborough's tenants were also tenants-in-chief in the abbey's shire.[48] Most of the magnates held land in several shires, including subinfeudated land held of the clergy. The new men, however, do not appear in as many surveys; and holdings by new men in more than one shire appear only in the later surveys. This should be expected in the case of men who first had to prove themselves to Henry. The one exception to this rule occurs in the *Liber Winton,* where several new men are listed as holding land within the first fifteen years of the reign. This may be due to the town's unique tie to the court where these men were getting their start. It seems natural that their first appearances would be found in court-related witness lists and Winchester town records. The lesser nobles and service families appear about equally in terms of holding in more than one shire, aside from the few outstanding cases already mentioned.

The surveys leave us with a complicated picture of the connections within the nobility in Henry I's reign. It is clear that the king played an important role in the fortunes of the various groups, but the relationships among the various categories were in part a function of the activity of their members.

The interconnections made by some of the lesser nobles (Category 2) benefited their families. Some members of this group, like the Newmarket family, married into great and rising families from the same geographical area, so that their descendants were major tenants in one part of the country. Several of the families achieved important connections through marriage. Many of these, such as the Lacy/Pontefracts, Paynels, and Percys, were from the northern counties and they intermarried with rising service families, as well as with families of already higher status.

The service families (Category 3) were very active in establishing complex networks. They accomplished this primarily by marriage, but also through subinfeudation both of and to others. Marriages were made by the more active members of this group between their families and all other categories, resulting in a network of connections extending in status both upward and downward, and geographically throughout England.

Some of the new men (Category 4) established familial ties, though in some cases (such as that of the Bassets) the ties were to other new families or service families and only occasionally to lesser nobles. As a group, the new men were far less successful than the service families during Henry I's lifetime in forming networks of feudal and especially familial connections, but some were able to expand their ties in the following generations. As will be seen, those families which survived the Anarchy did so more through marriages than as a result of direct patronage by Henry I. Therefore, the slight difference in the forms of patronage received from the king by the service families and the new men may have been the crucial difference in their ability to retain their new status.

Finally, as a group, the magnate families (Category 5) were highly interconnected, as they had already been by 1100. They continued throughout the reign to intermarry and make alliances among their own level of society.

One last observation before moving on. Even after thorough examination of the period, it is difficult to separate the nobles from the king. When we discuss advantageous alliances, we are far more certain of those gained through the king's patronage than of those independent of it. Part of this relative certainty, of course is due to the nature of the sources, but it also must be seen as a reflection of both the king's increasing control of the resources and the nobles' increasing reliance upon the court under Henry I.

Notes

1. See above, chapter 2.
2. West, *St. Benet of Holme, 1020–1210,* vol. 1, Appendix E, pp. 173–74.
3. See chapter 7 concerning the feudal ties in the *Cartae Baronum.*
4. Loyd, *Origins of Some Anglo-Norman Families,* p. 1; Heales, ed., *Records of Merton Priory,* pp. 13–14; *RB* I, p. 405.
5. Patterson, ed., *Earldom of Gloucester Charters,* p. 152.
6. *PR,* p. 121; *Lind. Surv.,* pp. 238–59 passim; *Reg.* II, #1816; *CDF* #921; Loyd, *Origins,* p. 51.
7. *Mon.Ang.,* vol. 4, p. 633 (I); *Reg.* II, #1307; Hollings, ed., *Red Book of Worcester,* part 2, p. 439; Vernier, ed., *Chartes de l'Abbaye de Jumièges,* p. 138.

For de la Haia's tenantry of Lincoln, fitz Goscelin, Meschin, Criol, Gant, and Vallo, see *Lind. Surv.*, L 3/1; L 2/9, 10, 11; L 3/19; L 6/2.

8. Ranulf held land which de la Haia held of Gloucester (*Reg.* II, #1307). Lovetot held the land which de la Haia held of Vallo (*Lind. Surv.*, L 6/2). For the other Lincolnshire land see *Lind. Surv.*, L3/4, L13/4, L14/11, L18/15.

9. Sanders, *English Baronies*, p. 75; Hollings, ed., *Red Book*, part 2, p. 432; *FE*, pp. 178–79; Loyd, *Origins*, p. 1; *FE*, pp. 170–75.

10. Patterson, ed., *Earldom of Gloucester Charters*, pp. 42, 95, 96; Maxwell-Lyte, ed., *Two Cartularies of the Augustinian Priory of Bruton and the Cluniac Priory of Montacute*, p. 184; *Mon.Ang.*, vol. 4, p. 633 (I); Barkly, "Remarks on the Liber Niger," p. 295; *RB* I, p. 288; *Chronicon Monasterii de Abingdon*, vol. 2, p. 96.

11. Clay and Greenway, *Early Yorkshire Families*, p. 10.

12. *PR*, p. 103.

13. B.L. Harley Ms. 3650, fol. 3r.

14. Holt, "Patronage and Politics," pp. 12–13.

15. B.L. Cotton Vesp. B. XXIV. fol. 31r.

16. B.L. Harley Ms. 3650, fol. 11r.

17. Wightman, *The Lacy Family in England*, geneological tables 1 and 2.

18. Loyd, *Origins*, pp. 47, 52.

19. D. Walker, ed., "Charters of the Earldom of Hereford," pp. 1–5.

20. *RB* I, p. 403.

21. DeAragon, "In Pursuit of Aristocratic Women," pp. 261–62.

22. Atkin, "The Bigod Family"; Bailey, "The Countess Gundred's Lands."

23. Ellis, "On the Landholders of Gloucestershire," p. 183. Ellis traced the family to the Tancarvilles. Robert gave land to St.Barbe-en-Auge, whose major patron was Rabel de Tancarville (*Reg.* III, #749).

24. Fleming, ed., *Cartulary of Boxgrove Priory*, pp. 17–20, and Salter, ed., *Cartulary of Oseney Abbey*, vol. 4, pp. 28–29.

25. *CDF*, #924, p. 330.

26. Bearman, "Charters of the Redvers Family," pp. 16 table 2, 17, 92–143.

27. Douglas, ed., *The Domesday Monachorum* , pp. 77–104. The families identified were Ros, Arches/Arques, Maminot, Port of Basing, and Hesdin. Arches/Arques' descendants married Monvilles, Tancarvilles, and d'Avranches. Hesdin's heir married Patrick de Chaources.

28. *RB* I, pp. 196, 192–93, 194–95.

29. "Descriptio," pp. 168–75.

30. Hollings, ed., *Red Book*, part 2, pp. 412–14; *RB* II, pp. 645–47.

31. Hollings, part 2, p. 435; *PR*, pp. 111, 121, 119; *Reg.* II, #1845; *RB* II, p. 646; "Descriptio," p. 174; *Leic. Surv.*, pp. 19–20, 23, 26; *Lind. Surv.* L1/3, L3/15, L8/17, L16/9, L18/14, L19/2; *FE*, p. 173; *Nhants. Surv.*, pp. 366, 367, 388; *Liber Winton*, p. 63,#230; *RB* I, pp. 187, 300, 326, 327.

32. *Lind. Surv.*, L18/14; *RB* I, p. 327.

33. *Liber Winton*, pp. 33–131.

34. *RB* I, pp. 204–10.

35. Patterson, "Bristol's Early Angevin Proprietary Society."

36. *Lind. Surv.*, L7/1 (St. Quentin/Aumale); Clay and Greenway, *Early Yorkshire Families*, p. 79; *Liber Winton*, pp. 42 (#50); 55 (#149); 55–56 (#150); 56 (#151).

37. *CDF*, #1264, p. 459 (Aumale/Mortimer); *Reg.* II, #1333 (Paynel/Aumale).

38. *Lind. Surv.*, L3/18.

39. Ibid., passim; *EYC* 4, pp. 84–91; Greenway, ed., *Charters of the Honour of Mowbray*, pp. 260–61; *EYC* 11, frontispiece; Wightman, *Lacy Family*, ge-

nealogical table (no page); OVC 4: 338–41; Tremlett and Blakiston, eds., *Stogursey Charters*, p. xxiv.

40. *PR*, p. 11.

41. William d'Albini Brito and Roger de Lisle shared the Toeni estates. Walter de Beauchamp and Roger Marmion shared the d'Abetot estates.

42. *Leic. Surv.*, pp. 21, 27, 23, 29.

43. Round, *Studies in Peerage*, pp. 195, 205; *RB* I, p. 296.

44. *Worc. Cart.*, #150, pp. 83–84.

45. *Heref. Dd.*, p. 7; Wightman, *Lacy Family*, p. 130.

46. *Nhants. Surv.*, pp. 365–89. The date of the survey is uncertain, though it definitely belongs to the second half of the reign.

47. Fowler, ed., *Cartulary of the Abbey of Old Wardon*, pedigree #2; *RB* I, pp. 269, 329.

48. Avenel, Engaine, fitz Ansketil, Marmion, Ridel/Basset, Eudo Dapifer, and Hugh the Poer Beaumont all held land in Northamptonshire.

CHAPTER 7

The Nobles After Henry I—
Success and Failure

Henry I died on December 1, 1135 while the court was in Normandy. While several of the nobles stayed in Normandy to prevent rebellion, the household officials and *familiares* accompanied the king's body to England. The question of succession was reopened. No legitimate heir had been produced by Henry's second marriage, and the oath of fealty made to the Empress Matilda in 1127 had not been publicly denied. However, earlier in 1135, Henry and his son-in-law Geoffrey of Anjou had quarrelled over control of Normandy, and the breach appeared to be growing rather than being resolved.[1]

When Henry died, his nephew Stephen of Blois quickly went from Boulogne to London, where he received support from the clergy and nobility for his claim to the throne. Stephen then proceeded—as Henry I had in 1100—to the treasury city of Winchester, where his brother Henry was bishop. The archbishop of Canterbury, who traditionally crowned the king, hesitated to accept Stephen because of the oath to Matilda. Then Hugh Bigod arrived from Normandy and swore that Henry, on his deathbed, had designated Stephen the heir. This would have been plausible in light of the relationship between Henry and Geoffrey. The archbishop accepted this and the coronation was planned. By his coronation on December 22, Stephen had also received the support of the justiciar, Roger of Salisbury, and the treasurer, William de Pont de l'Arche. Also, Robert, earl of Gloucester, the Empress' half-brother, initially swore fealty to Stephen.[2] By late spring, most of the nobles in England had declared their allegiance either to Stephen or to the Empress; while Stephen's forces controlled England, Matilda's were making gains in Normandy and her uncle supported her in Scotland.

The years from 1136 to 1141 were filled with military and diplomatic

errors on Stephen's part which led to the alienation of some of his sup-
porters, including his brother. In February 1141, Stephen lost a battle at
Lincoln; he was captured, and the Empress was recognized as "Lady of
England." For almost nine months, the Empress ruled England and proved
that she had an ability even greater than Stephen's to alienate supporters.
Particularly crucial was her expulsion from London, which William of
Malmesbury credited to her personal alienation of the Londoners.[3] Queen
Matilda, Stephen's wife, raised an army which captured the earl of
Gloucester, who was exchanged for the king. Following this setback, Ste-
phen ruled for ten more years marked by frequent rebellions by supporters
and disputes with the upper clergy. Meanwhile, the Angevin party, which
from the mid-1140s included the Empress' son, the young Duke Henry,
made fairly steady gains on the continent. In January 1153, Duke Henry
invaded England, and supporters of both sides forced negotiations. In
November, the final settlement was reached designating Duke Henry as
Stephen's heir. Within a year, the Empress' son was crowned Henry II.[4]

Historiographic arguments on the Anarchy have raised questions which
directly concern the nobility and their relations to Henry I, and these, as
well as the effects of the Anarchy on the major groups of nobles, are
relevant to our discussion. Beyond these, we can determine the lasting
effects of Henry I's favor by examining the standing in the *Cartae Baronum* (1166) of the families which were upwardly mobile in 1135. Finally,
from that vantage point, some general conclusions can be drawn concerning the Anglo-Norman nobility.

Whether there really was "anarchy," and if so, what its causes were,
are among the questions that historians have debated over the years.[5]
Whether one believes that all men acted as Geoffrey de Mandeville did—
changing sides several times because of promised rewards—or that Geoffrey was unique and that the situation was more peaceful than any modern
conception of anarchy, it cannot be disputed that there were divided loyalties, more warfare in England than there had been for a generation, and
many castles built without royal license. The initial choice of Stephen over
Matilda, which led to the Anarchy, is understandable—most men of the
noble class in England disliked the idea of a woman ruler, let alone this
particularly imperious woman,[6] and they hated her Angevin in-laws. Stephen was a man of royal blood, well known to the nobles, and was a
magnate in his lifestyle and outlook—a second generation noble in attitude and curial pattern. Bigod's testimony to Henry's deathbed designation of Stephen as his successor gave the nobles and the clergy an excuse
to break their oath of fealty to Matilda with a clear conscience.

The complicated questions concerning the Anarchy, of course, are those dealing with the motives behind individuals' choices of sides. Stephen's "mistakes" are undoubtedly among the reasons for choice of sides. He lacked the diplomatic touch with which Henry dealt with the nobility. As Davis has pointed out, Henry never arrested a noble at court, both because it would break the king's peace and because Henry could deal effectively with his enemies in subtler ways. When Stephen broke his own peace and attacked unarmed members of his court (especially some of his bishops in 1139), he engaged in "a clever but dishonest trick" which showed his own weakness.[7] Such actions, along with Stephen's undistinguished military record, caused many nobles to turn away from him to support the only alternative, the Empress. It is possible that the situation was made more serious because the nobles had had high expectations of Stephen. Stephen was a magnate like them, an "aristocratic noble" in lifestyle. He may also have been among the taller of the English kings (possibly about six feet tall),[8] giving him a regal look, especially after three "medium sized kings." The raised expectations for a man who "looked the part" would have made his "failures" seem even greater.

Discussions of Stephen's administration highlight his general weaknesses as a twelfth-century king. There appears to have been a breakdown of local government during the reign. Davis has argued that defections among administrators and lesser nobles caused Stephen to replace local officials with his military followers, and in particular with the seventeen men created earls by the king.[9] Unfortunately, most of the earls were more qualified to be military men than to be administrators.

Another major line of discussion treats the political situation in the Anarchy as a reaction to Henry I's reign. According to this viewpoint, the nobles were looking not for a strong leader but rather for the weakest one possible. Since Henry I's achievements included further centralization of the government, the nobles were reacting in an attempt to regain their independence.[10] Whether such independence ever existed is not the question here; rather, the question is what the second generation of nobles— those born to magnate status—believed their ancestors had possessed at the Conquest. Certainly the "aristocratic" types, the noncurial nobles, sided with Stephen at first.[11]

A more recent and complex discussion of the Anarchy involves certain nobles' complaint that they were disinherited or displaced from power by Henry I in favor of other nobles or new men.[12] Claims of disinheritance obviously were made and are found in the chronicles.[13] At one time, Davis believed that Henry's exercise of his right as lord to treat property as "tenements" led to a reaction by nobles,[14] but he later modified this point of view. "There were too many claimants for too few baronies, and do what one might there would always be some men complaining that they had been disinherited. They formed a ready-made opposition to any king, and flocked to the support of the empress."[15] Southern theorizes that the new men supported the Empress and the older part of the noble class supported Stephen,[16] but no strict division of this sort seems to have taken place, though many of the prominent servants did support Matilda. King has suggested three possible solutions to the question of disinheritance: (1) that the tenurial disputes caused the Anarchy (that is, the Anarchy was a reaction to Henry I's involvement in tenure); (2) that such disputes helped to fuel the Anarchy once it started; or (3) that the disputes were the result of the breakdown in lordship during the Anarchy. King prefers the third solution,[17] but an examination of events seems to indicate that while all three of King's solutions were true to some extent, no single one can be said to have predominated. Some men were fighting over land before 1135 and undoubtedly chose their side because of this. Miles of Gloucester and Gilbert de Lacy, for example, whose families were claimants to the Lacy/Hereford lands, were on opposing sides and switched sides in the same years, obviously insuring that if one should win, the other would lose. Many local disputes had not surfaced before—and possibly would not have done so if the opportunity created by the Anarchy had not occurred. Some disputes arose when the royal claimants raised a local landholder to earl of the shire. The evidence bearing on the reasons behind the various disputes has been analyzed by a number of historians, who have come to differing conclusions as to which motives were the most important. Some nobles undoubtedly were alienated by Henry I's actions, but most could have simply taken advantage of Stephen's weakness. As with most historical questions of motivation, there will always be several ways of reading each individual case, as indeed each person is motivated by several things at the same time.

If Stephen and his supporters did in fact symbolize the reaction against Henry and his "government of new men," then one would expect Stephen's administration to have been composed of different men; yet not all of Henry's administrators ever supported Matilda, and most did so only after several years had elapsed.[18] Two of Henry's administrators, Roger of Salisbury and William de Pont de l'Arche, were instrumental in turning the government over to Stephen. All of the ecclesiastical new men continued to support Stephen, and it is for this reason that the king's motives for arresting Roger in 1139 have been debated. Of the twenty most active new men alive in 1135, only five supported Matilda immediately.[19] A sixth, William Maltravers, was killed by a local knight as soon as the news of Henry I's death was received.[20] Geoffrey fitz Payn and Payn

fitz John died within the first two years of the reign after initially supporting the king. Baldwin de Redvers, son of a *familiaris,* was himself an
"aristocratic" noble but nevertheless sided with Matilda because it had
been "Henry's wishes." In 1141, Redvers joined the earl of Chester to
relieve their common relative, William de Roumare. He is a unique case.[21]
Where the loyalties of four of the twenty lay is hard to determine because
of their low profile, though one man witnessed twice for Stephen and
another once for Duke Henry.[22] Only one new family, the de la Haias,
supported Stephen actively through most of his reign. Both Robert de la
Haia's sons, Richard and Ralph, defended the Cotentin for Stephen and
served in their royal offices as dapifer and justice. When Normandy finally
was lost in the mid-1140s, however, Ralph returned to England to serve
Stephen, while Richard made peace with Duke Henry and served him in
Normandy.[23] Of the other seven new families, all supported the king at
first. The Courcys were with the Empress by 1138, and William fitz
Walter de Beauchamp, Richard Basset, Geoffrey (II) de Clinton, William
Mauduit, and William de Pont de l'Arche by 1141. William d'Albini Brito
did not switch allegiance until sometime before 1146. Of the seven, only
two, Beauchamp and Mauduit, seem to have switched because Stephen
would not let them hold the offices they had held under Henry, while the
Empress reinstated them. Pont de l'Arche even served as chamberlain for
all three principals—Stephen, Matilda, and Duke Henry. None of the new
men were *curiales* to any claimant, although those who continued to serve
(that is, the de la Haias and Pont de l'Arche) witnessed documents more
than a few times.[24] No new man obtained an earldom from either royal
party.

Of twenty-one members of service families active in 1135, seventeen
were fairly evenly split in the support of the combatants, while the preferences of the remaining four are unknown.[25] Eight of the twenty-one
servants active, including some of Henry I's closest *familiares,* were the
king's supporters. It would be simplistic to expect any one factor, like
generation, to determine the sides. Looking at just the service families we
see the variety of causes. Robert Marmion supported Stephen after his
cousin and rival for their mothers' inheritance, William de Beauchamp,
joined Matilda (before 1141). They were the same "generation"; the rivalry created the sides. Herbert the Chamberlain's heirs supported Stephen but were not active during the reign. William de Chesney, and two
younger sons of service families, Fulk d'Oilli and Robert de Vere, all
actively supported the king, as did Aubrey (II) de Vere, a first generation
noble, until his death in 1140. William (II) d'Albini Pincerna, a second
generation noble, was an active supporter of Stephen even though he was

married to the Empress' stepmother, Queen Adeliza. As I have indicated earlier, Roger de Mowbray was unsuccessful in most of his Anarchy ventures and was not active in politics for part of the reign, first because he was a minor, and later because he was on crusade, but during most of the reign Roger supported Stephen. Roger, the archetypal second generation noble, was a natural supporter for Stephen.

Only two members of service families, Montpinçon and Tancarville, sided with Matilda from 1135. Rabel de Tancarville is arguably second generation but both were based in Normandy, which Matilda held, their future clearly lay with her. Most of Matilda's supporters in this group as well as among the new men came through defections. Bohun, Cahaignes, John the Marshal, and Miles of Gloucester were all early defectors (before 1139), some probably having been persuaded to alter their allegiance by Robert of Gloucester, and all were men who had continued to perform royal service, not lead the baronial life. Hugh Bigod, whose testimony had persuaded the clergy to support Stephen, had switched to Matilda by 1141. Hugh was second generation but had been a younger son who inherited only after his noncurial brother died in the White Ship. His own career was curial. Also by 1141, Robert d'Oilli, Fulk's elder brother, had "defected." Robert had remained as curial as his father, though he may not have been given his father's office of constable (given by Stephen in 1136). Aubrey (III) de Vere, definitely a second generation noble, joined Matilda between 1141 and 1145, then returned to Stephen.

To sum up, of twenty-one servants, eight were mainly supporters of Stephen, nine were for Matilda, and one supported both at different times. The service families continued to be *curiales,* especially when supporting Stephen.[26] Among the service families, four obtained earldoms through their support. All four were second generation nobles, although two were curial and two were aristocratic. The title was the next logical step in status for all.[27] Looking at the generations of these men, their status as well as their curial lifestyle, does not unravel the knot of the Anarchy, but it does add to our understanding of both the social group and the politics of the time.

The magnates as a group supported Stephen. The Counts of Aumâle, Leicester (Beaumont), Huntingdon (Senlis), Surrey (Warenne), and Brittany, as well as most of the younger brothers such as Hugh the Poer Beaumont, were fairly consistent and active in their support, while the earl of Warwick and the many Clares were usually for Stephen but occasionally changed allegiance. Ranulf (II) earl of Chester, who was about 15 when his father unexpectedly acquired the earldom, defected to Matilda before 1139. However, Waleran of Meulan, already described as a second generation baron, also defected before 1141. Robert of Neufbourg, Warwick's younger brother, who held mainly Norman land, supported Matilda from 1135, with locus of tenure again obviously influencing the decision. Only Giffard, earl of Buckingham, did not support anyone. The magnates were moderately active as *curiales* during Stephen's reign, some witnessing as many as twenty times, a change in their behavior of the latter years of Henry's reign. Eight of the magnates received new earldoms from Stephen for their support, again, the only logical reward for the heavily landed.

Unlike the magnates, the royal family sided with Matilda, although they also changed sides at some point. Robert, earl of Gloucester, went to England after his father's death and stayed, apparently to try to secure his property and persuade some nobles to join him.[28] By 1138 he was with Matilda. Two other half-brothers, Reginald and Robert fitz Edith, supported their sister; and Reginald was rewarded with the earldom of Cornwall. Matilda's maternal uncle, David, King of Scotland, raided northern England persistently and usually effectively, though he switched to Stephen for a period after Scotland lost the Battle of the Standard (1138). David's son Henry was reinstated as earl of Northumberland for a time for his support of Stephen. While David's behavior during Henry I's reign was aristocratic, the additional bond of maternal uncle appears to have been a strong motivation. Gloucester's son Philip also supported Stephen for a year after an in-law was humiliated by Angevin supporters; but his support of the king was less active than it had been for the Empress, and he left on crusade shortly after his defection.

For the most part members of the untitled nobility were not active for either claimant during the period, though there were several exception. Gant and Ferrers[29] were with the king throughout the reign, more often as military leaders than as *curiales,* and received earldoms as rewards. Walter Espec, who had often served as a justice for Henry I in the northern counties, supported Stephen and defended his own land against the Scots, but was generally inactive after the Battle of the Standard. Gilbert de Lacy and William de Mohun supported the Empress at first but had switched to Stephen before 1141. Roger de Nonant and the sons of Alan fitz Flaad were among the few prominent untitled nobles who actively supported the Empress. The "fitz Flaads" present an interesting case: they are a familial political bloc yet also are brothers using different epithets as surnames, the name not symbolizing the family bond. Others in the category of lesser nobles were some of the obviously opportunistic ones: Geoffrey de Mandeville and William de Roumare both received earldoms from Stephen and rebelled and switched sides several times. In spite of these examples, few lesser nobles appeared at court a significant number of times.

Thus while the king's favor could provide wealth and influence for a family, the politics of Stephen's reign and the activities of the next generation could alter the family's position and power. Many motivations were operating at the time—those previously examined (political and economic) but also social and familial ones. What then was the lasting importance of Henry I's favor for the families who were rising in status during his reign? Who was able to use that favor to rise in power over time? Luckily, Henry II's great surveys provide snapshots of the descendants of Henry I's nobles.

Henry II's survey, the *Cartae Baronum* of 1166,[30] provides a way of gauging how the families of Henry I's servants and *familiares* fared during the generation after his death. Did the new forms of social mobility provide lasting benefits? Most of the new men can be traced into the second half of the century.

William Trussebut, one of Orderic's list, witnessed only twice, once for Henry I and once for Duke Henry,[31] and left no record of royal service; but he did marry into a prominent new family that ultimately provided his sons with inheritances: in 1166, William (II) Trussebut held ten fees in Yorkshire—land probably inherited from his maternal uncle, Geoffrey fitz Payn, rather than from his father.[32] Two of Orderic's new men—Geoffrey de Clinton and Ralph Basset—were among the most conspicuous and rewarded royal servants. While Geoffrey (I) de Clinton was ubiquitous in the 1120s and the early 1130s, and was exempt from the danegeld in fourteen counties, his heirs' power seems to have been based on their marital connections with the earl of Warwick. The Clintons had more than twenty-six fees in 1166, but none were held in chief, and seventeen were held of Geoffrey (II)'s in-law, the earl of Warwick.[33] Ralph Basset's descendants fared better than Clinton's but show little increase in wealth after 1135. At least two generations of Bassets performed service and were *curiales*. Through marriage, the Bassets united with an earlier new family, that of Ridel, and Richard Basset's heir took his name. In 1166, Geoffrey (II) Ridel held fifteen fees in chief in Northamptonshire—land originally held by Geoffrey (I) Ridel and Richard Basset. Among the tenants on this land were descendants of several service families, including the Engaines and the family of Herbert the Chamberlain.[34]

The other new men we have looked at, so characterized by their origins and actions rather than by Orderic's statement, also appear to have fared well or ill as much by reason of their marriage alliances as by their continued curial service or by their political actions, the side they took in the

Anarchy. William d'Albini Brito held 32½ fees in chief in Leicestershire, and almost half of these were subinfeudated to his family.[35] While this was a large holding, it is probably about equal in size to the land of Belvoir, which was gained through marriage in Henry I's reign. Walter de Beauchamp's descendants continued to hold sixteen fees in chief in Worcestershire, in which shire Walter's wife, Emmeline d'Abetot, inherited much land during the reign of Henry I. The Beauchamp family also held twenty-four fees of various churches in Worcester and four fees in three other shires; but some holdings which appear in the 1130 Pipe Roll do not appear in the *Cartae*.[36] Eustace fitz John's heirs appear to have maintained their hold on the land and status Eustace had acquired both through marriage and through direct royal favor. The principal heir, William de Vesci, held over twenty-six fees in chief in Yorkshire, the location both of his mother's land and of the barony created by Henry I for his father; in addition, he held more than eleven fees of other lords.[37] Eustace's other children became heirs of the Lacys and (through Eustace's second wife) of the constable of Chester. The heirs of both Beauchamp and Eustace fitz John had to struggle to preserve their land against encroachment. Beauchamp came into conflict with the powerful Waleran, count of Meulan, which may account for his apparent loss of land and his inability to gain more;[38] in a surviving Anarchy charter, Roger de Mowbray restored to William de Vesci Yorkshire land which Eustace fitz John had held of Nigel d'Albini. This land was accounted for in the *Cartae* as new land, acquired after 1135.[39]

The de la Haias were one of the few families new to England in Henry I's reign who retained their lands and offices through the Anarchy. The lands held by the principal heir were all in Lincolnshire—eleven fees held in chief and three held of other lords. Another de la Haia descendant held fewer than three fees of others. As I have noted, both brothers defended the Cotentin for Stephen, but Richard came to terms with Duke Henry and continued to serve as dapifer and justice in Normandy, while Ralph returned to England and continued to serve Stephen.[40] Members of the family have been classified as new men because of their late appearance in England as regards both land holding and service; but in fact, they were members of a rising service family in Normandy. Their ability to survive Henry I's death was due both to their continued service and to the land base obtained through marriage to a Lincolnshire heiress, made during Henry I's reign.

The Courcys were another service family mainly associated with Normandy, with a cadet line new to England early in Henry I's reign. They continued to serve as dapifers, especially in Normandy, through the Anarchy. In 1166 the direct heir, William (III) de Courcy, held twenty-five old fees and 5½ new fees in Somerset, and nine more which had been William Meschin's barony. Like the holdings of most new families, this holding was based on marriages made by Courcy ancestors. William (I) de Courcy married the heiress of a Somerset barony, William (II) was the first husband of the heiress of William Meschin, and William (III) the first husband of Gundreda de Warenne—the last two not only wealthy but from magnate families.[41]

The Pomeroys began subinfeudating to family members as soon as they gained land, and continued to do so. They made their major gain during Henry I's reign, especially with a marriage to Rohesia, one of the king's daughters. The family retained this status, though did not continue to rise until the rebellion of the eldest son against Richard I.[42]

The St. Johns made good marriages, and since only one of three in each of two generations had children, their acquired land was not divided; yet the family is barely mentioned in the Cartae, and one listing notes that the land was then (1166) held by Reginald de Sancto Walerico, a prominent servant of Henry II.[43]

The Redvers, we have seen, survived and thrived. Certainly, their marital and feudal networks helped—ties within two generations were extensive and through all categories including royal ones. Their land had been accumulated in small pieces as well as conspicuously large ones—no one obvious strategy was used. In addition, Baldwin's unique life as a non-curial, second generation noble who staunchly supported the Empress on ethical grounds (loyalty to Henry's wishes) helped his position in the long run since he retained his Angevin earldom.[44]

Three other major new families did not survive the Anarchy intact. Brian fitz Count's estates were forfeited to Stephen and were still in the king's hands in 1166.[45] There is no record of any children left to fight for their return—a sad note for the man who lives for us from his letter to Henry of Blois as the loyal Brian. Geoffrey fitz Payn's heir was his nephew William (II) Trussebut; but the Honour of Warter, created for Geoffrey by Henry I, was in the king's hands in 1166, and Geoffrey's other barony (Hunsingore) was held by the earl of Chester.[46] In other words, while lateral inheritance had been allowed, it was only partially so. Payn fitz John, whose fortune had been acquired through service and marriage, left two heiresses, the eldest of whom was married three times before dying without any direct heirs (ca. 1197).[47] None of Payn's descendants appear to have been holding much of his land in 1166.[48] A charter of the Abbey of St. Benet of Holme, dated ca. 1141–46, concerned land worth one-half fee which was to be regranted unless Payn's heir could recover it.[49] It would seem, therefore, that part of Payn's wealth was split among his heirs and part was lost.

As a group, the descendants of Henry I's new men as seen in the *Cartae Baronum* did not acquire lasting great fortunes. The traditional feudal factors—a good marriage and the production of an adult male heir who could fight actively for his status—were those which in the long run determined the family fortune. In terms of lasting benefits to their families, the new men profited most when Henry's reward for their curial service was granted in the form of good marriages—marriages which provided not only inheritance in land but status and helpful family connections.

The service families taken as a group fared better up to 1166. Herbert the Chamberlain, one of the lowest members of the group (in terms of status), in 1100, passed on to his heir Herbert fitz Herbert 3½ fees held in chief and 8½ held of others—about equal to the average acquisition of the new men.[50] However, this same heir was married to a daughter of Miles of Gloucester, and by chance their heir inherited both Herbert's land and all the land (though not the title) of Roger of Gloucester, earl of Hereford. The Tancarvilles, whose main allegiance was in Normandy, do not seem to have left heirs past 1140—or at least none who held their land in 1166.

Hugh de Bocland's heirs held four knight's fees, but only one of these was held in chief.[51] The family's great rise occurred as a result of Hugh's activity late in Rufus' reign and early in that of Henry I. Hugh's son succeeded him in only one of eight shrievalties and rarely appears in the records. Since the growth of the family's success had already slowed during Henry's reign, it is not surprising that the descendants held so little in 1166.

However, other service families discussed in previous chapters held substantial fees in 1166. The Northamptonshire forest families who intermarried, the Engaines and the Lisures, had two lines of descendants represented in the *Cartae*. Fulk de Lisures held the family lands in Northamptonshire by forestry service. His half-brother Richard Engaine held twelve fees of the Basset/Ridel heir in Northamptonshire together with a fee in Staffordshire and another in Bedfordshire held of other lords.[52] The forest families generally seem to have held their offices well into the Angevin period, though they do not seem to have often used the job as a springboard.[53]

Aubrey (II) de Vere's son became an earl during the Anarchy. In 1166, Aubrey (III) held about thirty fees in chief in Essex and more than ten additional fees held of other lords scattered through the country.[54] This curial family retained the lands obtained through service to the king, through advantagous marriage, and through Anarchy politics conducted by an adult, active heir. The d'Oilli heir was less active, though less controversial, and succeeded in maintaining and perhaps enhancing the family's wealth. In 1166, Henry d'Oilli held more than thirty-two fees in chief and more than two new fees in Oxfordshire in addition to six more fees held of others in other counties.[55]

Several curial families had acquired great fortunes by 1166. The Bigods, who had profited by two generations of men who had been *curiales* to Henry I, several advantageous marriages, and successful political maneuvering during the Anarchy, became earls of Norfolk, the shire where their central holdings were located. In 1166, Count Hugh held 125 fees in chief and 5½ of others, all in Norfolk and all *de veteri feffamento,* that is, held during the reign of Henry I.[56]

All three lines of d'Albini/Cainhoes were large landholders in 1166. Robert d'Albini was the heir of the least active member of the family, Henry d'Albini. In 1166, Robert held twenty-five fees in chief in Bedfordshire where his father's land had been, and twelve of these were new fees, acquired since 1135. Robert appears to have been more active that his father. Henry's younger son, Nigel, was provided for through family connections: Henry's marriage to Cecily de Chaources during Henry I's reign made Nigel a cousin of Payn de Muntdubel, heir of Patrick de Chaources; and in 1166, Nigel was listed as holding one manor worth £20 of Payn in Gloucester.[57] However, no mention is found of his mother's Wiltshire dowry. William d'Albini Pincerna's son, the first earl of Arundel, married the dowager queen, Adeliza, and was active throughout the Anarchy. In 1166, he held well over 100 fees in Norfolk, Suffolk and Kent. Three groups of fees are directly tied to marriages in three generations. Ten fees were held of Hugh Bigod *de maritagio*— that is, through the elder Pincerna's marriage to a Bigod. Arundel itself and the Sussex lands attached were the barony created from royal demesne as the *maritagium* for Queen Adeliza when she married Henry I, and were held by her husband, the earl, in 1166. The eleven fees in Kent were subinfeudated to the count of Eu as the *maritagium* of Arundel's daughter.[58] Therefore, there are two things to note here: the importance of the gain made by marriage, and the provision for the family members by subinfeudation. Additionally, in this case as in others, such marriages and the activity of a grown male heir allowed the family to retain or increase the fortune begun by the servant ancestor. The third major line of Albini/Cainhoe active in Henry I's reign was represented in 1166 by Roger de Mowbray. The family history[59] shows that Roger was not nearly so politically effective as his father had been, though in 1166 he had not as yet rebelled against Henry II. The only major account of his land, however, is that very compact Yorkshire holding in chief, eighty-eight fees which had been held by his father but which included over eleven newly subinfeudated ones. There was no record of his lands in other counties.[60]

As a group, the less active untitled nobility had retained in 1166 most of what they held earlier in the century. Marital connections appear to have been less important for the lesser noble families than they were for the new and service families. As with some of the servants, lesser nobles held on to their ancestors' more compact holdings, some of which had been obtained through Henry I's favor.[61]

Most lesser noble families were not curial. Hamelin de Ballon is recorded as witnessing three extant documents all of which were associated with his brother Winebald, who himself acted as witness only six times in twenty-one years. However, the family did marry well. Hamelin's heiress married Reginald fitz Count, son of the disinherited earl of Hereford. In 1166, their heir William fitz Reginald held one fee in Hereford and continued to hold his Ballon grandfather's honour of Abergavenny. His younger brother Hamelin held half a fee of his cousin, Henry de Newmarket. The latter, Winebald's eventual heir was the son of another advantageous marriage, that of his daughter to a Hereford and Gloucester heir, Bernard de Newmarket. Henry de Newmarket held more than fifteen fees in chief in Gloucester and enfeoffed his cousins.[62]

Another noncurial noble, Patrick de Chaources, was represented by his son Payn de Muntdubel in 1166. Payn retained his father's substantial 12½ fees in Gloucester but is not mentioned in connection with the lands in Oxfordshire, Buckinghamshire, or Berkshire which were his father's in 1130.[63] Similarly, Alfred of Lincoln's descendants retained his main Dorset holding of twenty-five fees held in chief as well as eight fees held of others. Alfred cannot be called a *curialis,* but appeared at court regularly (eighteen times in twenty-two years) and was used as a royal justice in Dorset where most of his land lay.[64] Gilbert de Laigle was a *curialis* during the first eighteen years of the reign and received the forfeited barony of Pevensey from Henry I. As I have noted, Henry I attempted to give this land to Gilbert's younger son until the heir, Richer, threatened rebellion at a crucial time. Richer never became a *curialis* nor performed service. The *Cartae* shows that he retained the fought-for Pevensey barony worth 35½ fees but nothing else in England.[65] The two families of Port also witnessed documents periodically during Henry I's reign, but both performed service in the shires where they held most of their land. These major holdings were retained—Adam de Port of Mapledurwell held over twenty-two fees in Hereford, and John de Port of Basing held fifty-five fees in Hampshire.[66] Neither family played a large part in the Anarchy. They obtained their land early, served in the same area, made no spectacular marriages until late in the twelfth century, and retained their holdings.

One example of a rear vassal surviving the Anarchy again shows the importance of land gained through marriage. In chapter 1, we met Pinceon, the steward of the bishop of Durham, who held land of the bishop in 1115–18 and who had given his son a Norman name. This son, Hugh, however, sided with Cumin against the bishop during the Anarchy, which probably led to the loss of his land, but was rewarded with a relative of Cumin to marry. In 1166, he still held seven knights' fees.[67]

It becomes clear from studying the long term effects of Henry I's administrative policies and distribution of favors that the king was indeed the springboard, or "the chief external impulse to social climbing in the twelfth century."[68] However, various other factors determined whether a family continued to rise or even retained wealth they had gained through favor; of these factors, marital connections appear to have been the most important. The major holdings derived from Henry I's favor which survived into Henry II's reign were acquired through marriage, and younger sons and cousins were provided for through these connections as well.

This study has concerned itself with the Anglo-Norman upper class in the reign of Henry I, and in particular with changes in the composition of the upper class and the factors which caused these changes, with special attention to royal favor as a factor. The general characteristics of the noble class did not change, but its composition was altered as new families entered the class and older families found ways to rise in status within it.

A major portion of this work has been concerned with an examination of royal favor—in part because of the special developments of Henry I's reign. Henry was apparently the first English king to create a professional administration—one composed of less wealthy individuals who were less likely to usurp royal authority—and in doing so, he provided an opportunity for individuals of lesser status to rise into or within the nobility. Royal favor provided some men with land (the basic unit of wealth and status), marriage to heirs of tenants-in-chief (with their lands), royal offices (sometimes with land or with the opportunity for other favors), exemptions from various assessments, or grants of various benefits on land already held. Attendance at Henry's court provided the opportunity to gain power which was associated with advising the king or helping to run the daily administration. Presence at court also allowed an individual to be available to serve the king or to receive other favors.

Attitudes toward royal favor varied among the different groups within the upper class. Some people—mainly the service families and new men—actively sought favor. Others—especially the younger magnates—felt it was their right to receive favor, a consequence of their position in life. Those who sought favor did so mainly by attending court, thus making themselves, their loyalty, and their abilities known to the king and serving him in various capacities. Indeed, the examination of witnessing at court in the later years of the reign (when Henry appears to have been experimenting with the administration) shows the court to have been composed mainly of new men, members of service families and ecclesiastical new men.

Favor, however, proved to be more important to individuals than to families. Many individuals started or strengthened fortunes through their service to the king, but the protection of their wealth and position after Henry's death and the continued enhancement of their family's status depended upon other factors. This may perhaps best be seen by looking at the situation of the new men, those who began their rise through Henry I's favor.

Despite some advantageous marriages and spectacular gains made by new men during Henry I's reign, no one made a major and lasting family fortune based on favor from this king. The few new families who did survive the Anarchy with their wealth intact had not extended their connections or their service enough to continue to rise either to a great height or at the same speed. In some cases, the problem was the lack of adult male heirs who would continue to serve or could fight the possibility of disinheritance. In other cases, there was an obvious reaction against the new man and his power. Henry I's actions, therefore, opened the upper class to new men, but in the long run such access did not drastically alter the composition of the class.

Many of the service families, on the other hand, made great fortunes, and their families continued to prosper. These families started with a larger base of wealth and connections, as well as a tradition of royal service. In many cases, royal service was performed by at least two generations after 1100. Starting with a higher status than the new men had, and enjoying the king's favor, members of service families made more advantageous marriages (in terms of both income and status) per generation, and thus established more intricate networks of familial and feudal ties. While these networks of families did not necessarily act as political blocs, they provided wealth and status for later generations. These alliances often made it possible for families to provide for younger children by allowing younger sons to hold land of, or inherit land from, a collateral relative.

Once status had been achieved, there were no apparent differences in patterns of life among the newly rich to set them apart from the rest of the upper class—their patronage of religious houses, their treatment of their relatives, and their households were similar to those of the magnates. Their behavior in their families was similar. Most of their descendants acted as other second generation nobles did—expecting certain privileges and relying for gain on their traditional feudal alliances than on royal favor. This behavior, too, is like that of the magnates—those who achieved their status from the Conquest and reared their heirs to be "aristocratic." While living in a changing world and participating in the new arts and styles of life, the noble who gained mobility through the new governmental means strove to fit into the established mold. The second generation noble saw the king as a rival, whether or not his wealth was based upon the king's professional administration.

Notes

1. Hollister and Keefe, "Making of the Angevin Empire," p. 16.
2. Malmesbury (*HN*, p. 18) wrote that Robert took the oath "conditionally" as long as his honor would let him, fully expecting Stephen to "break his word." For arguments concerning the validity of this point see Patterson, "William of Malmesbury's Robert of Gloucester," and Leedom, "William of Malmesbury."
3. *HN*, p. 56.
4. Two excellent modern histories survey the Anarchy, each written by an editor of the *Regesta* for the reign. R. H. C. Davis' *King Stephen,* the earlier of the works, is arranged chronologically and includes a discussion of the sources for the reign. H. A. Cronne's *Reign of Stephen* includes a chronological chapter but concentrates on topical analysis and as such discusses questions of social history which are relevant to this work. Either of these books is recommended for further reading and bibliographic information. The contemporary sources are similar to those for 1100–35—the collection of royal charters in *Reg.* III which also includes those charters of the Angevin courts, the various cartularies of churches, and chronicles. The chroniclers themselves showed characteristics of the Anarchy in their partisanship—*The Gesta Stephani* (*GS*) for the king, Malmesbury's *Historia Novella* (*HN*) for the Empress. For arguments about aspects of the Anarchy after these books see: Callahan, "Ecclesiastical Reparations," which discusses many of the nobles included in this study; King, "The Anarchy of King Stephen's Reign," which reexamines the question of "anarchy"; Schnith, "Regni et pacis inquietatrix," which reexamines Matilda's reputation; and Leedom, "The English Settlement of 1153," which analyzes the events from 1150 to 1153.
5. King, "King Stephen and the Anglo-Norman Aristocracy" provides a fine summary of the arguments and their proponents.
6. See the discussion in chapter 2.
7. Davis, *King Stephen,* pp. 33–34. Davis had previously stated this argument in his article "What Happened in Stephen's Reign."

8. Russell, "Tall Kings."

9. Davis, *King Stephen*, pp. 32–33 and Appendix I, pp. 129–32. An unsystematic survey of *Reg.* III bears this out. Strikingly few writs were addressed to a specific administrator rather than to an earl or even to all nobles of England and Normandy, even where specific orders concerning local matters were concerned. Duke Henry's charters seem to follow his grandfather's form: that is, they were addressed to whoever could carry out the order.

10. Davis, *King Stephen*, p. 1. This is the argument which developed out of the early studies of the Anarchy, especially Round's *Geoffrey de Mandeville*.

11. For example William, count of Aumâle, who had been reared at court (English, *Lords of Holderness*, p. 17).

12. Southern ("Place") and Davis ("What Happened") argue that the disinheritances were directly attributable to Henry I and his policies. Cronne (*Reign*, pp. 19–24) modifies this to include intrafamily claims and old Norman feuds. This argument has also been the subject of debates in articles by Holt, "Politics and Property," and "Politics and Property: A Rejoinder"; King, "The Tenurial Crisis of the Early Twelfth Century"; Le Patourel, "What Did Not Happen in Stephen's Reign"; and Crouch, "Geoffrey de Clinton and Roger, Earl of Warwick."

13. The *Gesta Stephani*, for example, describes Henry I's practice of disinheriting nobles and giving their land to "court pages" (*GS*, pp. 22–23). The less biased chroniclers refer more often to specific cases.

14. Davis, "What Happened," p. 12.

15. Davis, *King Stephen*, p. 41.

16. Southern, "Place," pp. 141–42.

17. King, "Tenurial," p. 113.

18. Patterson ("William," p. 997) has written that Stephen simply alienated the old *familiares* by replacing them with new ones. Stephen obviously did have a group of new men who formed the core of his court, including William of Ypres, Adam de Beaunay, Roger de Fraxineto, Henry of Essex, and Turgis of Avranches. Whether his use of these men alienated Henry I's servants is an open question.

19. The St. Johns, Robert de Sigillo (who accompanied Henry I's body to Reading), Baldwin de Redvers (son of Henry's pre-1100 supporters), Eustace fitz John, and Brian fitz Count (who eloquently defended his stance to Henry of Blois [Davis, "Henry of Blois and Brian fitz Count," pp. 297–303]) all supported Matilda.

20. *Reg.* III, #428n. Stephen pardoned the knight.

21. Bearman, "Charters of the Redvers Family," pp. 29–40.

22. Pomeroy and Houghton do not appear in Anarchy documents, although Orderic placed Pomeroy with Waleran of Meulan fighting for Stephen in 1136 (OVC 6:476). Eynesford witnessed twice for Stephen (*Reg.* III, #163, 406), Trussebut once for Duke Henry (*Reg.* III, #167).

23. *Reg.* III, p. xxxvi. Records of their service include #54, 66, and 86.

24. Ralph de la Haia witnessed six times for Stephen, Richard once for Stephen and six times for the Angevins. Far less can be written concerning the Anarchy from the witnessing because there are fewer extant documents and their dating is more precarious than it was for the previous reigns.

25. Those about whom little is known during the reign were Rualon d'Avranches, Henry d'Albini, William de Bocland, and Richard Engaine.

26. Robert de Vere witnessed 140 times for Stephen and his queen, Matilda, Aubrey (II) de Vere 40 times before his death in 1140, Fulk d'Oilli 25 times, Albini Pincerna 22, Bigod 36 before 1141. The low number of charters for the Empress' court make it more difficult to make comparisons.

27. William (II) d'Albini Pincerna (second generation) was given the earldom by Stephen and allowed to exchange it later. The Empress made Miles of Gloucester (second generation but curial), Aubrey (III) de Vere (second generation), and Hugh Bigod (second generation but curial) earls, although de Vere lost his earldom when he switched again.

28. Robert Patterson argues against this interpretation of Robert of Gloucester's early Anarchy behavior ("Robert of Gloucester: A Reappraisal), believing it to be genuine support of Stephen which William of Malmesbury concealed for political reasons after Robert's change of alliance after 1138.

29. M. Jones, "The Charters of Robert II de Ferrers."

30. The *Cartae Baronum* of 1166 and the 1172 Norman *Infeudationes militum* are analyzed by Keefe in *Feudal Assessment*. Keefe has found a surprisingly low percentage of subinfeudation occurring during the period after Henry I's death. See especially p. 43, Table 4.

31. *Reg.* II, #1442; *Reg.* III, #167.

32. William probably had married the sister of Geoffrey fitz Payn (*EYC* 10, p. 6). *RB* I, p. 435.

33. *RB* I, pp. 289, 295, 309, 325. Southern ("Place," pp. 135–40) has listed Geoffrey's connections during the reign. Green (*Government,* pp. 239–42) provides a summary of his career and holdings.

34. *RB* I, pp. 329–331. The Bassets also held one fee of the Honour of Wallingford and 2½ fees in Nottinghamshire of Hubert fitz Ralph (ibid., p. 334). Two other members of the family held a total of eight fees—Ralph and Gilbert Basset were relatives of Geoffrey (ibid., pp. 223, 308). Five men—Alan, Nicholas, Thustin, Osmund and Fulk—were probably relatives and held twenty-two fees, none in chief (ibid., pp. 198, 311, 319, 308, 309, 310). Green (*Government,* pp. 231–32) provides a summary of his career and holdings.

35. *RB* I, p. 328.

36. Ibid., pp. 299–300, 188, 302, 269, 278, 287. Walter was exempt from the danegeld for land in Wiltshire, Gloucestershire, Leicestershire, and Berkshire (*PR,* pp. 22, 80, 89, 126) but William held no land in Wiltshire, Leicestershire, or Berkshire in 1166 and only land held of an abbot in Gloucestershire.

37. *RB* I, pp. 428–29, 382, 407, 417, 433–34. Green (*Government,* pp. 250–53) provides a summary of his holdings.

38. Cronne, *Reign,* pp. 172–74; Crouch, *Beaumont Twins,* p. 50.

39. Greenway, #397; *RB* I, p. 420; *Reg.*II, #1722, 1730.

40. *RB* I, pp. 390–91, 385, 416, 355, 361, 380.*Reg.*III, p. xxxvi, #54, 66.

41. *RB* I, pp. 224–25.

42. Powley, p. 14. Henry (I) held more than thirty-three fees in chief in Devon (*RB* I, 260–61) as well as 3½ fees in Devon and Cornwall held of the bishop of Exeter and his in-laws the earls of Gloucester and Cornwall (ibid., pp. 249, 252, 262). His son held one fee of his maternal relation, the earl of Gloucester (ibid., p. 289).

43. *RB* I, p. 204. The Oxfordshire land which cost Thomas 160*m.* relief in 1130 (*PR,* p. 3) is not found in the hands of the family in 1166.

44. See above, chapter 6.

45. RB I, pp. 308–11 is the main entry for the honour of Wallingford.

46. Ibid., p. 435; Sanders, *English Baronies,* p. 56.

47. Payn's elder daughter Cecily was married during his lifetime to the future earl of Hereford, but the earl's wealth was claimed by his sisters' families since no child was produced.

48. Cecily's third husband, Walter de Mayenne, was listed as holding 1½ fees of churches and as holding in chief Kentish land which had belonged to Geoffrey

Tallebot temp. Henry I (*RB* I, pp. 187, 189, 195). Geoffrey Tallebot was Payn's wife's half-brother. The second daughter's line held twelve fees in Eye (her son Hubert) and eight fees in Berkshire and Norfolk (held by her second husband, Bidun) (ibid., pp. 411, 310, 395).

49. West, *St. Benet of Holme,* I, #143.

50. *RB* I, pp. 199, 205, 207, 291, 306, 413, 246, 307.

51. *RB* I, pp. 258, 306, 307.

52. Ibid., pp. 333, 371, 269, 322, 329.

53. Young, *Royal Forests,* p. 15.

54. *RB* I, pp. 352–55, 318, 358, 368, 393, 403, 410. In addition, Count Aubrey held three fees *de novo* (ibid., pp. 366, 420).

55. Ibid., pp. 305, 265, 269, 312, 375.

56. Ibid., pp. 395–97, 393, 400. Atkin's analysis ("Bigod Family," p. 29) shows the majority of the Bigod fortune to have come from the original marriage to the Toeni heiress.

57. *RB* I, pp. 324, 298.

58. Ibid., pp. 200–02, 395, 397–99. It should be noted that the entry regarding the Bigod land is repeated on p. 395 and pp. 397–98.

59. See above, chapter 3.

60. Ibid., pp. 418–21. Roger also held four parts of one fee of the archbishop of York and 1½ fees *de novo* in Northamptonshire of Robert Foliet (ibid., pp. 413, 332). Greenway, ed. (*Charters of the Honour of Mowbray,* pp. xx–xxi) lists nine counties in which Nigel held land.

61. Only the most active of this large category were traced into Henry II's reign.

62. *RB* I, pp. 281, 296–97. Hamelin's younger (?) son, Matthew, also held ten fees in Sussex of the count of Eu (ibid., p. 202).

63. Ibid., pp. 297–98; *PR,* pp. 5, 104, 125–26.

64. *RB* I, pp. 214–16, 212, 222, 236, 240; *PR,* p. 15; *Reg.*II, p. xviii.

65. *RB* I, pp. 203–04.

66. Ibid., pp. 279–80, 206.

67. *Durham Episcopal Charters,* pp. 97–100.

68. Southern, "Place," p. 132.

Appendix I: Charter Attestations, 1100–35

The following tables have been compiled from the witness lists of the charters in *Regesta* II (those charters indicated as spurious not being included). The dating follows that of the *Regesta* editors, using the earliest possible date. The categories, as summarized below, are more fully defined in chapter 4 in the discussion of court attendance and witnessing. Table A (Major Witnesses) indicates the location of the court for each year, the total number of individuals who witnessed documents, and the total number of attestations. This is followed by the "distribution," that is, the range of the number of attestations for individuals that year. The major witnesses, those attesting four or more times, have been listed, together with the number of their attestations and the category in which I have classified them, in order to give the reader an idea of the composition of the court. Abbreviations used are as follows: standard abbreviations for first names; chanc. for chancellor; e. for Earl; ct. for Count. Bishops are indicated by name/church. Table B (Major Witnesses by Category) rearranges Table A to give easy reference to these often-mentioned individuals by category. They are alphabetized strictly by first name for convenience. Table C (Witnessing) records the percentage of those attending constituted by each category, together with the percentage of total attestations which the group represented. This table is arranged so as to enable the reader to gauge how heavily Henry relied upon each category and whether, as a group, they were used as often as their representation at court warranted. Table D (Witnessing by Category) uses the same figures as Table C arranged to enable the reader to see changes throughout the reign in the frequency with which they were used as witnesses.

Summary of Categories

Category 1—Retainers, servants of other nobles, lesser clergy
Category 2—Lesser nobles: untitled and not associated with any office
Category 3—Service families: families identified with royal service, including those holding serjeanty tenures and shrievalties
Category 4—New men: families having no noticeable status in England before 1100, including royal clerks
Category 5—Magnates: titled nobility
Category 6—Royal family
Category 7—Upper clergy

TABLE A.   Major Witnesses*

1100, England

Totals: 41 men, 97 times
Distribution: 1–11

11	Walter Giffard/chanc.	(5)
8	Henry, e. Warwick	(5)
5	Robert fitz Hamon	(3)
	Gerard/Hereford	(7)
	Robt. Bloet/Lincoln	(7)
4	Wm. Warelwast/chap.	(4)
	Roger Bigod	(3)

1101, England

Totals: 103 men, 295 times
Distribution: 1–12

12	Walter Giffard/chanc.	(5)
11	Robt.Bloet/Lincoln	(7)
	Eudo Dapifer	(3)
10	Hamo Dapifer	(3)
	Henry e. Warwick	(5)
9	Robert/Chester	(7)
	Robert ct. Meulan	(5)
8	Robert fitz Hamon	(3)
7	Wm. d'Albini Pincerna	(3)
	Roger Bigod	(3)
6	Urse d'Abetot	(3)
	Roger/chancellor	(4)
	Anselm/Canterbury	(7)
5	Maurice/London	(7)
	Gundulf/Rochester	(7)

1102, England

Totals: 57 men, 131 times
Distribution: 1–12

12	Urse d'Abetot	(3)
11	Roger/chancellor	(4)
10	Eudo Dapifer	(3)
9	Robt. Bloet/Lincoln	(7)
8	Roger Bigod	(3)
	Robert ct. Meulan	(5)
6	Walter Giffard/Winch.	(7)
4	Robert fitz Hamon	(3)
	Henry e. Warwick	(5)

1103, England

Totals: 46 men, 114 times
Distributions: 1–11

11	Waldric/chancellor	(4)
10	Robt. Bloet/Lincoln	(7)
7	Robert fitz Hamon	(3)
6	Urse d'Abetot	(3)
5	Wm d'Albini Pincerna	(3)
	Roger Bigod	(3)
	Robert ct. Meulan	(5)
	Roger/Salisbury	(7)
4	Wm. Warelwast/chap.	(4)
	Anselm/Canterbury	(7)

*For each name, first column is number of attestations, third column is category.

1104, Normandy, 5 months

Totals: 38 men, 56 times
Distributions: 1–7

7	Waldric/chancellor	(4)

1105, Normandy, 5 months

Totals: 73 men, 194 times
Distribution: 1–16

16	Waldric/chancellor	(4)
13	Roger Bigod	(4)
	Robt. Bloet/Lincoln	(7)
11	Eudo Dapifer	(3)
10	Robert ct. Meulan	(5)
7	Robert fitz Hamon	(3)
6	Urse d'Abetot	(3)
	Hamo Dapifer	(3)
	Richard de Redvers	(4)
5	Robert Malet	(2)
	Nigel d'Oilli	(3)
	Ranulf/Durham	(7)
	Roger/Salisbury	(7)
4	Alan fitz Flaad	(2)
	Nigel d'Albini	(3)

1106, Normandy, 6 months

Totals: 64 men, 169 times
Distribution: 1–31

31	Waldric/chancellor	(4)
10	Robert ct. Meulan	(5)
9	Roger/Salisbury	(7)
	Roger Bigod	(3)
8	Eudo Dapifer	(3)
7	Robt. Bloet/Lincoln	(7)
6	Wm. d'Albini Pincerna	(3)

1107, Normandy, 4 months

Totals: 92 men, 242 times
Distributions: 1–18

18	Roger Bigod	(3)
16	Ranulf/chancellor	(4)
13	Robert ct. Meulan	(5)
12	Robt. Bloet/Lincoln	(7)
10	Eudo Dapifer	(3)
7	Wm. d'Albini Pincerna	(3)
	Roger/Salisbury	(7)
	Hamo Dapifer	(3)
6	Anselm/Canterbury	(7)
	Henry e. Warwick	(5)
	Wm. Giffard/Winchester	(7)
5	Roger fitz Richard	(5)
4	William de Warenne	(5)
	Simon e. Huntingdon	(5)
	Samson/Worcester	(7)
	Wm. Warelwast/Exeter	(7)
	Wm. Courcy	(4)

1108, Normandy, 6 months

Totals: 42 men, 100 times
Distribution: 1–15

15	Roger/Salisbury	(7)
8	Robert ct. Meulan	(5)
7	Wm. Warelwast/Exeter	(7)
6	Robt. Bloet/Lincoln	(7)
5	Ranulf/chancellor	(4)
4	Urse d'Abetot	(3)

1109, Normandy, 6 months

Totals: 41 men, 90 times
Distributions: 1–9

9	Ranulf/chancellor	(4)
7	Robert ct. Meulan	(5)
	Robt. Bloet/Lincoln	(7)
5	Gilbert de Laigle	(2)
	Roger/Salisbury	(7)
4	Nigel d'Albini	(3)
	Roger Brus	(2)

1110, England

Totals: 58 men, 136 times
Distribution: 1–13

13	Robt. Bloet/Lincoln	(7)
12	Ranulf/chancellor	(4)
10	Roger/Salisbury	(7)
9	Hamo Dapifer	(3)
8	Wm. d'Albini Pincerna	(3)
6	Wm. Courcy	(4)
	Gilbert de Laigle	(2)
4	Wm. de Houghton	(4)
	Robert ct. Meulan	(5)

1111, Normandy, 5 months

Totals: 52 men, 93 times
Distribution: 1–9

9	Roger/Salisbury	(7)
8	Ranulf/chancellor	(4)
	Robt. Bloet/Lincoln	(7)
4	John of Bayeux	(4)
	Gilbert de Laigle	(2)

1112, Normandy

Totals: 7 men, 9 times
Distribution: 1–3

1113, Normandy, 7 months

Totals: 80 men, 138 times
Distribution: 1–10

10	Hamo Dapifer	(3)
7	Ranulf/chancellor	(4)
5	Richard e. Chester	(5)
4	Nigel d'Albini	(3)
	Wm. d'Albini Pincerna	(3)
	Wm. de Tancarville	(3)

1114, Normandy, 4 months

Totals: 67 men, 163 times
Distribution: 1–13

13	Ranulf/chancellor	(4)
	Roger/Salisbury	(7)
11	Robt. Bloet/Lincoln	(7)
10	Hamo Dapifer	(3)
8	Nigel d'Albini	(3)
	Robert ct. Meulan	(5)
6	Thurstan/York	(7)
5	Wm. de Tancarville	(3)
	Wm. d'Albini Pincerna	(3)
4	Ralph/Canterbury	(7)
	Walter of Gloucester	(3)

1115, Normandy, 5 months

Totals: 71 men, 149 times
Distribution: 1–17

17	Ranulf/chancellor	(4)
7	Roger/Salisbury	(7)
6	Robert ct. Meulan	(5)
5	Nigel d'Albini	(3)
	William the Aethling	(6)
4	Adam de Port	(2)
	Walter of Gloucester	(3)
	Robt. Bloet/Lincoln	(7)
	John/Lisieux	(7)

1116, Normandy, 9 months

Totals: 42 men, 105 times
Distribution: 1–16

16	Ranulf/chancellor	(4)
13	Robert ct. Meulan	(5)
8	Wm. d'Albini Pincerna	(3)
7	Roger/Salisbury	(7)
	Nigel d'Albini	(3)
	Robt. Bloet/Lincoln	(7)
4	Wm. Warelwast/Exeter	(7)

1117, *Normandy*

Totals: 2 men, 2 times

1118, *Normandy*

Totals: 41 men, 71 times
Distribution: 1–8

8	Ranulf/chancellor	(4)
5	Roger/Salisbury	(7)
4	Wm. d'Albini Pincerna	(3)

1119, *Normandy*

Totals: 46 men, 88 times
Distribution: 1–8

8	Ranulf/Canterbury	(7)
7	Ranulf/chancellor	(4)
5	Nigel d'Albini	(3)
4	Roger fitz Richard	(5)

1120, *Normandy, 11 months*

Totals: 38 men, 55 times
Distribution: 1–6

6	Ranulf/chancellor	(4)
4	Nigel d'Albini	(3)

1121, *England*

Totals: 129 men, 420 times
Distribution: 1–32

32	Ranulf/chancellor	(4)
28	Nigel d'Albini	(3)
23	Roger/Salisbury	(7)
18	Geoffrey de Clinton	(4)
14	Wm. de Tancarville	(3)
	Wm. Giffard/Winchester	(7)
13	Bernard/St. David's	(7)
12	Robt. Bloet/Lincoln	(7)
11	Walter of Gloucester	(3)
	Richard/Lincoln	(7)
10	Ralph Basset	(4)
	Robert e. Gloucester	(6)
8	Payn fitz John	(4)
	Ralph/Canterbury	(7)
7	Geoffrey fitz Payn	(4)
	Geoffrey/Rouen	(7)
6	Wm. d'Albini Pincerna	(3)
	David of Scotland	(6)
5	John of Bayeux	(4)
	Ranulf/Durham	(7)
4	Adam de Port	(2)
	Hamo Peverel	(4)
	William de Warenne	(5)
	Ranulf e. Chester	(5)
	Theowulf/Worcester	(7)

1122, *England*

Totals: 104 men, 219 times
Distribution: 1–27

27	Ranulf/chancellor	(4)
17	Nigel d'Albini	(3)
8	Robt. Bloet/ Lincoln	(7)
7	Ralph Basset	(4)
	Thurstan/York	(7)
6	Walter Espec	(2)
	Wm. de Tancarville	(3)
	Geoffrey de Clinton	(4)
4	William de Warenne	(5)
	Eustace fitz John	(4)

1123, Normandy, 6 months

Totals: 78 men, 141 times
Distribution: 1–8

8	Roger/Salisbury	(7)
7	Geoffrey Rufus/chanc.	(4)
	Nigel d'Albini	(3)
5	Wm. d'Albini Pincerna	(3)
4	Thomas St. John	(4)
	Hugh Bigod	(3)
	Geoffrey de Clinton	(4)

1124, Normandy

Totals: 11 men, 20 times

1125, Normandy

Totals: 43 men, 84 times
Distribution: 1–5

5	Bernard/ St. David's	(7)
	William/Canterbury	(7)
4	Nigel d'Albini	(3)
	William de Warenne	(5)
	Audin/Evreux	(7)
	Geoffrey/Rouen	(7)
	Wm.Giffard/Winchester	(7)
	Thurstan/York	(7)

1126, Normandy, 9 months

Totals: 89 men, 162 times
Distribution: 1–9

9	Geoffrey Rufus/chanc.	(4)
7	Robert de Sigillo	(4)
	Geoffrey de Clinton	(4)
6	Audin/Evreux	(7)
4	Brian fitz Count	(4)
	Robert e. Gloucester	(6)
	Alexander/Lincoln	(7)
	Roger/Salisbury	(7)
	Thurstan/York	(7)
	Nigel d'Albini	(3)

1127, Normandy, 5 months

Totals: 60 men, 246 times
Distribution: 1–29

29	Geoffrey Rufus/chanc.	(4)
22	Roger/Salisbury	(7)
17	Nigel d'Albini	(3)
16	Geoffrey de Clinton	(4)
12	Wm. de Tancarville	(3)
	Robert de Sigillo	(4)
10	Payn fitz John	(4)
9	Wm. de Pont de l'Arche	(4)
	Ralph Basset	(4)
8	Wm. d'Albini Pincerna	(3)
	Miles of Gloucester	(3)
7	Bernard/ St. David's	(7)
	Alexander/Lincoln	(7)
5	William/Canterbury	(7)
	Seffrid/Chichester	(7)
4	Aubrey de Vere	(3)
	Robert e. Gloucester	(6)

1128, Normandy

Totals: 64 men, 90 times
Distribution: 1–3

1129, Normandy, 7 months

Totals: 94 men, 250 times
Distribution: 1-18

18	Nigel d'Albini	(3)
17	Wm. de Tancarville	(3)
15	Geoffrey Rufus/chanc.	(4)
12	Geoffrey fitz Payn	(4)
11	Geoffrey de Clinton	(4)
	Robert de Sigillo	(4)
9	Robert e. Gloucester	(6)
	Thurstan/York	(7)
8	John/Lisieux	(7)
	Wm. d'Albini Pincerna	(3)
6	Richard/Bayeux	(7)
4	Robert de la Haia	(4)
	Wm. de Pont de l'Arche	(4)
	William de Warenne	(5)
	Roger/Salisbury	(7)

1130, Normandy, 5 months

Total: 71 men, 144 times
Distribution: 1–16

16	Geoffrey Rufus/chanc.	(4)
8	Roger/Salisbury	(7)
	Robert e. Gloucester	(6)
6	Robert de Vere	(3)
	Wm. d'Albini Brito	(4)
	Brian fitz Count	(4)
5	Miles of Gloucester	(3)
4	Henry of Blois/Winch.	(7)
	Wm. de Pont de l'Arche	(4)
	Hugh Bigod	(3)

1131, Normandy, 8 months

Totals: 108 men, 374 times
Distribution: 1–17

17	Robert e. Gloucester	(6)
16	Robert de Sigillo	(4)
13	Geoffrey Rufus/chanc.	(4)
	Hugh Bigod	(3)
12	Robert de la Haia	(4)
	Brian fitz Count	(4)
	Geoffrey fitz Payn	(4)
10	John/Lisieux	(7)
	Miles of Gloucester	(3)
	Alexander/Lincoln	(7)
9	Payn fitz John	(4)
	Nigel/Ely	(7)
	Hugh/Rouen	(7)
8	Roger e. Warwick	(5)
	William/Canterbury	(7)
	Audin/Evreux	(7)
7	Waleran ct. Meulan	(5)
	Humphrey de Bohun	(3)
	John/Sées	(7)
	Thurstan/York	(7)
6	Geoffrey de Clinton	(4)
	Roger/Salisbury	(7)
	Henry of Blois/Winch.	(7)
5	William fitz Odo	(3)
	Rabel de Tancarville	(3)
	Richard Basset	(4)
	Robert de Courcy	(4)
	William Mauduit	(4)
	Wm. de Pont de l'Arche	(4)
	Gilbert/London	(7)
4	Robert e. Leicester	(5)

1132, England

Totals: 50 men, 127 times
Distribution: 1–9

9	Geoffrey Rufus/chanc.	(4)
8	Robert de Sigillo	(4)
7	Payn fitz John	(4)
6	Roger/Salisbury	(7)
	Aubrey de Vere	(3)
	Miles of Gloucester	(3)
5	Robert de Vere	(3)
	Humphrey de Bohun	(3)
4	William/Canterbury	(7)
	Alexander/Lincoln	(7)
	Robert e. Gloucester	(6)

1133, Normandy, 5 months

Totals: 75 men, 383 times
Distribution: 1–44

44	Geoffrey Rufus/chanc.	(4)
31	Roger/Salisbury	(7)
22	Richard Basset	(4)
15	Robert de Vere	(3)
14	Aubrey de Vere	(3)
13	Miles of Gloucester	(3)
	Robert de Courcy	(4)
	Robert de Sigillo	(4)
12	Eustace fitz John	(4)
10	Henry of Blois/Winch.	(7)
	Hugh Bigod	(3)
9	Wm. d'Albini Brito	(4)
	Bernard/St. David's	(7)
8	Robert e. Gloucester	(6)
	Payn fitz John	(4)
7	Nigel/Ely	(7)
	Geoffrey de Clinton	(4)
	Thurstan/York	(7)
6	John the Marshal	(3)
	William de Warenne	(5)
5	Alexander/Lincoln	(7)
	Brian fitz Count	(4)
	Wm. de Pont de l'Arche	(4)
4	Wm. d'Albini Pincerna	(3)
	Stephen of Blois	(6)

1134, Normandy

Totals: 34 men, 47 times

1135, Normandy

Totals: 55 men, 138 times
Distribution: 1–13

13	Robert de Vere	(3)
12	Robert e. Gloucester	(6)
10	Robert de Sigillo	(4)
	John/Lisieux	(7)
8	Robert de Courcy	(4)
	Geoffrey fitz Payn	(4)
5	Aubrey de Vere	(3)
4	William fitz Odo	(3)
	Brian fitz Count	(4)
	Stephen of Blois	(6)
	Adelulf/Carlisle	(7)

TABLE B.   Major Witnesses by Category

Category 2	Category 4
Adam de Port	Brian fitz Count
Alan fitz Flaad	Eustace fitz John
Gilbert de Laigle	Geoffrey de Clinton
Robert Malet	Geoffrey fitz Payn
Roger Brus	Geoffrey Rufus
Walter Espec	Hamo Peverel
	John of Bayeux
	Payn fitz John
Category 3	Ralph Basset
	Ranulf the Chancellor
	Richard Basset
Aubrey de Vere	Richard de Redvers
Eudo Dapifer	Robert de Courcy
Hamo Dapifer	Robert de la Haia
Hugh Bigod	Robert de Sigillo
Humphrey de Bohun	Roger the Chancellor
John the Marshal	Thomas St. John
Miles of Gloucester	Waldric the Chancellor
Nigel d'Albini	William de Courcy
Nigel d'Oilli	William d'Albini Brito
Rabel de Tancarville	William de Houghton
Robert de Vere	William de Pont de l'Arche
Robert fitz Hamon	William Mauduit
Roger Bigod	William Warelwast (as chaplain)
Urse d'Abetot	
Walter of Gloucester	
William d'Albini Pincerna	
William de Tancarville	
William fitz Odo	

Category 5

Henry, earl of Warwick
Ranulf, earl of Chester
Richard, earl of Chester
Robert, count of Meulan
Robert, earl of Leicester
Robert, earl of Warwick
Roger fitz Richard
Simon, earl of Huntingdon
Waleran, count of Meulan
Walter Giffard
William de Warenne

Category 6

David of Scotland
Robert, earl of Gloucester
Stephen of Blois
William the Aethling

Category 7

Adelulf / Carlisle
Alexander / Lincoln
Anselm / Canterbury
Audin / Evreux
Bernard / St.David's
Geoffrey / Rouen
Gerard / Hereford
Gilbert / London
Gundulf / Rochester
Henry of Blois / Winchester
Hugh / Rouen
John / Lisieux
John / Sées
Maurice / London
Nigel / Ely
Ralph / Canterbury
Ranulf / Durham
Richard / Bayeux
Richard / London
Robert / Chester
Robert Bloet / Lincoln
Roger / Salisbury
Seffrid / Chichester
Samson / Worcester
Walter Giffard / Winchester
William / Canterbury
William Warelwast / Exeter
Theowulf / Worcester
Thurstan / York

TABLE C.   Witnessing by Category: Year by Year*

1100: 41 men 97 times		
1–	—	—
2–	27%	12%
3–	21	22
4–	10	10
5–	27	39
6–	—	—
7–	17	16

1101: 103 men 295 times		
1–	—	—
2–	11	4
3–	21	23
4–	21	14
5–	21	24
6–	1	1
7–	25	33

1102: 57 men 131 times		
1–	9	4
2–	18	9
3–	21	32
4–	23	21
5–	14	14
6–	—	—
7–	16	20

1103: 46 men 114 times		
1–	—	—
2–	15	7
3–	30	37
4–	17	20
5–	17	13
6–	4	2
7–	15	21

1104: 38 men 56 times		
1–	—	—
2–	5	5
3–	24	29
4–	16	23
5–	16	13
6–	—	—
7–	39	30

1105: 73 men 194 times		
1–	11	4
2–	23	11
3–	23	36
4–	23	23
5–	8	9
6–	1	2
7–	10	14

1106: 64 men 169 times		
1–	22	10
2–	19	10
3–	17	25
4–	14	27
5–	9	11
6–	2	1
7–	17	17

1107: 92 men 242 times		
1–	11	4
2–	14	6
3–	15	25
4–	17	17
5–	13	16
6–	1	1
7–	28	31

1108: 42 men 100 times		
1–	2	1
2–	21	9
3–	14	12
4–	12	10
5–	24	24
6–	2	1
7–	24	43

a. Less than .5%.
*For each entry, first column is category, second column is percentage of men witnessing, third column is percentage of attestations.

1109: 41 men
90 times

1–	2	1
2–	15	14
3–	22	16
4–	12	16
5–	15	17
6–	2	1
7–	32	36

1110: 58 men
136 times

1–	10	4
2–	19	13
3–	22	24
4–	21	25
5–	12	8
6–	—	—
7–	16	26

1111: 52 men
93 times

1–	6	3
2–	17	15
3–	17	15
4–	25	28
5–	13	10
6–	—	—
7–	21	29

1112: 7 men
9 times

1113: 80 men
133 times

1–	26	16
2–	19	13
3–	15	25
4–	18	23
5–	11	12
6–	3	2
7–	9	9

1114: 67 men
163 times

1–	1	1
2–	25	12
3–	15	23
4–	22	22
5–	13	10
6–	4	2
7–	18	29

1115: 71 men
149 times

1–	7	3
2–	11	7
3–	16	20
4–	23	27
5–	11	11
6–	6	6
7–	27	25

1116: 42 men
105 times

1–	—	—
2–	19	10
3–	24	25
4–	17	23
5–	12	17
6–	7	3
7–	21	22

1117: 2 men
2 times

1118: 41 men 65 times		
1–	12	8
2–	22	17
3–	10	12
4–	25	31
5–	20	15
6–	5	3
7–	7	14

1119: 46 men 88 times		
1–	9	5
2–	17	11
3–	9	11
4–	22	22
5–	17	17
6–	7	3
7–	20	31

1120: 38 men 55 times		
1–	5	4
2–	21	15
3–	11	13
4–	21	31
5–	21	16
6–	3	2
7–	18	20

1121: 128 men 420 times		
1–	13	4
2–	22	9
3–	16	20
4–	18	26
5–	10	6
6–	2	4
7–	18	30

1122: 104 men 219 times		
1–	36	17
2–	16	11
3–	9	16
4–	19	30
5–	4	4
6–	3	2
7–	13	19

1123: 78 men 141 times		
1–	9	5
2–	14	10
3–	14	21
4–	21	25
5–	10	8
6–	3	3
7–	29	29

1124: 11 men 20 times		

1125: 43 men 84 times		
1–	5	2
2–	2	2
3–	14	14
4–	10	8
5–	12	11
6–	2	4
7–	56	60

1126: 89 men 162 times		
1–	17	9
2–	19	15
3–	12	11
4–	21	33
5–	10	6
6–	3	4
7–	17	22

1127: 60 men 246 times		
1–	2	a
2–	15	4
3–	22	25
4–	23	40
5–	7	2
6–	2	2
7–	30	26

1128: 64 men 90 times		
1–	25	18
2–	13	9
3–	19	20
4–	25	30
5–	6	7
6–	2	2
7–	11	14

1129: 94 men 250 times		
1–	21	8
2–	18	9
3–	15	25
4–	22	30
5–	7	5
6–	3	4
7–	13	18

1130: 61 men 144 times		
1–	10	4
2–	16	8
3–	16	18
4–	30	40
5–	10	6
6–	3	8
7–	15	16

1131: 108 men 374 times		
1–	8	2
2–	18	7
3–	10	14
4–	18	30
5–	16	10
6–	2	5
7–	29	31

1132: 50 men 127 times		
1–	—	—
2–	6	2
3–	12	20
4–	30	36
5–	8	6
6–	4	4
7–	40	31

1133: 75 men 383 times		
1–	15	3
2–	13	4
3–	13	20
4–	31	43
5–	5	3
6–	3	3
7–	20	25

1134: 34 men 47 times		
1–	6	4
2–	18	13
3–	9	13
4–	18	21
5–	12	11
6–	6	6
7–	32	32

1135: 55 men 138 times		
1–	11	4
2–	11	7
3–	20	24
4–	26	30
5–	7	4
6–	5	13
7–	20	17

TABLE D.   Witnessing by Category: A Tabulation

	% MEN								% WITNESSED						
Year	#	1	2	3	4	5	6	7	#	1	2	3	4	5	6	7
1100	41	—	27	20	10	27	—	17	97	—	12	22	10	39	—	16
1101	103	—	11	20	21	21	1	25	295	—	4	23	14	24	1	33
1102	57	9	18	21	23	14	—	16	131	4	9	32	21	14	—	20
1103	46	—	15	30	17	17	4	15	114	—	7	37	20	13	2	21
1104	38	—	5	24	16	16	—	40	56	—	5	29	24	13	—	30
1105	73	11	23	23	23	8	1	10	194	4	11	36	23	9	2	14
1106	64	22	19	17	14	9	2	17	169	10	10	25	27	11	1	17
1107	92	11	14	15	17	13	1	28	242	4	6	25	17	16	1	31
1108	42	2	21	14	12	24	2	24	100	1	9	12	10	24	1	43
1109	41	2	15	22	12	15	2	32	90	1	14	16	16	17	1	36
1110	58	10	19	22	21	12	—	16	136	4	13	24	25	8	—	26
1111	52	6	17	17	25	13	—	21	93	3	15	15	28	10	—	29
1112	7	—	—	—	—	—	—	—	9	—	—	—	—	—	—	—
1113	80	26	19	15	18	11	3	9	133	16	13	25	23	12	2	9
1114	67	1	25	15	22	13	4	18	163	1	12	23	22	10	2	29
1115	71	7	11	16	23	11	6	27	149	3	7	20	27	11	6	25
1116	42	—	19	24	17	12	7	21	105	—	10	25	23	17	3	22
1117	2	—	—	—	—	—	—	—	2	—	—	—	—	—	—	—
1118	41	12	22	10	24	20	5	7	65	8	17	12	31	15	3	14
1119	46	9	17	9	22	17	7	20	88	5	11	11	22	17	3	31
1120	38	5	21	11	21	21	3	18	55	4	15	13	31	16	2	20
1121	128	13	22	16	18	10	2	18	420	4	9	20	25	6	4	30
1122	104	36	16	9	19	4	3	13	219	17	11	16	30	4	2	19
1123	78	9	14	14	21	10	3	29	141	5	10	21	25	8	3	29
1124	11	—	—	—	—	—	—	—	20	—	—	—	—	—	—	—
1125	43	5	2	14	9	12	2	56	84	2	1	14	8	11	4	60
1126	89	17	19	12	21	10	3	17	162	9	15	11	33	6	4	22
1127	60	2	15	22	23	7	2	30	246	a	4	25	40	2	2	26
1128	64	25	13	19	25	6	2	11	90	18	9	20	30	7	2	14
1129	94	21	18	15	22	7	3	13	250	8	9	25	30	5	4	18
1130	61	10	16	16	30	10	3	15	144	4	8	18	40	6	8	16
1131	108	8	18	10	18	16	2	29	374	2	7	14	30	10	5	31
1132	50	—	6	12	30	8	4	40	127	—	2	20	36	6	4	31
1133	75	15	13	13	31	5	3	20	383	3	4	20	43	3	3	25
1134	34	6	18	9	18	12	6	32	47	4	13	13	21	11	6	32
1135	55	11	11	20	25	7	5	20	138	4	7	24	30	4	13	17

a. Less than .5%.

Appendix II: The Problem of the Bastard

Bastardy was a common theme in the history of the ducal/royal family. William the Conqueror was illegitimate, and two of his three sons (Robert Curthose and Henry I) as well as grandsons (including Stephen) had recognized natural children. Henry I holds the English royal record, with twenty-one having been identified. Another group of acknowledged bastards are found among the curial nobles. However, there are very few identifiable illegitimates beyond the curial group, bringing the numbers for the nobility well below the percentage found among the peasants. Only seven of the 250 non-royal families represented in this study had identifiable acknowledged bastards while the peasant births average between 0.6% and 3.4%.[1] This finding is contrary to expectations. Chroniclers, clergy, and troubadours say that nobles were not living up to the virtue of chastity—there must have been by-products, but where are they? Are those "verifiable bastards" the only ones who were acknowledged or is this a problem of sources? Why were some acknowledged and others not? Those we know of as being recognized by their fathers were termed son or daughter, provided with land and marriage, and were visible at public occasions. We have seen how they fit into the noble's family, perhaps this can provide clues to why some were acknowledged and others not.

Surprisingly, there is almost nothing relevant to this issue in the work of historians of other eras in which there were "prominent bastards," or in that of sociologists of the family. Certainly, politically powerful bastards are the subjects of biographical works,[2] and a recent work which attempted to give an analysis of royal illegitimacy really gave a biographical collection,[3] but there is a lack of work on noble illegitimacy generally. Actually in the work which has been done, there is a reverse snobbery. The medieval and early modern historians of the *Annales* school and the sociologists have done enormous quantitative and analytical studies of peasant illegitimacy, not only approaching the questions of "who," and "why," but also "how often," "when," "where," and "what seasons of the year were most conducive to."[4] From these studies, it appears that peasant illegitimacy was part of a fairly loose system of marriage in the Middle Ages. Monogamous cohabitation, especially by couples who post-poned marriage for economic reasons, seems to have been fairly accepted in the villages except by the clergy.[5] All efforts were made to get the couples to the church, and when they were married, their children could become legitimate retroactively.[6] The questions are somewhat different for the nobles however. There it was rare at any time for the children to be a product of a prenuptial union with the future bride and therefore could not be legitimized even when acknowledged.

Why can we find so few in the extant sources? It is possible that they did not exist beyond the small group belonging to the top of the society. Perhaps the royals and their friends had a different view of morality or family than the rest of the nobility, or the sexual behavior was accepta-ble only when the man was above a certain status.[7] That is, perhaps the lesser nobles were sexually virtuous. This seems unlikely. The chronicle condemnations of "licentious" behavior were not leveled at only the high-est nobles but rather at men of all ranks.[8] Also, since we know that some of the high nobles had natural children, it seems unlikely that the rest of the nobles were different when they were not different in other behavior. As seen in the body of this work, the only major differences in the behavior of the nobles was their attitude towards curial attendance and service. This difference was not based exclusively on wealth and does not coincide with the appearance of verifiable bastards in any statistically significant sense.

A more plausible explanation is that while noblemen of all levels were sexually active outside of marriage, the lesser nobles did not acknowledge the resulting children. If so, this nonacknowledgment could be explained by two conditions—the father's wealth and/or the mother's rank. The father's landed wealth, or his friends' and relatives' connections, affected his ability to provide for his children. Perhaps only the wealthiest nobles or those with wealthy connections could provide for extra children and indulge in recognizing more offspring. The question of the mother's rank may also have affected the possibility of acknowledgment. Though we do not know the origin of most of the mothers, those we do know were referred to as "ladies."[9] Perhaps only the greatest nobles had noble women as mistresses while the rest utilized peasant women. It seems, then that the known acknowledged children had the possibility of provision and acceptable lineage on both sides.

However, another plausible explanation for the failure of the search is that while there were more acknowledged, they are not recognizable to historians because they were not designated by anything that set them apart from their half-siblings. Those we know to have been bastards were mentioned in some chronicle reference as such, yet are *not* recorded as such in our other records of them.[10] As was described in chapter 2, illegitimates were designated simply as *filius, filia, frater,* and *soror* in charters. This type of evidence indicates that natural children were integrated into the family, not set off as a separate part. Those who were politically powerful, related to the king or simply close to him, commanded a greater share of the narrative evidence, so the likelihood of recording illegitimacy increased. This problem of designation, then, might explain why most of the verifiable bastards cluster around the royal house and the king's close friends. Because of their power, we simply know more about these families. We may be identifying natural children as younger, noninheriting legitimate children. Indeed, except for the royal family, we rarely know the birth order of a family beyond assuming that the heir of the patrimony was the eldest surviving son. It is possible, therefore, that the acceptance of noble bastards as part of the cognatic family has hidden them from us in the sources.

Whether or not we can ever know the extent of the phenomenon, we know that noble bastardy sometimes was accepted. Perhaps this is evidence of a premarital double standard, the young nobleman "sowing his oats." Duby, who has given us most of our concepts of twelfth-century noble youth, believes this to be the case. He argues that the *juvenes* postponed marriage until they came into their inheritance but did not attempt to be celibate.[11] This would parallel the peasant experience except for the crucial issue that the woman in this case was not the future bride. Most of the Anglo-Norman bastards, except for Henry I's brood, appear to have been older than their legitimate siblings.[12] It is possible that in Anglo-Norman society this was behavior appropriate to a life stage and its consequences could be acceptably recognized, whereas, unless one was royal,[13] most extra-marital affairs were not as openly acknowledged by recognizing their products.

Although we saw in chapter 2 that the natural children were accepted as part of the family in designation and were provided for in the usual ways available for younger children, although they were treated differently from the heir, the quality of their lives may have been affected by their birth status. William the Conqueror is the only bastard we know to have received verbal abuse because of being illegitimate.[14] However, only two verifiable bastards had verifiable bastards and these two were the most rewarded (financially and personally) of Henry I's sons. Many other bastards had enough wealth to have provided for more children and were considered high nobles by their contemporaries. Perhaps natural children were not as accepted and life as pleasant as the impersonal records of designation and patronage indicate. Perhaps an acknowledged bastard would not put another child through the experience.

Notes

1. Oosterveen and Smith, "Bastardy and Family Reconstruction," pp. 96–97.
2. For example, see Douie, *Archbishop Geoffrey Plantagenet.*
3. Given-Wilson and Curteis, *The Royal Bastards of Medieval England;* see also Newman, "Review Essay of Royal Bastards."
4. For example, see the collections edited by Laslett, et al, *Bastardy,* and by Forster and Ranum, *Family and Society.*
5. Stone, *The Family, Sex and Marriage in England,* p. 58.
6. Helmholz, "Bastardy Litigation in Medieval England," p. 362. The peasant situation did not markedly change until the early modern period, when increased peasant mobility and abandonment of the mother and child, and with it an increase in recorded infanticide, became scandalously evident. See Shorter, "Illegitimacy, Sexual Revolution and Social Change in Modern Europe"; Laslett, *Family Life.*
7. Both MacFarlane ("Illegitimacy and Illegitimates in English History," p. 71) and Laslett (*Family Life,* p. 102) raise the issue of whether bastardy was a symbol of a behavioral rule or of the breach of one.
8. For example, William (II) de Roumare, not yet magnate though wealthy, "had in his youth been lewd and too much given to lust" until illness caused him to repent. (OVC 6:381). No bastards are known to have been acknowledged. Robert fitz Hildebrand, who seduced the wife of William de Pont de l'Arche and was "lustful, drunken and unchaste," was "of low birth" though high enough to make a treaty with the king. (GS, pp. 150–53).
9. All the women whom White ("Henry I's Illegitimate Children") identified, with the exception of Edith, were known to be noble.
10. See chapter 2 for the examples of the designation of Robert of Gloucester and Brian fitz Count.
11. Duby, *Medieval Marriage,* pp. 95–96, 110.
12. Henry recognized children born while he was a landless *juvenes* but also after he had gained the throne. Five listed by White definitely were born before 1100 (Robert, Richard, Mauds #1 and #2, and Juliana). William de Tracey and "unknown woman #4" probably were born before 1100. Gilbert was "still young and unmarried" in 1142 and Rohese married for the first time around 1146, so both are definitely post-1100 products. Others are probably after 1100, though perhaps close to the date judging by marriage and death years. Reginald and Robert fitz Roy lived into the 1170s and were younger than Robert of Gloucester; they were probably born shortly after 1100 while Henry was married to Edith/Maud. Henry fitz Roy died in battle in 1157 but had not been active before 1135. William #9 was still alive in 1187.
13. William of Malmesbury (GR, 2:488) says that Henry's high number of natural children was due to his political foresight, knowing that children were important in building political networks. Duby credits the count of Guines with the same reason for recognizing 23 children (*Medieval Marriage,* p. 48). In Malmes-

bury's case, it seems to have been a tactful way to be truthful while avoid either criticizing the king, whom he otherwise praised, or worse, insulting his own patron, one of the king's natural sons, Robert of Gloucester. Duby simply postulates this as an excuse which the count may have made. Was this excuse necessary? Even the clerical commentators credit it to youth and rarely condemn it as long as the father took responsibility and stopped such behavior as an adult. Orderic described Robert Curthose as having to be publicly confronted by his children's mother before accepting them. He is condemned only for denying paternity which was proven by an ordeal, not for siring the children. (OVC 5:282–83).

    14. OVC 4:83–85.

BIBLIOGRAPHY

Manuscript Sources (Unprinted)

London. British Library. Additional Manuscripts 6040, 14250, 29436, 37022, 46701.
———. Cotton Manuscripts: Cleopatra E.I., Tiberius C.I., Tiberius C.IX., Titus C.VII., Vespasian B.XXIV., Vespasian D.X., Vespasian E.V.
———. Egerton Manuscripts 3031, 3058.
———. Harley Manuscripts 1708, 2110, 3650, 3667, 3697.
———. Loan Manuscript no. 30.
———. Sloane Manuscript 2839.
———. Stowe Manuscript 937.
London. Public Record Office. D.L. 34/1, 41/10/12, E.41/388.

Printed Contemporary Sources

Ancient Charters, Royal and Private, Prior to A.D. 1200. Edited and annotated by J. H. Round. ("Publications of the Pipe Roll Society," vol. 10.) London: Pipe Roll Society, 1888; reprinted by Kraus, 1966.
Anglo-Saxon Chronicle. Two of the Saxon Chronicles Parallel. Edited by Charles Plummer on the basis of an edition by John Earle. 2 vols. Oxford: Clarendon Press, 1899; reprinted by Oxford, 1965.
———. Edited by Dorothy Whitelock, with David C. Douglas and Susie I. Tucker. New Brunswick: Rutgers University Press, 1961.
Annales monastici. Edited by Henry R. Luard. 5 vols. ("Rolls Series," #36.) London: HMSO, 1864–69; reprinted by Kraus, 1965.
Atkinson, John C., ed. *Cartularium abbathiae de Rievalle.* ("Surtees Society," vol. 88.) Durham: Surtees Society, 1889.
———. *Cartularium abbathiae de Whiteby.* 2 vols. ("Surtees Society," vols. 69, 72.) Durham: Surtees Society, 1879–81.
Atkinson, John C., and Brownbill, John, eds. *The Coucher Book of Furness Abbey.* 6 vols. ("Chetham Society, New Series," vols. 9, 11, 14, 74, 76, 78.) Manchester: Chetham Society, 1886–1919.
Biddle, Martin, ed. *Winchester in the Early Middle Ages: An Edition and Discussion of the Winton Domesday.* Vol. 1 of Winchester Studies. Oxford: Clarendon Press, 1976. [Cited as *Liber Winton.*]
Blake, E. O., ed. *The Cartulary of the Priory of St. Denys near Southampton.* 2 vols. ("Southampton Record Series," vols. 24 and 25.) Southampton: University Press, 1981.
Bourienne, Valentin V. A., ed. *Antiquus cartularius ecclesiae Baroncensis (Livre*

Noir). 2 vols. ("Société de l'Histoire de Normandie.") Rouen: A. Lestringant, 1902–03.

Bracton, Henry de. *Bracton's Note-Book.* Edited by F. W. Maitland. 3 vols. London: C. J. Clay and Sons, 1887.

Bridgeman, Charles G. O., ed. "The Burton Abbey Twelfth Century Surveys," *William Salt Archaelogical Society Collections,"* 3rd series. 41 (1918 for 1916), 209–300.

Brown, William, ed. *Cartularium prioratus de Gyseburne.* 2 vols. ("Surtees Society," vols. 86, 89.) Durham: Surtees Society, 1889–94.

Cartularium monasterii de Rameseia. Edited by William H. Hart and A. Lyons Ponsonby. 3 vols. ("Rolls Series," #79.) London: HMSO, 1884–94; reprinted by Kraus, 1965.

Cartulary of Cirencester Abbey, Gloucestershire. 3 vols. Vols. 1–2 edited by Charles D. Ross; vol. 3 edited by Mary Devine. London: Oxford University Press, 1964.

Cartulary of Worcester Cathedral Priory. Edited by R. R. Darlington. ("Publications of the Pipe Roll Society," vol. 76a,"New Series," vol. 38.) London: Pipe Roll Society, 1968. [Cited as *Worc.Cart.*]

Charters and Documents Illustrating the History of the Cathedral, City and Diocese of Salisbury. Edited by W. H. Richard and William Dunn Macray. ("Rolls Series," #97.) London: HMSO, 1891; reprinted by Kraus, 1965.

Charters of Norwich Cathedral Priory, Part One. Edited by Barbara Dodwell. ("Publications of the Pipe Roll Society," vol. 78,"New Series," vol. 40.) London: Pipe Roll Society, 1974.

Chibnall, Marjorie, ed. *Charters and Custumnals of the Abbey of Holy Trinity, Caen.* ("Records of Social and Economic History. New Series 5.") London: for the British Academy by Oxford University Press, 1982.

———. *Select Documents of the English Lands of the Abbey of Bec.* ("Camden Society, Third Series," vol. 73.) London: Camden Society, 1951.

Chronicle of Battle Abbey. Edited and translated by Eleanor Searle. ("Oxford Medieval Texts" Series.) Oxford: Clarendon Press, 1980.

Chronicon Monasterii de Abingdon. Edited by Joseph Stevenson. 2 vols. ("Rolls Series, #2.) London: Longman, Brown, Green, Longmans and Roberts, 1858; reprinted by Kraus, n.d.

Clark, Andrew, ed. *The English Register of Godstow Priory.* 3 vols. ("Early English Text Society, Original Series," vols. 129–30, 142.) London: Early English Text Society, 1905–11.

"Constitutio Domus Regis. The Establishment of the Royal Household." Edited and translated by Charles Johnson with corrections by F. E. L. Carter and D. E. Greenway. In Richard, fitz Nigel, *Dialogus de Scaccario. The Course of the Exchequer.* ("Oxford Medieval Texts.") Oxford: Clarendon Press, 1983.

Coss, Peter R., ed. *The Langley Cartulary.* ("Dugdale Society Publications," #32.) Stratford-upon-Avon: The Dugdale Society, 1980.

"Descriptio militum de Abbatia de Burgo." Edited by Thomas Stapleton. In *Chronicon Petroburgense.* ("Camden Society, Original Series," vol. 47.), pp. 168–75. London: Camden Society, 1849.

Devine, Mary, ed. *The Cartulary of Cirencester Abbey, Gloucestershire,* vol. 3. Oxford: 1977.

Douglas, David C., ed. *The Domesday Monachorum of Christ Church Canterbury.* London: Royal Historical Society, 1944.

―――. *Feudal Documents from the Abbey of Bury St. Edmunds.* ("Records of the Social and Economic History of England and Wales," no. 8.) London: British Academy, 1932.

Duckett, George F., ed. *Charters and Records Among the Archives of the Ancient Abbey of Cluni, 1077–1534.* 2 vols. Lewes: R. Wolff, 1888.

Dugdale, William. *Monasticon Anglicanum.* Edited by John Caley, Henry Ellis, and Bulkeley Bandinel. 6 vols. in 8. London: Longman's, 1817–30.

Durham Episcopal Charters, 1071–1152. Edited by H. S. Offler. ("Surtees Society," vol. 179.) Gateshead: Surtees Society, 1968.

Eadmer. *Eadmeri Historia Novorum in Anglia.* Edited by Martin Rule. ("Rolls Series," #81.) London: HMSO, 1884; reprinted by Kraus, 1965.

Elvey, G.R., ed. *Luffield Priory Charters,* vol. 2. Buckingham Record Society 18 (1975) and Northampton Record Society 26 (1975).

Farrer, Willliam and Clay, Charles T., eds. *Early Yorkshire Charters.* 12 vols. Vols. 1–3: Edinburgh: Ballantyne, Hanson and Co., 1914–16. Vols. 4–12: "Yorkshire Archaeological Society, Record Series, Extra Series, Nos. 1–10." Wakefield: Yorkshire Archaeological Society, 1935–65. [Cited as [*EYC*].

Fleming, Lindsay, ed. *Cartulary of Boxgrove Priory.* ("Sussex Record Society," vol. 59.) Lewes: Sussex Record Society, 1960.

Foster, Charles W. and Longley, Thomas, eds. *The Lincolnshire Domesday and the Lindsey Survey.* ("Lincolnshire Record Society," vol. 19.) Horncastle: Lincolnshire Record Society, 1924. [Cited as *Lind.Surv.*]

Foster, Charles W. and Major, Kathleen, eds. *The Registrum Antiquissimum of the Cathedral Church of Lincoln.* 10 vols. ("Lincolnshire Record Society," vols. 27–29, 32, 34, 41, 46, 51, 62, 67.) Horncastle: Lincolnshire Record Society, 1931―.

Fowler, Herbert, ed. *Cartulary of the Abbey of Old Wardon.* ("Bedfordshire Historical Record Society," vol. 13.) Bedford: Bedfordshire Historical Record Society, 1930.

―――. *A Digest of the Charters Preserved in the Cartulary of Dunstable.* ("Bedfordshire Historical Record Society," vol. 10.) Bedford: Bedfordshire Historical Record Society, 1926.

Gaimar, Geoffrey. *The Anglo-Norman Metrical Chronicle of Geoffrey Gaimar.* Edited by Thomas Wright. ("Publications of the Caxton Society," vol. 9.) N.p.: Caxton Society, 1850; reprinted by Burt Franklin, 1967.

Geoffrey of Monmouth. *Historia Regum Brittaniae: A Variant Version Edited from the Manuscripts.* Edited by Jacob Hammer. Cambridge, Mass.: The Mediaeval Academy of America, 1951.

Gesta Stephani. Edited and translated by K. R. Potter, with new introduction and notes by R. H. C. Davis. ("Oxford Medieval Texts" Series.) Oxford: Clarendon Press, 1976. [Cited as *GS.*]

Gibbs, Marion, ed. *Early Charters of the Cathedral Church of St. Paul's, London.* ("Camden Society, Third Series," vol. 58.) London: Camden Society, 1939.

Giraldus Cambrensis. *Giraldi Cambrensis opera.* Vol. 4: *Itinerarium Kambriae.* Edited by James F. Dimock. ("Rolls Series," #21.) London: HMSO, 1868; reprinted by Kraus, 1964.

Great Britain. Public Record Office. *Liber feodorum; The Book of Fees, Commonly Called the Testa de Nevill.* Reformed from the earliest MSS. by the Deputy Keeper of the Records [H. C. Maxwell-Lyte]. 2 vols. in 3. London: HMSO, 1920–31; reprinted by Kraus, 1971.

————. *Lists and Indexes.* Vol. 9: *List of Sheriffs for England and Wales from the Earliest Times to A.D. 1831.* London: HMSO, 1897; reprinted by Kraus, 1963.

Great Britain. Record Commission. *Magnum rotulum scaccarii, vel magnum rotulum pipae, de anno tricesimo-primo regni Henrici primi (ut videtur;) quem plurimi hactenus laudarunt pro rotulo quinti anni Stephani regis.* Edited by Joseph Hunter. London: Record Commissioners, 1833; reprinted by HMSO, 1929. [Cited as *PR.*]

Greenway, D. E., ed. *Charters of the Honour of Mowbray, 1107–1191.* ("Records of Social and Economic History, New Series," no. 1.) London: for the British Academy at Oxford University Press, 1972.

Harper-Bill, Christopher, ed. *Blythburgh Priory Cartulary.* ("Suffolk Record Society. Suffolk Charters," vol. 2.) Woodbridge, Suffolk: Boydell and Brewer Ltd., 1980.

Harper-Bill, Christopher and Mortimer, Richard, eds. *Stoke by Clare Cartulary.* 3 vols. ("Suffolk Record Society, Suffolk Charters," vols. 4–6.) Woodbridge, Suffolk: Boydell and Brewer, Ltd., 1982–84.

Hart, Cyril E., ed. *Early Charters of Essex: The Norman Period.* ("University of Leicester, Department of English Local History, Occasional Papers," no. 2.) Leicester: University of Leicester, 1957.

Hassall, William O., ed. *Cartulary of St. Mary Clerkenwell.* ("Camden Society, Third Series," vol. 71.) London: Camden Society, 1949.

————. *Wheatley Records.* ("Oxfordshire Record Society, Record Series," vol. 37.) Oxford: Oxfordshire Record Society, 1956.

Heales, Alfred C., ed. *Records of Merton Priory in the County of Surrey.* London: Henry Froude, 1898.

Henry of Huntingdon. *Henrici Huntendunensis. Historia Anglorum et Epistola de Contemptu Mundi.* Edited by Thomas Arnold. ("Rolls Series," #74.) London: HMSO, 1879; reprinted by Kraus, 1965.

————. *The Chronicle of Henry of Huntingdon.* Edited and translated by Thomas Forester. London: Henry G. Bohn, 1853.

Herefordshire Domesday. Edited by James Tait and V.H. Galbraith. ("Publications of the Pipe Roll Society," vol. 62, "New Series," vol. 25.). London: Pipe Roll Society, 1950. [Cited as *Heref. Dd.*].

Historia et cartularium monasterii Sancti Petri Gloucestriae. Edited by William H. Hart. 3 vols. ("Rolls Series," #33.) London: HMSO, 1863–67; reprinted by Kraus, 1965.

Hodgett, Gerald A. J., ed. *The Cartulary of Holy Trinity, Aldgate.* ("London Record Society," vol. 7.) London: London Record Society, 1971.

Holdsworth, C. J., ed. *Rufford Charters.* 2 vols. ("Thoroton Society Record Series," vols. 29–30.) Nottingham: Derry and Sons, 1972, 1974.

Hollings, Marjory, ed. *The Red Book of Worcester.* 1 vol. in 4 parts. ("Worcestershire Historical Society," vol. 42.) London: Worcestershire Historical Society, 1934–50.

Holmes, Richard, ed. *Chartulary of St. John of Pontefract.* 2 vols. ("Yorkshire

Archaeological Society, Record Series," vols. 25, 30.) Wakefield: Yorkshire Archaeological Society, 1899–1902.

Hugh the Chantor. *History of the Church of York, 1066–1127*. Edited and translated by Charles Johnson. ("Medieval Texts" Series.) London: Thomas Nelson and Sons, 1961.

Hulton, William A., ed. *Documents Relating to the Priory of Penwortham and Other Possessions in Lancashire of the Abbey of Evesham*. ("Chetham Society, Original Series," vol. 30.) Manchester: Chetham Society, 1853.

Hunt, William, ed. *Two Chartularies of the Priory of St. Peter at Bath*. ("Somerset Record Society," vol. 7.) London: Somerset Record Society, 1893.

Hunter, Joseph, ed. *Ecclesiastical Documents*. ("Camden Society, Original Series," vol. 8.) London: Camden Society, 1840.

Ingulf. *Ingulph's Chronicle of the Abbey of Croyland with Continuations by Peter of Blois and Anonymous Writers*. Translated by Henry T. Riley. London: Henry G. Bohn, 1854.

Ivo of Chartres. *Epistolae*, vol. 162. *Patrologia Cursus Completus Completus, Serie Latina*. Edited by J.-P. Migne. 221 volumes. Paris, 1844–64.

Jenkins, John G., ed. *The Cartulary of Missenden Abbey*. 3 vols. ("Buckinghamshire Record Society," vols. 2, 10.) Jordans: Buckinghamshire Record Society, 1938–46; ("Historical Manuscripts Commission, Joint Publications Series," no. 1.) London: HMSO, 1962.

Kemp, B. R., ed. *Reading Abbey Cartularies*. 2 vols. ("Camden Society, 4th series," vols. 31, 33.) London: Offices of the Royal Historical Society, 1986–87.

Lancaster, William T., ed. *Abstracts of the Charters and Other Documents Contained in the Chartulary of the Cistercian Abbey of Fountains*. 2 vols. Leeds: J. Whitehead and Son, 1915–18.

Leach, Arthur F., ed. *Visitations and Memorials of Southwell Minster*. ("Camden Society, New Series," vol. 48.) London: Camden Society, 1891.

Leges Henrici Primi. Edited and translated by L. J. Downer. Oxford: Clarendon Press, 1972.

Liber Eliensis. Edited by E. O. Blake. ("Camden Society, Third Series," vol. 92.) London: Camden Society, 1962.

Liber Monasterii de Hyda. Edited by Edward Edwards. ("Rolls Series," #45.) London: HMSO, 1866; reprinted by Kraus, 1964.

Loyd, Lewis C. and Stenton, Doris M., eds. *Sir Christopher Hatton's Book of Seals*. Oxford: Clarendon Press, 1950.

Magni Rotuli Scaccarii Normanniae sub Regibus Angliae. Edited by Thomas Stapleton. 2 vols. London: Society of Antiquaries of London, 1840–44.

Mason, Emma, ed. *The Beauchamp Cartulary Charters, 1100–1268*. ("Pipe Roll Society," vol. 81, "New Series," vol. 43.) London: for the Pipe Roll Society by J. W. Ruddock and Sons, Ltd., 1980.

Maxwell-Lyte, Henry C., ed. *Two Cartularies of the Augustinian Priory of Bruton and the Cluniac Priory of Montacute*. ("Somerset Record Society," vol. 8.) London: Somerset Record Society, 1894.

Mayr-Harting, Henry, ed. *Acta of the Bishops of Chichester, 1075–1207*. ("Canterbury and York Society," vol. 56.) Torquay: Canterbury and York Society, 1964.

Memorials of St. Edmund's Abbey. Edited by Thomas Arnold. 3 vols. ("Rolls Series," #96.) London: HMSO, 1890–96; reprinted by Kraus, 1965.

Moore, Stuart A., ed. Cartularium monasterii Sancti Johannis Baptiste de Colecestria. 2 vols. ("Roxburghe Club.") London: Chiswick Press, 1897.

Napier, A. S. and Stevenson, W. H., eds. The Crawford Collection of Early Charters and Documents now in the Bodleian Library. Oxford: Clarendon Press, 1895.

"Northamptonshire Survey." Edited by John Horace Round. In The Victoria County History of Northamptonshire. Edited by W. Ryland, D. Adkins, and R. M. Serjeantson. ("The Victoria History of the Counties of England," vol. 1.) London: University of London, Institute for Historical Research, 1902; reprinted by Dawson, 1970. Pp. 365–89. [Cited as Nhants Surv.]

Orderic Vitalis. The Ecclesiastical History of Orderic Vitalis. Edited and translated by Marjorie Chibnall. 6 vols. ("Oxford Medieval Texts.") Oxford: Clarendon Press, 1968–1980. [Cited as OVC].

———. The Ecclesiastical History of England and Normandy. Translated by Thomas Forester. 4 vols. London: Henry G. Bohn, 1854. [Cited as OVB].

———. Historiae Ecclesiasticae. Edited by August le Prévost. 5 vols. ("Société de l'Histoire de France.") Paris: Julius Renouard, 1838–55; reprinted by Johnson, 1965.

Patterson, Robert B., ed. Earldom of Gloucester Charters to A.D 1217. Oxford: Clarendon Press, 1973.

Peckham, Walter D., ed. Chartulary of the High Church of Chicester. ("Sussex Record Society," vol. 46.) Lewes: Sussex Record Society, 1946.

Placita Anglo-Normannica: Law Cases From William I to Richard I. Edited by Melville Madison Bigelow. Boston: Soule and Bugbee, 1881; reprinted by Rothman, 1970.

Ransome, Gwenllian C., ed. Chartulary of Tockwith alias Scokirk, Cell to the Priory of Nostell. ("Yorkshire Archaeological Society, Record Series," vol. 80.) Wakefield: Yorkshire Archaeological Society, 1931.

Red Book of the Exchequer. Edited by Hubert Hall. 3 vols. ("Rolls Series," #99.) London: HMSO, 1896; reprinted by Kraus, 1965. [Cited as RB].

Rees, Una, ed. The Cartulary of Shrewsbury Abbey. 2 vols. Aberystwyth: National Library of Wales, 1975.

Regesta regum Anglo-Normannorum, 1066–1154. Vol. 1: Regesta Willelmi Conquestoris et Willelmi Rufi, 1066–1100. Edited by H. W. C. Davis with R. J. Whitwell. Vol. 2: Regesta Henrici Primi, 1100–1135. Edited by Charles Johnson and H. A. Cronne from the collections of the late H. W. C. Davis. Vol. 3: Regesta Regis Stephani ac Mathildis Imperiatricis ac Gaufridi et Henrici Ducum Normannorum, 1135–1154. Edited by H. A. Cronne and R. H. C. Davis. Vol. 4: Facsimiles of Original Charters and Writs of King Stephen, the Empress Matilda and Dukes Geoffrey and Henry, 1135–1154. Edited by H. A. Cronne and R. H. C. Davis. Oxford: Clarendon Press, 1913–69. [Cited as Reg. I, Reg. II, Reg. III and Reg. IV].

Registrum Malmesburiense; The Register of Malmesbury Abbey, Preserved in the Public Record Office. 2 vols. Vol. 1 edited by J. S. Brewer. Vol. 2 edited by J. S. Brewer and Charles T. Martin. ("Rolls Series," #72.) London: HMSO, 1879–80; reprinted by Kraus.

Richard, fitz Nigel. *Dialogus de Scaccario. The Course of the Exchequer.* Edited and translated by Charles Johnson with corrections by F. E. L. Carter and D. E. Greenway. ("Oxford Medieval Texts.") Oxford: Clarendon Press, 1983.

Robert of Torigni. *Chronicle of Robert of Torigni, Abbot of the Monastery of St. Michael-in-Peril-of-the-Sea.* In *Chronicles of Stephen, Henry II and Richard I.* Vol. 4. Edited by R. Howlett. ("Rolls Series," #82.) London: HMSO, 1890; reprinted by Kraus, 1964.

————. *King Henry I.* In *Church Historians of England.* Vol. 5, part 1. Edited by Joseph Stevenson. London: Seeley's, 1858.

Round, John Horace, ed. *Calendar of Documents Preserved in France, A.D. 918–1206.* London: HMSO, 1899. [Cited as *CDF.*]

————. *Rotuli de dominibus et pueris et puellis de XII comitatibus (1185).* ("Pipe Roll Society," vol. 35.) London: St. Catherine's Press for the Pipe Roll Society, 1913; reprinted by Kraus, 1966.

Royce, David, ed. *Landboc sive registrum monasterii B.M. Virginis et Sancti Cenhelmi de Winchelcumba.* 2 vols. Exeter: no publisher, 1892–93.

Salter, Herbert, ed. *Cartulary of Oseney Abbey.* 6 vols. ("Oxfordshire Historical Society," vols. 89–91, 97–98, 101.) Oxford: Oxfordshire Historical Society, 1929–36.

————. *Eynsham Cartulary.* 2 vols. ("Oxfordshire Historical Society," vols. 48, 51.) Oxford: Oxfordshire Historical Society, 1907–08.

————. *The Thame Cartulary.* 2 vols. ("Oxfordshire Historical Society, Record Series," vols. 25–26.) Oxford: Oxfordshire Historical Society, 1947–48.

Salzman, Louis F., ed. *Chartulary of the Priory of St. Pancras of Lewes.* 2 vols. ("Sussex Record Society," vols. 38, 40.) Lewes: Sussex Record Society, 1933–35.

————. *The Chartulary of the Priory of St. Peter at Sele.* Cambridge: W. Heffer and Sons, Ltd., 1923.

Saunders, Herbert W., ed. *The First Register of Norwich Cathedral Priory.* ("Norfolk Record Society," vol. 11.) Norfolk: Norfolk Record Society, 1939.

Savage, Henry E., ed. *The Great Register of Lichfield Cathedral.* ("William Salt Archaeological Society, Third Series," vol. for 1924.) London: William Salt Archaeological Society, 1926.

Slade, Cecil F., ed. and trans. *The Leicestershire Survey c. A.D. 1130.* ("University of Leicester, Department of English Local History, Occasional Papers, no. 7.) Leicester: University of Leicester, 1956. [Cited as *Leic. Surv.*]

Smith, David, ed. *English Episcopal Acta. I: Lincoln, 1067–1185.* London: British Academy at the Oxford University Press, 1980.

Stenton, Frank M., ed. *Documents Illustrative of Social and Economic History of the Danelaw (Danelaw Charters).* ("Records of the Social and Economic History of England and Wales," no. 5.) London: British Academy, 1920.

————. *Facsimiles of Early Charters from Northamptonshire Collections.* ("Northamptonshire Record Society," vol. 4.) Kettering: Northamptonshire Record Society, 1930.

Suger. *Vie de Louis le Gros.* Edited and translated by Henri Waquet. ("Les Classiques de l'histoire de France au Moyen Age," tôme 11.) Paris: Librairie Ancienne Honoré Champion, 1929.

Symeon of Durham. *Historia Ecclesiae Dunhelmensis.* In *Symeon of Durham:*

Historical Works. Vol.1. Edited by Thomas Arnold. ("Rolls Series," #75.) London: HMSO, 1882; reprinted by Kraus, 1965.

―――. *Historia Regum.* In *Symeon of Durham: Historical Works.* Vol. 2. Edited by Thomas Arnold. ("Rolls Series," #75.) London: HMSO, 1885; reprinted by Kraus, 1965.

Tait, James, ed. *The Chartulary or Register of the Abbey of St. Werburgh, Chester.* 2 vols. ("Chetham Society, New Series," vols. 79, 82.) Manchester: Chetham Society, 1920–23.

―――. *The Foundation Charter of Runcorn (later Norton) Priory.* ("Chetham Society, New Series," vol. 100, "Miscellanies," vol. 7.) Manchester: Chetham Society, 1939; reprinted by Johnson, 1968.

Thomson, Rodney M., ed. *The Archives of the Abbey of Bury St. Edmunds.* ("Suffolk Record Society," vol. 21.) Woodbridge, Suffolk: Boydell Press for the Suffolk Record Society, 1980.

Timson, R. T., ed. *Cartulary of Blyth Abbey.* 2 vols. ("Thoroton Society," vols. 27, 28.) London: Thoroton Society and HMSO, 1973.

Tremlett, John D. and Blakiston, Noel, eds. *Stogursey Charters.* ("Somerset Record Society," vol. 61.) London: Somerset Record Society, 1949.

Turner, George J. and Salter, Herbert, eds. *The Register of St. Augustine's Abbey, Canterbury, commonly called the Black Book.* 2 vols. ("Records of the Social and Economic History of England and Wales," nos. 2–3.) London: British Academy, 1915–24.

Vernier, J. J., ed. *Chartes de l'Abbaye de Jumièges (825 à 1204).* ("Société de l'Histoire de Normandie, Publications.") Rouen: A. Lestringant, 1916.

Wace. *Le Roman de Rou de Wace.* Edited by A.J. Holden. Paris: Picard, 1970.

Walbran, John R., ed. *Memorials of the Abbey of Fountains.* 2 vols. in 3 parts. ("Surtees Society," vols. 42, 47, 130.) Durham: Surtees Society, 1853–78.

Walker, David, ed. "The Charters of the Earldom of Hereford." ("Camden Society, Fourth Series," vol. 1. *Camden Miscellany,* vol. 22.) London: Camden Society, 1964. Pp. 1–75.

Watkin, Aelred, ed. *The Great Chartulary of Glastonbury.* 3 vols. ("Somerset Record Society," vols. 59, 63–64.) Frome: Somerset Record Society, 1947–56.

Watkin, Hugh R., ed. *History of Totnes Priory and Medieval Town, Devonshire.* 3 vols. Torquay: 1904–19.

West, James R., ed. *St. Benet of Holme, 1020–1210.* 2 vols. ("Norfolk Record Society," vols. 2–3.) Fakenham: Norfolk Record Society, 1932.

Wigram, S. Robert, ed. *Cartulary of the Monastery of St. Fridewide at Oxford.* 2 vols. ("Oxfordshire Historical Society," vols. 28, 31.) Oxford: Oxfordshire Historical Society, 1895–96.

William of Malmesbury. *Chronicle of the Kings of England.* Translated by J. A. Giles. London: Henry G. Bohn, 1847.

―――. *Historia Novella.* Edited by K. R. Potter. ("Medieval Texts" Series.) London: Thomas Nelson and Son, 1955. [Cited as *HN.*]

―――. *Willelmi Malmesbiriensis monachi de gestis pontificum Anglorum libri quinque.* Edited by N. E. S. A. Hamilton. ("Rolls Series," #52.) London: HMSO, 1870; reprinted by Kraus, 1964. [Cited as *GP.*]

―――. *Willelmi Malmesbiriensis monachi de gestis regum Anglorum libri quinque; Historia novellae libri tres.* Edited by William Stubbs. 2 vols. ("Rolls

Series," #90.) London: Printed for HMSO by Eyre and Spottiswoode, 1887–89; reprinted by Kraus, 1964. [Cited as *GR*.]

Wilson, James, ed. *Register of the Priory of St. Bees.* ("Surtees Society," vol. 126.) Durham: Surtees Society, 1915.

Woodcock, Audrey, ed. *Cartulary of the Priory of St. Gregory, Canterbury.* ("Camden Society, Third Series," vol. 88.) London: Camden Society, 1956.

Wrottesley, George, ed. *The Burton Chartulary.* ("William Salt Archaeological Society, Collection of the History of Staffordshire," vol. 5, part 1.) London: William Salt Archaeological Society, 1884.

———. *The Stone Chartulary.* ("William Salt Archaeological Society, Original Series," vol. 6 part 1.) London: William Salt Archaeological Society, 1885.

Modern Works

Books

Adams, George B. *Councils and Courts in Anglo-Norman England.* ("Yale Historical Publications," no. 5.) New York: Russell and Russell, 1926.

Allan, Graham A. *A Sociology of Friendship and Kinship.* ("Studies in Sociology," no. 10.) London: George Allen and Unwin, 1979.

Altschul, Michael, ed. *Anglo-Norman England, 1066–1154.* ("Conference on British Studies. Bibliographic Handbooks.") Cambridge: Cambridge University Press, 1969.

———. *A Baronial Family in Medieval England: the Clares, 1217–1314.* ("Johns Hopkins University. Studies in historical and political science," vol. 83, no. 2.) Baltimore: Johns Hopkins University Press, 1965.

Atkin, Susan A. J. "The Bigod Family. An Investigation into Their Lands and Activities, 1066–1306." Unpublished Ph.D. diss. University of Reading, 1979.

Barlow, Frank. *The English Church, 1066–1154.* ("A History of the Anglo-Norman Church.") London: Longman's, 1979.

———. *William Rufus.* London: Methuen, 1983.

Barnes, Patricia M. and Slade, C. F., eds. *A Medieval Miscellany for Doris Mary Stenton.* ("Pipe Roll Society," vol. 76. "New Series," vol. 36.) London: Pipe Roll Society, 1960.

Barrow, G. W. S. *The Anglo-Norman Era in Scottish History.* Oxford: Clarendon Press, 1980.

———. *Kingship and Unity: Scotland 1000–1306.* ("The New History of Scotland," no. 2.) Toronto: University of Toronto Press, 1981.

Bates, David. *Normandy Before 1066.* London: Longman's, 1982.

Bearman, Robert. "Charters of the Redvers Family and Earldom of Devon in the Twelfth Century." Unpublished Ph.D. diss., University of London, 1981.

Beckwith, John. *Ivory Carvings in Early Medieval England.* London: Harvey Miller and Medcalf, 1972.

Bémont, Charles, ed. *Chartes des libertés anglaises 1100–1305.* Paris: Picard, 1892.

Bloch, Marc. *Feudal Society.* 2 vols. Translated by L. A. Manyon. Chicago: University of Chicago Press, 1961.

Boase, T. S. R. *English Art 1100–1216.* ("The Oxford History of English Art," vol. 3.) Oxford: Clarendon Press, 1953.

Boston, E. J. R. "The Territorial Interests of the Anglo-Norman Aristocracy c. 1086–1135." Unpublished Ph.D. diss., Cambridge University, 1979.

Boutruche, Robert. *Seigneurie et féodalité.* 2 vols. Paris: Aubier, 1959.

Brett, M. *The English Church Under Henry I.* Oxford: Clarendon Press, 1975.

Cantor, Norman F. *Church, Kingship and Lay Investiture in England, 1089–1135.* Princeton, N.J.: Princeton University Press, 1958.

Charbonnel, Josèphe (Chartrou). *L'Anjou de 1109 à 1151.* Paris: Les Presses Universitaires de France, 1928.

Charlton, Anne R. "A Study of the Mandeville Family and Its Estates." Unpublished Ph.D. diss., University of Reading, 1977.

Chibnall, Marjorie. *Anglo-Norman England, 1066–1166.* Oxford: Basil Blackwell, 1986.

——. *The World of Orderic Vitalis.* Oxford: Clarendon Press, 1984.

Chrimes, S.B. *An Introduction to the Administrative History of Mediaeval England.* 3d. ed. Oxford: Basil Blackwell, 1966.

Cipolla, Carlo M., ed. *The Fontana Economic History of Europe.* Vol. 1: *The Middle Ages.* Glasgow: Collins, 1972.

Clanchy, M. T. *England and Its Rulers, 1066–1272: Foreign Lordship and National Identity.* Oxford: Basil Blackwell, 1983.

——. *From Memory to Written Record: England, 1066–1307.* Cambridge, Mass.: Harvard University Press, 1979.

Clapham, A. W. *English Romanesque Architecture after the Conquest.* Oxford: Clarendon Press, 1964.

Clay, Charles and Greenway, Diana E. *Early Yorkshire Families.* ("Yorkshire Archaeological Society, Record Series," vol. 135.) Wakefield: Yorkshire Archaeological Society, 1973.

Clay, Charles T. *Notes on the Family of Clare with a Bibliography of His Writings.* Wakefield: privately printed, 1975.

——. *York Minister Fasti.* 2 vols. ("Yorkshire Archaeological Society, Record Series," vols. 123–24.) York: Yorkshire Archaeological Society, 1958–59.

Clayton, Richard. *The Family, Marriage and Social Change.* 2d ed. Lexington, Mass.: D. C. Heath and Co., 1979.

Cokayne, George Edward. *The Complete Peerage of England, Scotland, Ireland, Great Britain and the United Kingdom.* 13 vols. Edited by Vicary Gibbs. London: St. Catherine's Press, 1910.

Crane, Susan. *Insular Romance. Politics, Faith, and Culture in Anglo-Norman and Middle English Literature.* Berkeley: University of California Press, 1986.

Cronne, H. A. *The Reign of Stephen. Anarchy in England, 1135–1154.* London: Weidenfeld and Nicolson, 1970.

Crouch, David. *The Beaumont Twins. The Roots and Branches of Power in the Twelfth Century.* ("Cambridge Studies in Medieval Life and Thought, Fourth Series," no. 1.) Cambridge: Cambridge University Press, 1986.

David, Charles Wendell. *Robert Curthose Duke of Normandy.* ("Harvard Historical Studies," vol. 15.) Cambridge, Mass.: Harvard University Press, 1920.

Davis, G. R. C. *Medieval Cartularies of Great Britain, A Short Catalogue.* London: Longman's, Green and Co., 1958.

Davis, R. H. C. *King Stephen, 1135–1154.* Berkeley: University of California Press, 1967.

———. *The Normans and Their Myth*. London: Thames and Hudson, 1976.

Davis, R. H. C. and Wallace-Hadrill, J. M., eds. *The Writing of History in the Middle Ages. Essays Presented to Richard William Southern*. Oxford: Clarendon Press, 1981.

Denholm-Young, N. *Seigneurial Administration in England*. New York: Barnes and Noble, 1937.

Denton, J. H. *English Royal Free Chapels, 1100–1300. A Constitutional Study*. Manchester: Manchester University Press, 1970.

Dickinson, J. C. *The Origins of the Austin Canons and Their Introduction into England*. London: S.P.C.K., 1950.

Dodwell, Charles R. *The Canterbury School of Illumination, 1066–1200*. Cambridge: Cambridge University Press, 1954.

Dolley, Reginald Hugh Michael. *Anglo-Norman Ireland, 1100–1318*. Dublin: Gill and Macmillan, 1973.

Douglas, David C. *The Social Structure of Medieval East Anglia*. ("Oxford Studies in Social and Legal History," vol. 9.) Oxford: Clarendon Press, 1927; reprinted by Octagon, 1974.

———. *William the Conqueror*. Berkeley: University of California Press, 1967.

Douie, D. L. *Archbishop Geoffrey Plantagenet and the Chapter of York*. York: St. Anthony's Press, 1960.

Du Boulay, F. R. H. *The Lordship of Canterbury: an Essay on Medieval Society*. New York: Barnes and Noble, 1966.

Duby, Georges. *Medieval Marriage: Two Models from Twelfth-Century France*. Translated by Elborg Forster. Baltimore: Johns Hopkins University Press, 1978.

———. *The Knight, the Lady and the Priest: The Making of Modern Marriage in Medieval France*. Translated by Barbara Bray. New York: Pantheon, 1983.

Duby, Georges and LeGoff, Jacques, eds. *Famille et parenté dans l'occident médiéval*. ("Actes des Colloque de Paris, 6–8 Juin 1974.") Rome: Ecole Française de Rome, 1977.

English, Barbara. *The Lords of Holderness 1086–1260: A Study in Feudal Society*. Oxford: Oxford University Press, 1979.

Farnsworth, William Oliver. *Uncle and Nephew in the Old French Chansons de Geste. A Study in the Survival of Matriarchy*. New York: Columbia University Press, 1913; reprinted AMS Press, 1966.

Finberg, H. P. R. *Lucerna*. London: Macmillan, 1964.

Foner, Nancy. *Ages in Conflict. A Cross-Cultural Perspective on Inequality Between Young and Old*. ("Columbia Studies of Social Gerontology and Aging.") New York: Columbia University Press, 1984.

Forster, Robert and Ranum, Orest, eds. *Family and Society*. ("Selections from *Annales*.") Translated by Elborg Forster and Patricia Ranum. Baltimore: Johns Hopkins University Press, 1976.

Freed, John B. *The Counts of Falkenstein: Noble Self-Consciousness in Twelfth-Century Germany*. Transactions of the American Philosophical Society 74, part 6 (1984).

Freeman, Edward A. *The Reign of William Rufus and the Accession of Henry I*. 2 vols. Oxford: Clarendon Press, 1882.

Gillingham, John and Holt, J. C., eds. *War and Government in the Middle Ages: Essays in Honour of J. O. Prestwich*. Woodbridge, Suffolk: Boydell Press, 1984.

Given-Wilson, Chris and Curteis, Alice. *The Royal Bastards of Medieval England.* London: Routledge and Kegan Paul, 1984.

Goldy, Robert G. "The Question of Jewish Theology in America since the Second World War. An Intellectual History." Unpublished Ph.D. diss. Hebrew University, Jerusalem, 1987.

Goody, Jack, ed. *The Character of Kinship.* Cambridge: Cambridge University Press, 1973.

———. *Comparative Studies in Kinship.* Stanford, Calif.: Stanford University Press, 1969.

———. *The Development of the Family and Marriage in Europe.* Cambridge: Cambridge University Press, 1983.

Gransden, Antonia. *Historical Writing in England c. 550–c. 1307.* Ithaca, N.Y.: Cornell University Press, 1974.

Green, Judith A. *The Government of England Under Henry I.* ("Cambridge Studies in Medieval Life and Thought, Fourth Series," no. 3.) Cambridge: Cambridge University Press, 1986.

Hanawalt, Barbara. *The Ties That Bound.* New York: Oxford University Press, 1986.

Hansen, Marcus Lee. *The Immigrant in American History.* Cambridge, Mass.: Harvard University Press, 1940.

———. *The Problem of the Third Generation Immigrant.* ("Augustana Historical Society Publications.") Rock Island, Ill.: Augustana Historical Society, 1938.

Haskins, Charles Homer. *Norman Institutions.* New York: Frederick Ungar, 1918.

———. *The Renaissance of the Twelfth Century.* Cambridge, Mass.: Harvard University Press, 1927.

Helmholz, R. H. *Marriage Litigation in Medieval England.* Cambridge: Cambridge University Press, 1975.

Herlihy, David. *Medieval Households.* ("Studies in Cultural History,") Cambridge, Mass.: Harvard University Press, 1985.

———. *The Social History of Italy and Western Europe: Collected Studies.* London: Variorum Reprints, 1978.

Hill, Bennett D. *English Cistercian Monasteries and Their Patrons in the Twelfth Century.* Urbana: University of Illinois Press, 1968.

Hill, Sir Francis. *Medieval Lincoln.* Cambridge: Cambridge University Press, 1965.

Hill, Mary C. *The King's Messengers. 1199–1377: A Contribution to the History of the Royal Household.* London: Edward Arnold Ltd., 1961.

Hockey, S. F. *Quarr Abbey and Its Lands. 1132–1631.* Leicester: Leicester University Press, 1970.

Hollister, C. Warren. *Monarchy, Magnates and Institutions in the Anglo-Norman World.* London: Hambledon Press, 1986.

Holt, J. C. *The Northerners: A Study in the Reign of King John.* Oxford: Clarendon Press, 1961.

Houlbrooke, R. A. *The English Family, 1450–1700.* ("Themes in British Social History Series.") London: Longman's, 1984.

Hoyt, Robert S. *The Royal Demesne in English Constitutional History, 1066–1275.* Ithaca, N.Y.: Cornell University Press, 1950.

Ibn Khaldun, *The Muqaddimah*. Translated by Franz Rosenthal. New York: Pantheon Books, 1958.

Kapelle, William E. *The Norman Conquest of the North. The Region and Its Transformation, 1000–1135*. Chapel Hill: University of North Carolina Press, 1979.

Kauffmann, C. M. *Romanesque Manuscripts, 1066–1190*. ("A Survey of Manuscripts Illuminated in the British Isles," vol. 3.) London: Harvey Miller, 1975.

Kealey, Edward J. *Harvesting the Air*. Berkeley: University of California Press, 1987.

———. *Medieval Medicus*. Baltimore: Johns Hopkins University Press, 1981.

———. *Roger of Salisbury: Viceroy of England*. Berkeley: University of California Press, 1972.

Keefe, Thomas K. *Feudal Assessments and the Political Community Under Henry II and His Sons*. Berkeley: University of California Press, 1983.

Ker, N. R. *English Manuscripts in the Century After the Norman Conquest*. ("Lyell Lectures 1952–1953.") Oxford: Clarendon Press, 1960.

Kimball, Elisabeth G. *Serjeanty Tenure in Medieval England*. New Haven, Conn.: Yale University Press, 1936.

King, Edmund. *Peterborough Abbey, 1086–1310: A Study in the Land Market*. ("Cambridge Studies in Economic History.") Cambridge: Cambridge University Press, 1973.

Knowles, David; Brooke, C. N. L.; and London, V. C. M., eds. *Heads of Religious Houses. England and Wales 940–1216*. Cambridge: Cambridge University Press, 1972.

Laslett, Peter. *Family Life and Illicit Love in Earlier Generations*. Cambridge: Cambridge University Press, 1977.

Laslett, Peter; Oosterveen, Karla; and Smith, Richard M., eds. *Bastardy and Its Comparative History*. Cambridge, Mass.: Harvard University Press, 1980.

Legge, M. Dominica. *Anglo-Norman in the Cloisters*. Edinburgh: Edinburgh University Press, 1950.

———. *Anglo-Norman Literature and Its Background*. Oxford: Clarendon Press, 1963.

Le Neve, John. *Fasti Ecclesiae Anglicanae, 1066–1300*. 3 vols. Compiled by Diana E. Greenway. London: University of London. Institute of Historical Research, 1968–77.

Le Patourel, John. *Feudal Empires. Norman and Plantagenet*. London: Hambledon Press, 1984.

———. *Norman Barons*. ("1066 Commemoration Series," no. 4.) Hastings: The Historical Association, 1966.

———. *The Norman Empire*. Oxford: Clarendon Press, 1976.

———. *Normandy and England, 1066–1144*. ("Stenton Lectures," no. 4.) Reading: University of Reading Press, 1971.

Loyd, Lewis C. *The Origins of Some Anglo-Norman Families*. Edited by Charles T. Clay and David C. Douglas. ("Harlean Society," vol. 103.) Leeds: Harlean Society, 1951.

Mariás, Julián. *Generations: A Historical Method*. Translated by Harold C. Raley. University, Ala.: University of Alabama Press, 1970.

Mason, J. F. A. *William the First and the Sussex Rapes*. ("1066 Commemoration Series, no. 3.) Hastings: The Historical Association, 1966.

Meisel, Janet. *Barons of the Welsh Frontier*. Lincoln: University of Nebraska Press, 1980.

Meiss, Millard. *Painting in Florence and Siena after the Black Death*. Princeton, N.J.: Princeton University Press, 1951.

Miller, Edward. *Abbey and Bishopric of Ely*. Cambridge: Cambridge University Press, 1950.

Milsom, S. F. C. *The Legal Framework of English Feudalism*. ("Cambridge Studies in English Legal History.") Cambridge: Cambridge University Press, 1976.

Mitterauer, Michael and Sieder, Reinhard. *The European Family: Patriarchy to Partnership, 1400 to the Present*. Translated by Karla Oosterveen and Manfred Horzinger. Chicago: University of Chicago Press, 1982.

Morgan, Marjorie M. *The English Lands of the Abbey of Bec*. Oxford: Clarendon Press, 1968.

Murray, Alexander C. *Germanic Kinship Structure. Studies in Law and Society in Antiquity and the Early Middle Ages*. ("Studies and Texts," no. 65.) Toronto: Pontifical Institute of Mediaeval Studies, 1983.

Musset, Lucien. *Normandie Romane*. 2 vols. Translated by Alan McLeer. Zodiaque, 1974.

Nicholl, David. *Thurstan, archbishop of York (1114–1140)*. York: The Stonegate Press, 1964.

Orme, Nicholas. *From Childhood to Chivalry*. London: Methuen, 1984.

Painter, Sidney. *Studies in the History of the English Feudal Barony*. ("Studies in Historical and Political Sciences," series 61, no. 3.) Baltimore: Johns Hopkins University Press, 1943.

———. *William Marshal: Knight-Errant, Baron and Regent of England*. Baltimore: Johns Hopkins University Press, 1933.

Partner, Nancy. *Serious Entertainments: The Writing of History in Twelfth-Century England*. Chicago: University of Chicago Press, 1977.

Pollock, Frederick and Maitland, Frederic William. *The History of English Law Before the Time of Edward I*. 2 vols. 2d ed. Cambridge: Cambridge University Press, 1968.

Poole, Austin Lane. *Obligations of Society in the XII and XIII Centuries*. ("Ford Lectures," 1944.) Oxford: Clarendon Press, 1946.

Poole, Reginald Lane. *The Exchequer in the Twelfth Century*. ("Ford Lectures," 1911.) Oxford: Clarendon Press, 1912.

Powicke, F. M. *The Loss of Normandy, 1189–1204: Studies in the History of the Angevin Empire*. Manchester: Manchester University Press, 1913.

Powicke, Michael. *Military Obligation in Feudal England*. Oxford: Clarendon Press, 1962.

Powley, Edward B. *The House of De La Pomeroi*. Liverpool: University Press of Liverpool, 1944.

Reuter, Timothy, ed. *The Medieval Nobility: Studies on the Ruling Classes of France and Germany from the Sixth to the Twelfth Century*. ("Europe in the Middle Ages. Selected Studies, no. 14.") New York: Oxford University Press, 1978.

Richardson, H. G. and Sayles, G. O. *The Governance of Mediaeval England from the Conquest to Magna Carta.* Edinburgh: Edinburgh University Press, 1963.

Ritchie, R. L. Graeme. *The Normans in Scotland.* Edinburgh: Edinburgh University Press, 1954.

Rosenthal, Joel T. *Purchase of Paradise.* London: Routledge and Kegan Paul, 1972.

Rössler, Oskar. *Kaiserin Mathilde.* Berlin: G. Shade, 1897; reprinted by Kraus, 1965.

Round, John Horace. *The Commune of London and Other Studies.* Westminster: Archibald Constable and Co., 1899.

————. *Family Origins and Other Studies.* Edited by William Page. London: Constable and Co., Ltd., 1930.

————. *Feudal England: Historical Studies on the XIth and XIIth Centuries.* London: Swan Sonnenschein and Co., 1909. [Cited as *FE.*]

————. *Geoffrey de Mandeville: A Study of the Anarchy.* London: n.p., 1892; reprinted by Burt Franklin, n.d.

————. *The King's Serjeants and Officers of State.* London: James Nisbet and Co., 1911; reprinted by Barnes and Noble, 1970.

————. *Studies in Peerage and Family History.* Westminster: Archibald Constable and Co., 1907; facsimile ed. by Tabard Press, 1970.

————. *Studies on the Red Book of the Exchequer.* Np.: privately printed by the author, n.d.

Rowley, Trevor. *The Norman Heritage, 1055–1200.* ("The Making of Britain, 1066–1939" series.) London: Routledge and Kegan Paul, 1983.

Russell, Josiah C. *British Medieval Population.* Albuquerque: University of New Mexico Press, 1948.

————. *Late Ancient and Medieval Population Control. Memoirs of the American Philosophical Society,* vol. 160, 1985.

Sanders, I. J. *English Baronies: A Study of Their Origins and Descent, 1087–1327.* Oxford: Clarendon Press, 1960.

————. *Feudal Military Service in England: A Study of Constitutional and Military Powers of the Barones in Medieval England.* ("Oxford Historical Series, British Series.") London: Geoffrey Cumberlege/Oxford University Press, 1956.

Stenton, Frank M. *The First Century of English Feudalism, 1066–1166.* 2d ed. Oxford: Clarendon Press, 1961.

Stone, Lawrence. *The Family, Sex and Marriage in England, 1500–1800.* New York: Harper and Row, 1977.

Stringer, K. J. *Earl David of Huntingdon 1152–1219. A Study in Anglo-Scottish History.* Edinburgh: Edinburgh University Press, 1985.

Thomson, Rodney. *William of Malmesbury.* Woodbridge, Suffolk: Boydell Press, 1987.

Tout, T. F. *Chapters in the Administrative History of Mediaeval England.* 6 vols. 3d ed. Manchester: Manchester University Press, 1967.

Vaughn, Sally N. *The Abbey of Bec and the Anglo-Norman State, 1034–1136.* Woodbridge, Suffolk: Boydell Press, 1982.

————. *Anselm of Bec and Robert of Meulan. The Innocence of the Dove and the Wisdom of the Serpent.* Berkeley: University of California Press, 1987.

Voss, Lena. *Heinrich von Blois, Bischof von Winchester, 1129–71.* ("Historische Studien," vol. 210.) Berlin: 1932; reprinted by Kraus, 1965.

Walker, David. *The Norman Conquerors.* ("A New History of Wales.") Swansea: Christopher Davies, 1977.

Wall, Richard with Robin, Jean and Laslett, Peter. *Family Forms in Historic Europe.* Cambridge: Cambridge University Press, 1983.

Ward, Jennifer. "The Estates of the Clare Family, 1066–1317." Unpublished Ph.D. diss., University of London, 1962.

Warren, W. L. *Henry II.* Berkeley: University of California Press, 1973.

West, F. J. *The Justiciarship in England, 1066–1232.* Cambridge: Cambridge University Press, 1966.

Wightman, W. E. *The Lacy Family in England, 1066–1194.* Oxford: Clarendon Press, 1966.

Wolfe, B. P. *The Royal Demesne in English History: The Crown Estate in the Governance of the Realm from the Conquest to 1509.* London: Allen and Unwin, 1971.

Wootten, William W. "A Study of Henry I: King of England 1068–1107." Unpublished Ph.D. diss., University of Minnesota, 1964.

Young, Charles R. *The Royal Forests of Medieval England.* Philadelphia: University of Pennsylvania Press, 1979.

Zarnecki, George. *English Romanesque Sculpture, 1066–1140.* London: Alec Tiranti Ltd., 1951.

———. *Later English Romanesque Sculpture, 1140–1210.* London: Alec Tiranti Ltd., 1953.

Zarnecki, George; Holt, Janet; and Holland, Tristram, eds. *English Romanesque Art 1066–1200.* ("Hayward Gallery, London 5 April–8 July, 1984.") London: Weidenfeld and Nicolson for the Arts Council of Great Britain, 1984.

Zupko, Ronald Edward. *A Dictionary of English Weights and Measures: From Anglo-Saxon Times to the Nineteenth Century.* Madison: University of Wisconsin Press, 1968.

Articles and Papers

Alexander, James W. "The Alleged Palatinates of Norman England." *Speculum* 56 (1981): 17–27.

———. "Herbert of Norwich, 1091–1119: Studies in the History of Norman England." *Studies in Medieval and Renaissance History* 6 (1969): 115–232.

Bachrach, Bernard S. "The Idea of the Angevin Empire." *Albion* 10 (1978): 293–99.

Bailey, S. J. "The Countess Gundred's Lands." *Cambridge Law Journal* 10 (1948–1950): 84–104.

Barkly, Henry. "Remarks on the Liber Niger, or Black Book of the Exchequer." *Bristol and Gloucestershire Archaeological Society: Transactions* 14 (1889–1890): 285–320.

Barraclough, Geoffrey. "Some Charters of the Earls of Chester." In *A Medieval Miscellany for Doris Mary Stenton.* Edited by Patricia M. Barnes and C. Slade. ("Publications of the Pipe Roll Society," vol. 76, New Series, vol. 36.) London: Pipe Roll Society, 1960. Pp. 5–43.

Bartlett, Robert. "Rewriting Saints' Lives: The Case of Gerald of Wales." *Speculum* 58 (1983): 598–613.

Bates, David R. "The Character and Career of Odo, Bishop of Bayeux." *Speculum* 50 (1975): 1–20.

———. "The Earliest Norman Writs." *English Historical Review* 100 (1985): 266–84.

———. "The Origins of the Justiciarship." *Anglo-Norman Studies* 4 (1981): 1–12.

Beech, George. "Prosopography." In *Medieval Studies: An Introduction*. Edited by James M. Powell. Syracuse, N.Y.: Syracuse University Press, 1976. Pp. 151–84.

Bernstein, David. "The Englishness of the Bayeux Tapestry." Paper presented at the International Congress on Medieval Studies, Western Michigan University, May 11, 1985.

Blair, J. "The Surrey Endowments of Lewes Priory before 1200." *Surrey Archaeological Collections* 72 (1980): 97–126.

Bouchard, Constance. "The Structure of a Twelfth-Century French Family: The Lords of Seignelay." *Viator* 10 (1979): 39–56.

Boyd-Franklin, Nancy. "Black Family Life-Styles: A Lesson in Survival." In *Class, Race, and Sex: The Dynamics of Control*. Edited by Amy Swerdlow and Hanna Lessinger. Boston: G. K. Hall and Co., 1983. Pp. 189—99.

Brett, Martin. "John of Worcester and His Contemporaries." In *The Writing of History in the Middle Ages*. Edited by R. H. C. Davis and J. M. Wallace-Hadrill. Oxford: Clarendon Press, 1981. Pp. 101–26.

Brooke, Christopher. "The Archbishops of St. David's, Llandaff and Caerleon-on-Usk." In *Studies in the Early British Church*. Edited by Nora Chadwick, Kathleen Hughes, Christopher Brooke, and Kenneth Jackson. Hamden, Conn.: Archon Books, 1958. Pp. 201–42.

———. "Gregorian Reform in Action: Clerical Marriage in England, 1050–1200." In *Medieval Church and Society* by Christopher Brooke. London: Sidgewick and Jackson, 1971. Pp. 69—99.

Brooke, C. N. L.; Keir, G.; and Reynolds, S. "Henry I's Charter for the City of London." *Journal of the Society of Archivists* 4 (1973): 558–78.

Brown, R. Allen. "Early Charters of Sibton Abbey, Suffolk." In *A Medieval Miscellany for Doris Mary Stenton*. Edited by Patricia M. Barnes and C. F. Slade. ("Publications of the Pipe Roll Society," vol. 76, New Series, vol. 36.) London: Pipe Roll Society, 1960. Pp. 65–76.

Brownbill, J. "The Countess Lucy," *Complete Peerage*, vol. 7, Appendix J, pp. 743–46.

Bullough, D. A. "Early Medieval Social Groupings: The Terminology of Kinship." *Past and Present* 45 (1969): 3–18.

Bullough, Vern. "Medical and Scientific Views of Women." *Viator* 4 (1973): 485–501.

Callahan, Thomas. "Ecclesiastical Reparations and the Soldiers of the Anarchy." *Albion* 10 (1978): 300–18.

———. "The Impact of the Anarchy on English Monasticism, 1135–1154." *Albion* 6 (1974): 218–32.

———. "A Reevaluation of the Anarchy." *Revue Bénédictine* 84 (1974): 338–51.

Cazel, F. A. "Norman and Wessex Charters of the Roumare Family." In *A Me-*

dieval Miscellany for Doris Mary Stenton. Edited by Patricia M. Barnes and C. F. Slade. ("Publications of the Pipe Roll Society," vol. 76, "New Series," vol. 36.) London: Pipe Roll Society, 1960. Pp. 77–88.

Chandler, Victoria. "Ada de Warenne, Queen Mother of Scotland (c. 1123–1178)." *Scottish Historical Review* 60 (1981): 119–39.

———. "Family Histories: An Aid in the Study of the Anglo-Norman Aristocracy" *Medieval Prosopography* 6 (1985): 1–24.

———. "Historical Revision and the English Monarchs: The Case of William II and His Barons." *Indiana Social Studies Quarterly* 33 (1980): 41–48.

———. "Intimations of Authority: Notes on Three Anglo-Norman Countesses." *Indiana Social Studies Quarterly* 31 (1978): 5–17.

———. "Politics and Piety: Influences on Charitable Donations During the Anglo-Norman Period." *Revue Bénédictine* 90 (1980): 63–71.

Chaplais, Pierre. "The Original Charters of Herbert and Gervase, Abbots of Westminster (1121–1157)." In *A Medieval Miscellany for Doris Mary Stenton.* Edited by Patricia M. Barnes and C. F. Slade. ("Publications of the Pipe Roll Society," vol. 76,"New Series," vol. 36.) London: Pipe Roll Society, 1960. Pp. 89–110.

———. "The Seals and Original Charters of Henry I." *English Historical Review* 30 (1960): 260–75.

Chibnall, Marjorie. "Feudal Society in Orderic Vitalis." *Anglo-Norman Studies* 1 (1978): 35–48.

———. "Mercenaries and the *Familia Regis* under Henry I." *History* 62 (1977): 15–23.

Chojnacki, Stanley, "Mothers as Fathers: Widows in Early Renaissance Venice." Paper presented at the International Congress on Medieval Studies, Western Michigan University, May 9, 1986.

Clark, Cecily. "Women's Names in Post-Conquest England: Observations and Speculations." *Speculum* 53 (1978): 223–51.

Clay, Charles. "The Family of Meaux: I Meaux of Bewick and II Meaux of Owthorne." *Yorkshire Archaeological Journal* 43 (1971): 99–111.

———. "The Origin of Eustace Fitz John." *Complete Peerage,* vol. 12, part 2, Appendix B, pp. 7–11.

Cooke, Kathleen. "Kings, Knights, and Abbesses: Shaftesbury Abbey in the Twelfth Century." Paper presented at the International Congress on Medieval Studies, Western Michigan University, May 12, 1984.

Corbett, William John. "The Development of the Duchy of Normandy and the Norman Conquest of England." *Cambridge Medieval History* vol. 5, pp. 502–50. New York: Macmillan, 1926.

Coss, P. P. "Sir Geoffrey de Langley and the Crisis of the Knightly Class in Thirteenth-Century England." *Past and Present* 68 (1975): 3–37.

Cronne, H. A. "Ranulf de Gernons, Earl of Chester, 1129–1153," *Transactions of the Royal Historical Society,* 4th ser. 20 (1937): 103–34.

———. "The Royal Forest in the Reign of Henry I." In *Essays in British and Irish History in Honour of James Eadie Todd.* Edited by H. A. Cronne, T. W. Moody and D. B. Quinn. London: Frederick Muller, Ltd., 1949. Pp. 1–23.

Crook, David. "The Early Keepers of Sherwood Forest." *Transactions of the Thoroton Society* 84 (1980): 14–20.

Crosby, Everett U. "The Origins of the English Episcopate under Henry I." *Studies in Medieval and Renaissance History* 4 (1967): 1–88.

Crouch, David. "Geoffrey de Clinton and Roger, Earl of Warwick: New Men and Magnates in the Reign of Henry I." *Bulletin of the Institute of Historical Research* 55 (1982): 113–24.

David, Charles Wendell. "The Claim of King Henry I to be Called Learned." In *Haskins Anniversary Essays in Medieval History*. Edited by C. H. Taylor and J. L. LaMonte. Boston: Houghton-Mifflin Co., 1929. Pp. 45–56.

Davis, H.W.C. "The Anarchy of Stephen's Reign." *English Historical Review* 18 (1903): 630–41.

———. "Henry of Blois and Brian fitz Count." *English Historical Review* 24 (1910): 297–303.

Davis, R. H. C. "The Production and Breeding of the Medieval War Horse," Paper presented at the Haskins Society Conference, University of Houston, November 8, 1985.

———. "What Happened in Stephen's Reign." *History* 49 (1964): 1–12.

———. "William of Jumièges, Robert Curthose and the Norman Succession." *English Historical Review* 95 (1980): 597–606.

———. "William of Poitiers and his *History of William the Conqueror*." In *The Writing of History in the Middle Ages*. Edited by R. H. C. Davis and J. M. Wallace-Hadrill. Oxford: Clarendon Press, 1981. Pp. 71–100.

DeAragon, RaGena. "The Growth of Secure Inheritance in Anglo-Norman England." *Journal of Medieval History* 8 (1982): 381–93.

———. "In Pursuit of Aristocratic Women: A Key to Success in Norman England." *Albion* 14 (1982): 259–67.

Denholm-Young, N. "Eudo Dapifer's Honour of Walbrook." In *Collected Papers of N. Denholm-Young*. Cardiff: University of Wales Press, 1969. Pp. 205–12.

Dodwell, Barbara. "Some Charters Relating to the Honour of Bacton." In *A Medieval Miscellany for Doris Mary Stenton*. Edited by Patricia M. Barnes and C. F. Slade. ("Publications of the Pipe Roll Society," vol. 76, "New Series," vol. 36.) London: Pipe Roll Society, 1960. Pp. 147–65.

Douglas, Andrew W. "Tenure *in elemosina*: Origins and Establishment in Twelfth-Century England." *American Journal of Legal History* 24 (1980): 95–132.

Douglas, D. C. "Companions of the Conqueror." *English Historical Review* 28 (1943): 129–47.

Duby, Georges. "Youth in Aristocratic Society." In *The Chivalrous Society*. Translated by Cynthia Postan. Berkeley: University of California Press, 1977. Pp. 112–22.

Dyson, A. G. "The Monastic Patronage of Bishop Alexander." *Journal of Ecclesiastical History* 26 (1975): 1–24.

Edgington, Susan. "Pagan Peverel: An Anglo-Norman Crusader." In *Crusade and Settlement*. Edited by Peter Edbury. Cardiff: University College, 1985. Pp. 90–93.

Ellis, Alfred E. "On the Landholders of Gloucestershire named in Domesday Book," *Bristol and Gloucestershire Archaeological Society: Transactions* 4 (1879–1880): 86–198.

Farmer, Sharon. "Persuasive Voices: Clerical Images of Medieval Wives." *Speculum* 61 (1986): 517–43.

Farrer, William. "An Outline Itinerary of King Henry the First." *English Historical Review* 34 (1919): 303–82, 505–79.

———. "The Sheriffs of Lincolnshire and Yorkshire, 1066–1130." *English Historical Review* 30 (1915): 277–85.

Fox, Levi. "The Honour and Earldom of Leicester." *English Historical Review* 54 (1939): 385–402.

Freeman, J. D. "On the Concept of Kindred." *Journal of the Royal Anthropological Institute* 91 (1961): 192–220.

Galbraith, V. H. "Girard the Chancellor." *English Historical Review* 46 (1931): 77–79.

Gem, R. D. H. "The Romanesque Rebuilding of Westminster Abbey." *Anglo-Norman Studies* 3 (1980): 33–60.

Genicot, Leopold. "La Noblesse au Moyen Age dans l'ancienne 'Francie' : continuité, rupture ou évolution?" *Comparative Study of Society and History* 5 (1962/1963): 52–59.

Gibson, Margaret. "History at Bec in the Twelfth Century." In *The Writing of History in the Middle Ages*. Edited by R. H. C. Davis and J. M. Wallace-Hadrill. Oxford: Clarendon Press, 1981. Pp. 167–86.

Golding, Brian. "The Coming of the Cluniacs." *Anglo-Norman Studies* 3 (1980): 61–77.

Goody, Jack. "Under the Lineage's Shadow." *Proceedings of the British Academy* 70 (1984): 189–208.

Green, Judith. "The Lords of the Norman Vexin." In *War and Government in the Middle Ages*. Edited by John Gillingham and J. C. Holt. Woodbridge, Suffolk: Boydell, 1984. Pp. 46–62.

———. " 'Praeclarum et Magnificum Antiquitatis Monumentum': The Earliest Surviving Pipe Roll." *Bulletin of the Institute of Historical Research* 55 (1982): 1–17.

———. "William Rufus, Henry I and the Royal Demesne." *History* 64 (1979): 337–52.

Gunner, W. H. "The Alien Priory of Andwell." *Archaeological Journal* (London) 9 (1852): 246–61.

Harper-Bill, C. "The Piety of the Anglo-Norman Knightly Class," *Anglo-Norman Studies* 2 (1979): 63–77.

Harvey, Sally. "The Knight and the Knight's Fee in England." *Past and Present* 49 (1970): 3–43.

Helmholz, R. H. "Bastardy Litigation in Medieval England." *American Journal of Legal History* 13 (1969): 360–83.

Herlihy, David. "The Generation in Medieval History." *Viator* 5 (1974): 346–64; reprinted in *The Social History of Italy and Western Europe 700–1500*. London: Variorum Reprints, 1978. No. XII.

———. "The Making of the Medieval Family: Symmetry, Structure, and Sentiment." *Journal of Family History* 8 (1983): 116–30.

———. "The Medieval Marriage Market." *Medieval and Renaissance Studies* 6 (1976): 3–27; reprinted in *The Social History of Italy and Western Europe 700–1500*. London: Variorum Reprints, 1978. No. XIV.

Hicks, Sandy Burton. "The Anglo-Papal Bargain of 1125: The Legatine Mission of John of Crema." *Albion* 8 (1976): 301–10.

————. "England's King Henry I and the Flemish Succession Crisis of 1127–28." *Journal of the Rocky Mountain Medieval and Renaissance Association* 2 (1981): 41–49.

————. "The Impact of William Clito upon the Continental Policies of Henry I of England." *Viator* 10 (1979): 1–21.

Hill, Bennett. "The Counts of Mortain and the Origins of the Norman Congregation of Savigny." In *Order and Innovation in the Middle Ages: Essays in Honor of Joseph R. Strayer*. Edited by W. C. Jordan, B. McNab, and T. F. Ruiz. Princeton: Princeton University Press, 1976, Pp. 237–53.

Hockey, S. F. "William fitz Osbern and the Endowment of His Abbey of Lyre." *Anglo-Norman Studies* 3 (1980): 90–105.

Hodson, J. H. "Medieval Charters: The Last Witness." *Journal of the Society of Archivists* 5 (1974): 71–89.

Hollister, C. Warren. "The Anglo-Norman Civil War of 1101," *English Historical Review* 88 (1973): 315–34; reprinted in Monarchy, *Magnates and Institutions*. London: Hambledon Press, 1986.

————. "The Anglo-Norman Succession Debate of 1126: Prelude to Stephen's Anarchy." *Journal of Medieval History* 1 (1975): 19–41; reprinted in *Monarchy, Magnates and Institutions*. London: Hambledon Press, 1986.

————. "Henry I and Robert Malet." *Viator* 4 (1973): 115–22; reprinted in *Monarchy, Magnates and Institutions*. London: Hambledon Press, 1986.

————. "Henry I and the Anglo-Norman Magnates." *Anglo-Norman Studies* 2 (1979): 93–107; reprinted in *Monarchy, Magnates and Institutions*. London: Hambledon Press, 1986.

————. "International War and Diplomacy in the Anglo-Norman World: The Reign of Henry I." In *Monarchy, Magnates and Institutions*. London: Hambledon Press, 1986.

————. "London's First Charter of Liberties: Was it Genuine?" *Journal of Medieval History* 6 (1980): 289–306; reprinted in *Monarchy, Magnates and Institutions*. London: Hambledon Press, 1986.

————. "Magnates and *Curiales* in Early Norman England." *Viator* 8 (1977): 63–81; reprinted in *Monarchy, Magnates and Institutions*. London: Hambledon Press, 1986.

————. "The Misfortune of the Mandevilles." *History* 58 (1973): 18–28; reprinted in *Monarchy, Magnates and Institutions*. London: Hambledon Press, 1986.

————. "Normandy, France and the Anglo-Norman *Regnum*." *Speculum* 51 (1976): 202–42; reprinted in *Monarchy, Magnates and Institutions*. London: Hambledon Press, 1986.

————. "The Origins of the English Treasury." *English Historical Review* 93 (1978): 262–75; reprinted in *Monarchy, Magnates and Institutions*. London: Hambledon Press, 1986.

————. "Royal Acts of Mutilation: The Case Against Henry I." *Albion* 10 (1978): 330–40; reprinted in *Monarchy, Magnates and Institutions*. London: Hambledon Press, 1986.

————. "The Significance of Scutage Rates in Eleventh- and Twelfth-Century England." *English Historical Review* 75 (1960): 577–88.

————. "Stephen's Anarchy." *Albion* 6 (1974): 233–39.

———. "The Strange Death of William Rufus." *Speculum* 48 (1973): 637–53; reprinted in *Monarchy, Magnates and Institutions*. London: Hambledon Press, 1986.

———. "The Taming of a Turbulent Earl: Henry I and William of Warenne." *Historical Reflections (Réflexions Historiques)* 3 (1976):, 83–91; reprinted in *Monarchy, Magnates and Institutions*. London: Hambledon Press, 1986.

Hollister, C. Warren and Baldwin, John W. "The Rise of Adminstrative Kingship: Henry I and Philip Augustus." *American Historical Review* 83 (1978): 867–905; reprinted in *Monarchy, Magnates and Institutions*. London: Hambledon Press, 1986.

Hollister, C. Warren and Keefe, Thomas K. "The Making of the Angevin Empire." *Journal of British Studies* 12 (1973): 1–20; reprinted in *Monarchy, Magnates and Institutions*. London: Hambledon Press, 1986.

Holt, J. C. "Politics and Property in Early Medieval England. *Past and Present* 57 (1972): 3–52.

———. "Politics and Property: A Rejoinder." *Past and Present* 68 (1974): 127–35.

———. "Presidential Address: Feudal Society and the Family in Early Medieval England: I. Revolution of 1066." *Transactions of the Royal Historical Society,* 5th ser. 32 (1982): 193–212.

———. "Presidential Address: Feudal Society and the Family in Early Medieval England: II. Notions of Patrimony." *Transactions of the Royal Historical Society,* 5th ser. 33 (1983): 193–220.

———. "Presidential Address: Feudal Society and the Family in Early Medieval England: III. Patronage and Politics." *Transactions of the Royal Historical Society,* 5th ser. 34 (1984): 1–26.

———. "Presidential Address: Feudal Society and the Family in Early Medieval England: IV. The Heiress and the Alien." *Transactions of the Royal Historical Society,* 5th ser. 35 (1985): 1–28.

———. "Willoughby Deeds." In *A Medieval Miscellany for Doris Mary Stenton*. Edited by Patricia M. Barnes and C. F. Slade. ("Publications of the Pipe Roll Society," vol. 76, "New Series," vol. 36.) London: Pipe Roll Society, 1960.

Hyams, Paul. "The Common Law and the French Connection." *Anglo-Norman Studies* 4 (1981): 77–92.

———. "Henry II and Ganelon." *Syracuse Scholar* 4 (1983): 23–35.

———. "Trial by Ordeal: The Key to Proof in Early Common Law." In *On the Laws and Customs of England*. Edited by M. S. Arnold, T. A. Green, S. A. Scully and S. D. White. Chapel Hill: University of North Carolina Press, 1981. Pp. 90–126.

Johnson, Charles. "Waldric, the Chancellor of Henry I." *English Historical Review* 51 (1936): 103–04.

Jones, Michael. "The Charters of Robert II de Ferrers, Earl of Nottingham, Derby and Ferrers." *Nottingham Mediaeval Studies* 24 (1980): 7–26.

Jones, Thomas M. "The Generation Gap of 1173–74: The War Between the Two Henrys." *Albion* 5 (1973): 24–40.

Kealey, Edward J. "Anglo-Norman Policy and the Public Welfare." *Albion* 10 (1978): 341–51.

———. "King Stephen: Government and Anarchy." *Albion* 6 (1974): 201–17.

Kedar, Benjamin Z. "Toponymic Surnames as Evidence of Origin: Some Medieval Views." *Viator* 4 (1973): 123–29.

Keefe, Thomas K. "Geoffrey Plantagenet's Will and the Angevin Succession." *Albion* 6 (1974): 266–74.

King, Edmund. "The Anarchy of King Stephen's Reign." *Transactions of the Royal Historical Society,* 5th ser. 34 (1984): 133–54.

———. "King Stephen and the Anglo-Norman Aristocracy." *History* 59 (1974): 180–94.

———. "The Tenurial Crisis of the Early Twelfth Century." *Past and Present* 68 (1974): 110–17.

———. "Waleran, Count of Meulan, Earl of Worcester (1104–1166)." In *Traditions and Change.* Edited by D. E. Greenway, C. Holdsworth, and J. Sawyer. Cambridge: Cambridge University Press, 1985. Pp. 165–82.

Knowles, David. "The Case of St. William of York." *Cambridge Historical Journal* 5 (1936): 162–77, 212–14; reprinted in *Historian and Character.* Cambridge: Cambridge University Press, 1963. Pp. 76–97.

Lally, J. E. "Secular Patronage at the Court of King Henry II." *Bulletin of the Institute of Historical Research* 49 (1976): 159–84.

Lancaster, Lorraine. "Kinship in Anglo-Saxon Society." *British Journal of Sociology* 9 (1958): 230–50, 359–77.

Leedom, J. W. "The English Settlement of 1153." *History* 65 (1980): 347–64.

———. "William of Malmesbury and Robert of Gloucester Reconsidered." *Albion* 6 (1974): 251–63.

Legge, M. Dominica. "Anglo-Norman as a Spoken Language." *Anglo-Norman Studies* 2 (1979): 108–17.

———. "L'influence littéraire de la cour d'Henri Beauclerc." In *Mélanges offerts à Rita Lejeune.* Edited by Fred Dethier. Gembloux, 1969. Pp. 679–87.

———. "The Rise and Fall of Anglo-Norman Literature." *Mosaic* 8 (1975): 1–6.

Leyser, K. "England and the Empire in the Early Twelfth Century." *Transactions of the Royal Historical Society,* 5th ser. 10 (1960): 61–83.

Le Patourel, John. "The Norman Conquest of Yorkshire." *Northern History* 6 (1971): 1–21.

———. "The Norman Conquest, 1066, 1106, 1154?" *Anglo-Norman Studies* 1 (1978): 103–20, 216–20.

———. "The Norman Succession, 996–1135." *English Historical Review* 86 (1971): 225–50.

———. "What Did Not Happen in Stephen's Reign." *History* 58 (1971): 1–17.

Liebermann, Felix. "The Text of Henry I's Coronation Charter." *Transactions of the Royal Historical Society,* ns. 8 (1894): 19–48.

Lohrmann, Dietrich. "Der Tod König Heinrichs I. von England in der mittellateinischen Literatur Englands und der Normandie." *Mittellateinisches Jahrbuch* 8 (1973): 90–107.

Loyd, Lewis C. "The Norman Earls of Warwick." *Complete Peerage,* vol. 12, part 2, Appendix A, pp. 2–6.

———. "The Origin of the Family of Aubigny of Cainhoe." *Publications of the Bedfordshire Historical Society* 19 (1937): 101–09.

Lynch, Joseph. "Sponsorship Among the Anglo-Saxons." Paper presented at the

American Society of Church Historians Conference, Miami University, April 26, 1985.

MacFarlane, Alan. "Illegitimacy and Illegitimates in English History." In *Bastardy and Its Comparative History*. Edited by Peter Laslett, et al. Cambridge, Mass.: Harvard University Press, 1980. Pp. 71–85.

Mason, Emma. "Magnates, Curiales and the Wheel of Fortune." *Anglo-Norman Studies* 2 (1979): 118–40.

———. "The Mauduits and the Chamberlainship of the Exchequer." *Bulletin of the Institute of Historical Research* 49 (1976): 1–23.

———. "*Pro Statu et Incolumnitate Regni Mei*: Royal Monastic Patronage 1066–1154." *Studies in Church History* 18 (1982): 99–117.

———. "Timeo Barones et Donas Ferentes." *Studies in Church History* 15 (1978): 61–75.

———. "William Rufus: Myth and Reality." *Journal of Medieval History* 3 (1977): 1–20.

Mason, J. F. A. "Roger de Montgomery and His Sons (1067–1102)." *Transactions of the Royal Historical Society,* 5th ser. 13 (1963): 1–28.

Meekings, C. A. F. "Notes on the de Abernon Family Before 1236." *Surrey Archaeological Collections* 72 (1980): 157–73.

Milsom, S. F. C. "Inheritance by Women in the Twelfth and Early Thirteenth Century." In *On the Laws and Customs of England*. Edited by M. S. Arnold, T. A. Green, S. A. Scully, and S. D. White. Chapel Hill: University of North Carolina Press, 1981. Pp. 60–89.

Mooers, Stephanie, "'Backers and Stabbers': Problems of Loyalty in Robert Curthose's Entourage." *Journal of British Studies* 21 (1981): 1–17.

———. "Familial Clout and Financial Gain in Henry I's Later Reign." *Albion* 14 (1982): 268–91.

———. "Networks of Power in Anglo-Norman England." *Medieval Prosopography* 7 (1986): 25–54.

———. "Patronage in the Pipe Roll of 1130." *Speculum* 59 (1984): 282–307.

Moor, Charles. "The Bygods, Earls of Norfolk," *Yorkshire Archaeological Journal* 32 (1935): 172–213.

Moriarty, G. A., Loyd, L. C. and White, G. H. "Waleran, Count of Meulan, and His Successors." *Complete Peerage,* vol. 7, Appendix 1, pp. 737–42.

Moriarty, G. A.; White, G. H.; and Stokes, E. "Leicester." *Complete Peerage,* vol. 7, pp. 521–30.

Morris, W. A. "The Sheriffs and the Administrative System of Henry I." *English Historical Review* 37 (1922): 161–72.

Mortimer, Richard. "The Beginnings of the Honour of Clare." *Anglo-Norman Studies* 3 (1980): 119–41.

———. "The Family of Rannulf de Glanville." *Bulletin of the Institute of Historical Research* 54 (1981): 1–16.

Newman, Charlotte A. "Anglo-Norman Romanesque Architecture and the Conquest." *Medievalia* 7 (1984 for 1981): 265–79.

———. "Family and Royal Favor in Henry I's England." *Albion* 14 (1982): 292–306.

———. "Review Essay of *Royal Bastards*." *Medieval Prosopography* 7 (1986): 87–97.

Oggins, Robin S. "Population Growth, Inheritance and European Expansion." *Acta: The Eleventh Century* 1 (1974): 31–38.

Oosterveen, Karla and Smith, Richard M. "Bastardy and Family Reconstruction." In *Bastardy and Its Comparative History.* Edited by Peter Laslett, et al. Cambridge, Mass.: Harvard University Press, 1980.

Painter, Sidney, "Castle Guard." *American Historical Review* 40 (1935): 450–59.

———. "English Castles in the Middle Ages." *Speculum* 10 (1935): 321–32.

———. "The Family and the Feudal System in Twelfth-Century England." *Speculum* 35 (1960): 3–16.

Patterson, Robert B. "Anarchy in England, 1135–1154: The Theory of the Constitution." *Albion* 6 (1974): 189–200.

———. "Bristol's Early Angevin Proprietary Society." Paper presented at the Haskins Society Conference, University of Houston, November 16, 1986.

———. "Robert of Gloucester: A Reappraisal." Paper presented at the Haskins Society Conference, University of Houston, November 10, 1985.

———. "William of Malmesbury's Robert of Gloucester: A Re-evaluation of the *Historia Novella.*" *American Historical Review* 70 (1965): 983–97.

Phillpotts, Bertha. "The Germanic Kindreds." In *Early Medieval Society.* Edited by Sylvia L. Thrupp. New York: Appleton-Century-Crofts, 1967. Pp. 3–16.

Pitt-Rivers, Julian. "The Kith and Kin." In *The Character of Kinship.* Edited by Jack Goody. Cambridge: Cambridge University Press, 1973. Pp. 89–105.

Poole, R. L. "The Appointment and Deprivation of St. William, Archbishop of York." *English Historical Review* 45 (1930): 273–81.

Prestwich, John O. "The Military Household of the Norman Kings." *English Historical Review* 96 (1981): 1–35.

———. "War and Finance in the Anglo-Norman State." *Transactions of the Royal Historical Society,* 5th ser. 4 (1954): 19–44.

Reedy, William T. "The First Two Bassets of Weldon." *Northamptonshire Past and Present* 4 (1969–70): 241–45; 5 (1970–71): 295–98.

———. "Origins of the General Eyre in the Reign of Henry I." *Speculum* 41 (1966): 688–724.

———. "Were Ralph and Richard Basset Really Chief Justiciars of England in the Reign of Henry I?" *Acta: The Twelfth Century* 2 (1975): 74–103.

Reiss, Ira. "Universality of the Family: A Conceptual Analysis." *Journal of Marriage and the Family* 27 (1965): 443–53.

Renouard, Yves. "La notion de génération en histoire." *Revue Historique* 209 (1953): 1–23.

Reynolds, Susan. "The Rulers of London in the Twelfth Century." *History* 57 (1972): 337–53.

Richardson, Henry G. "Henry I's Charter to London." *English Historical Review* 42 (1927): 80–87.

———. "A Norman Lawsuit." *Speculum* 7 (1932): 383–93.

Ridyard, S. J. "*Condigna Veneratio*: Post-Conquest Attitudes to the Saints of the Anglo-Saxons." *Anglo-Norman Studies* 9 (1986): 179–208.

Riess, Ludwig. "The Reissue of Henry I's Coronation Charter," *English Historical Review* 14 (July 1926): 321–31.

Rogozinski, Jan. "Ennoblement by the Crown and Social Stratification in France

1285–1322: A Prosopographical Survey." In *Order and Innovation in the Middle Ages: Essays in Honor of Joseph R. Strayer.* Edited by W. C. Jordan, B. McNab, and T. F. Ruiz. Princeton, N.J.: Princeton University Press, 1976. Pp. 273–91.

Round, John Horace. "The Barony of Daubeney." *The Genealogist,* n.s. 4, pp. 42–46.

———. "Bernard the Scribe." *English Historical Review* 14 (1899): 417–30.

———. "The Burton Abbey Surveys." *English Historical Review* 20 (1905): 275–89.

———. "The Colchester Mint in Norman Times." *English Historical Review* 18 (1903): 305–15.

———. "Countess Lucy." *The Academy* 32 (1887): 391.

———. "A D'Aubeney Cadet." *The Ancestor* 12 (1905): 149–51.

———. "Families of St. John and of Port." *The Genealogist,* n.s. 16, pp. 1–13.

———. "The Family of Clare." *Archaeological Journal* 56 (1899): 221–31.

———. "Henry I as an English Scholar." *The Academy* 31 (1884): 168.

———. "King Stephen and the Earl of Chester." *English Historical Review* 10 (1895): 87–91.

———. "Mauduit of Hartley Mauduit." *The Ancestor* 48 (1903): 207–10.

———. "Nigel, Bishop of Ely." *English Historical Review* 8 (1893): 515–19.

———. "Notes on Anglo-Norman Genealogy." *The Genealogist,* n.s. 17, pp. 1–4.

———. "Notes on the Pedigree of D'Oilli." *The Genealogist,* n.s. 5, pp. 80–81.

———. "Odard of Carlisle." *The Genealogist,* n.s. 8, pp. 200–04.

———. "Odard the Sheriff." *The Genealogist,* n.s. 5, pp. 25–28.

———. "The Pedigree of Baynard." *The Genealogist,* n.s. 12, p. 211.

———. "The Ports of Basing and Their Priory." *The Genealogist,* n.s. 18, pp. 137–39.

———. "Robert, Earl of Leicester." *The Genealogist,* n.s. 9, 219–20; 10, pp. 131–34.

———. "Twelfth Century Notes: (1) An Unknown Mistress of Henry I." *English Historical Review* 5 (1890): 745–46.

———. "Who was Alice of Essex?" *Essex Archaeological Society Transactions,* n.s. 3 (1889): 242–51.

Rousset, Paul. "La femme et la famille dans *l'Histoire ecclésiastique* d'Orderic Vital." *Zeitschrift fur Schweizerische Kirchengeschichte. Revue d'histoire ecclésiastique suisse* 63 (1969): 58–66.

Rowlands, I. W. "The Making of the March: Aspects of Norman Settlement in Dyfed." *Anglo-Norman Studies* 3 (1980): 142–57.

Russell, Josiah C. "Death Along the Deer Trails. *Medievalia* 1 (1977): 89–95; reprinted in *Twelfth Century Studies.* New York: AMS Press, 1978. Pp. 76–82.

———. "Demographic Aspects of the Norman Invasion." In *Seven Studies in Medieval English History and Other Historical Essays Presented to Harold S. Snellgrove.* Edited by Richard H. Bowers. Jackson: University Press of Mississippi, 1983. Pp. 3–20.

———. "Samson, King's Clerk and Compiler of Domesday Book." Paper presented at the Haskins Society Conference, University of Houston, November 11, 1986.

——. "Social Status at the Court of King John." *Speculum* 12 (1937): 319–29; reprinted in *Twelfth Century Studies.* New York: AMS Press, 1978. Pp. 203–218.

——. "Tall Kings: The Height of Medieval English Kings." In *Twelfth Century Studies.* New York: AMS Press, 1978. Pp. 62–82.

Sawyer, Peter. "Domesday Book: Limitations and Potential." Paper presented at the Haskins Society Conference, University of Houston, November 14, 1986.

Schnith, Karl. "Regni et pacis inquietatrix: zur Rolle der Kaiserin Mathilde in der 'Anarchie,'" *Journal of Medieval History* 2 (1976): 135–58.

Searle, Eleanor. "Women and the Legitimisation of Succession at the Norman Conquest." *Anglo-Norman Studies* 3 (1980): 159–70.

Sherman, Richard. "The Continental Origins of the Ghent Family of Lincolnshire." *Nottingham Mediaeval Studies* 22 (1978): 23–35.

Short, Ian. "On Bilinguilism in Anglo-Norman England." *Romance Philology* 33 (1979–80): 467–79.

Shorter, Edward. "Illegitimacy, Sexual Revolution and Social Change in Modern Europe." In *The Family in History.* Edited by T. K. Rabb and R. I. Rotberg. New York: Harper and Row, 1971. Pp. 48–94.

Southern, R.W. "Aspects of the European Tradition of Historical Writing: 4. The Sense of the Past." *Transactions of the Royal Historical Society,* 5th ser. 23 (1973): 246–56.

——. "The Place of England in the Twelfth-Century Renaissance." In *Medieval Humanism and Other Studies.* New York: Harper and Row, 1970. Pp. 158–80.

——. "The Place of Henry I in English History." *Proceedings of the British Academy* 48 (1962): 127–69; reprinted without appendix in *Medieval Humanism and Other Studies.* New York: Harper and Row, 1970. Pp. 206–33.

——. "Ranulf Flambard and Early Anglo-Norman Administration." *Transactions of the Royal Historical Society,* 4th ser. 16 (1933): 95–128; reprinted in revised form in *Medieval Humanism and Other Studies.* New York: Harper and Row, 1970. Pp. 183–205.

Spear, David S. "Une famille ecclésiastique Anglo-Normande: L'Evêque Ouen et l'Archevêque Thurstan d'York." *Etudes Normandes* 3 (1986): 21–27.

——. "Les Archdiacres de Rouen au cours de la période ducale." *Annales de Normandie* 34 (1984): 15–50.

——. "Les Doyens du chapitre cathédral de Rouen durant la période ducale." *Annales de Normandie* 33 (1983): 91–119.

——. "Membership in the Norman Cathedral Chapters during the Ducal Period: Some Preliminary Findings." *Medieval Prosopography* 5 (1984): 1–18.

——. "The Norman Empire and the Secular Clergy, 1066–1204." *Journal of British Studies* 20 (1982): 1–10.

Spitzer, Alan B. "The Historical Problem of Generations." *American Historical Review* 78 (1973): 1353–85.

Stapleton, Thomas. "Observations upon the Succession to the Barony of William of Arques." *Archaeologia* 31 (1846): 216–37.

Stenton, F. M. "St. Benet of Holme and the Norman Conquest." *English Historical Review* 37 (1922): 225–35.

Stone, Lawrence. "Prosopography." In *Historical Studies Today*. Edited by Felix Gilbert and Stephen Graubard. New York: Norton, 1972. Pp. 107–140.

Tabuteau, Emily Z. "Definitions of Feudal Military Obligations in Eleventh-Century Normandy." In *On the Laws and Customs of England*. Edited by M. S. Arnold, T. A. Green, S. A. Scully and S. D. White. Chapel Hill: University of North Carolina Press, 1981. Pp. 18–59.

Tatlock, John S. P. "The Date of Henry I's Charter to London." *Speculum* 2 (1936): 461–69.

———. "The English Journey of the Laon Canons." *Speculum* 8 (1933): 454–65.

Teunis, Henry B. "The Coronation Charter of 1100: A Postponement of Decision: What Did Not Happen in Henry I's Reign." *Journal of Medieval History* 4 (1978): 135–44.

Thomas, Hugh. "A Yorkshire Thegn and His Descendants after the Conquest." *Medieval Prosopography* 8 (1987): 1–22.

Thomson, Rodney. "Twelfth-Century Documents from Bury St. Edmunds Abbey." *English Historical Review* 92 (1977): 806–19.

Thorne, S. E. "Henry I's Coronation Charter, Chapter 6." *English Historical Review* 93 (1978): 794; reprinted in *Essays in English Legal History*. London: Hambledon Press, 1985.

———. "English Feudalism and Estates in Land." *Cambridge Law Journal* (1959): 193–209; reprinted in *Essays in English Legal History*. London: Hambledon Press, 1985.

Thurlby, Malcolm. "Romanesque Sculpture at Tewkesbury Abbey." *Bristol and Gloucestershire Archaeological Society Transactions* 98 (1980): 89–94.

Turner, Ralph V. "The *Miles Literatus* in Twelfth- and Thirteenth-Century England: How Rare a Phenomenon?" *American Historical Review* 83 (1978): 928–45.

Van Houts, Elisabeth, "Latin Poetry as a Source for Anglo-Norman History, 1066–1135." Paper presented at the Haskins Society Conference, University of Houston, November 14, 1987.

Vaughn, Sally. "Robert of Meulan and Raison d'Etat in the Anglo-Norman State, 1093–1118." *Albion* 10 (1978): 352–73.

———. "St. Anselm and the English Investiture Controversy Reconsidered." *Journal of Medieval History* 6 (1980): 61–86.

———. "St. Anselm of Canterbury: the Philosopher-Saint as Politician." *Journal of Medieval History* 1 (1975): 279–306.

———. "Saint Anselm: Reluctant Archbishop?" *Albion* 6 (1974): 240–50.

Walker, Barbara MacDonald. "King Henry I's 'Old Men.'" *Journal of British Studies* 8 (1968): 1–21.

Walker, Curtis. "Sheriffs in the Pipe Roll of 31 Henry I." *English Historical Review* 37 (1922): 67–79.

Walker, David. "Miles of Gloucester, Earl of Hereford." *Bristol and Gloucestershire Archaeological Society Transactions* 77 (1958): 66–84.

———. "The Norman Settlement in Wales." *Anglo-Norman Studies* 1 (1978): 131–43.

————. "Some Charters Relating to St. Peter's Abbey, Gloucester." In *A Medieval Miscellany for Doris Mary Stenton*. Edited by Patricia M. Barnes and C. F. Slade. ("Publications of the Pipe Roll Society," vol. 76, "New Series," vol. 36.) London: Pipe Roll Society, 1960. Pp. 347–62.

Walker, Sue Sheridan. "The Marrying of Feudal Wards in Medieval England." *Studies in Medieval Culture* 4 (1974): 209–24.

Ward, J. C. "Fashions in Monastic Endowment: The Foundations of the Clare Family 1066–1314." *Journal of Ecclesiastical History* 32 (1981): 427–51.

Warren, W.L. "The Myth of Norman Administrative Efficiency." *Transactions of the Royal Historical Society*, 5th ser. 34 (1984): 113–32.

White, G. H. "The Career of Waleran, Count of Meulan and Earl of Worcester (1104–1166)." *Transactions of the Royal Historical Society*, 4th ser. 17 (1934): 19–48.

————. "Financial Administration under Henry I." *Transactions of the Royal Historical Society*, 4th ser. 8 (1925): 56–78.

————. "Henry I's Illegitimate Children." *Complete Peerage*, vol. 11, Appendix D, pp. 105–21.

————. "The Household of the Norman Kings." *Transactions of the Royal Historical Society*, 4th ser. 30 (1948): 127–55.

————. "King Stephen's Earldoms." *Transactions of the Royal Historical Society*, 4th ser. 13 (1930): 51–82.

————. "The Royal Household Under Henry I." *Notes and Queries* 151 (1926): 399–402.

————. "Warwick." *Complete Peerage*, vol. 12, part 2, pp. 357–63.

White, Graeme. "King Stephen, Duke Henry and Ranulf, Earl of Chester." *English Historical Review* 91 (1976): 555–65.

White, Stephen. "Succession to Fiefs in Early Medieval England." *Past and Present* 68 (1974): 118–26.

Zarnecki, George. "Romanesque Sculpture in Normandy and England in the Eleventh Century." *Anglo-Norman Studies* 1 (1978): 168–89.

INDEX

"Surnames" are used for references to families. Individuals are indexed by first name.

University of Pennsylvania Press
MIDDLE AGES SERIES
Edward Peters, General Editor

Edward Peters, ed. *Christian Society and the Crusades, 1198–1229.* Sources in Translation, including The Capture of Damietta by Oliver of Paderborn. 1971

Edward Peters, ed. *The First Crusade: The Chronicle of Fulcher of Chartres and Other Source Materials.* 1971

Katherine Fischer Drew, trans. *The Burgundian Code: The Book of Constitutions or Law of Gundobad and Additional Enactments.* 1972

G. G. Coulton. *From St. Francis to Dante: Translations from the Chronicle of the Franciscan Salimbene (1221–1288).* 1972

Alan C. Kors and Edward Peters, eds. *Witchcraft in Europe, 1110–1700: A Documentary History.* 1972

Richard C. Dales, *The Scientific Achievement of the Middle Ages.* 1973

Katherine Fischer Drew, trans. *The Lombard Laws.* 1973

Henry Charles Lea. *The Ordeal.* Part III of Superstition and Force. 1973

Henry Charles Lea. *Torture.* Part IV of Superstition and Force. 1973

Henry Charles Lea (Edward Peters, ed.). *The Duel and the Oath.* Parts I and II of Superstition and Force. 1974

Edward Peters, ed. *Monks, Bishops, and Pagans: Christian Culture in Gaul and Italy, 500–700.* 1975

Jeanne Krochalis and Edward Peters, ed. and trans. *The World of Piers Plowman.* 1975

Julius Goebel, Jr. *Felony and Misdemeanor: A Study in the History of Criminal Law.* 1976

Susan Mosher Stuard, ed. *Women in Medieval Society.* 1976

James Muldoon, ed. *The Expansion of Europe: The First Phase.* 1977

Clifford Peterson. *Saint Erkenwald.* 1977

Robert Somerville and Kenneth Pennington, eds. *Law, Church, and Society: Essays in Honor of Stephan Kuttner.* 1977

Donald E. Queller. *The Fourth Crusade: The Conquest of Constantinople, 1201–1204.* 1977

Pierre Riché (Jo Ann McNamara, trans.). *Daily Life in the World of Charlemagne.* 1978

Charles R. Young. *The Royal Forests of Medieval England.* 1979

Edward Peters, ed. *Heresy and Authority in Medieval Europe.* 1980

Suzanne Fonay Wemple. *Women in Frankish Society: Marriage and the Cloister, 500–900.* 1981

R. G. Davies and J. H. Denton, eds. *The English Parliament in the Middle Ages.* 1981

Edward Peters. *The Magician, the Witch, and the Law.* 1982

Barbara H. Rosenwein. *Rhinoceros Bound: Cluny in the Tenth Century.* 1982

Steven D. Sargent, ed. and trans. *On the Threshold of Exact Science: Selected Writings of Anneliese Maier on Late Medieval Natural Philosophy.* 1982

Benedicta Ward. *Miracles and the Medieval Mind: Theory, Record, and Event, 1000–1215.* 1982

Harry Turtledove, trans. *The Chronicle of Theophanes: An English Translation of anni mundi 6095–6305 (A.D. 602–813).* 1982

Leonard Cantor, ed. *The English Medieval Landscape.* 1982

Charles T. Davis. *Dante's Italy and Other Essays.* 1984

George T. Dennis, trans. *Maurice's Strategikon: Handbook of Byzantine Military Strategy.* 1984

Thomas F. X. Noble. *The Republic of St. Peter: The Birth of the Papal State, 680–825.* 1984

Kenneth Pennington. *Pope and Bishops: The Papal Monarchy in the Twelfth and Thirteenth Centuries.* 1984

Patrick J. Geary. *Aristocracy in Provence: The Rhône Basin at the Dawn of the Carolingian Age.* 1985

C. Stephen Jaeger. *The Origins of Courtliness: Civilizing Trends and the Formation of Courtly Ideals, 939–1210.* 1985

J. N. Hillgarth, ed. *Christianity and Paganism, 350–750: The Conversion of Western Europe.* 1986

William Chester Jordan. *From Servitude to Freedom: Manumission in the Sénonais in the Thirteenth Century.* 1986

James William Brodman. *Ransoming Captives in Crusader Spain: The Order of Merced on the Christian-Islamic Frontier.* 1986

Frank Tobin. *Meister Eckhart: Thought and Language.* 1986

Daniel Bornstein, trans. *Dino Compagni's Chronicle of Florence.* 1986

James M. Powell. *Anatomy of a Crusade, 1213–1221.* 1986

Jonathan Riley-Smith. *The First Crusade and the Idea of Crusading.* 1986

Susan Mosher Stuard, ed. *Women in Medieval History and Historiography.* 1987

Avril Henry, ed. *The Mirour of Mans Saluacioune.* 1987

Maria Menocal. *The Arabic Role in Medieval Literary History.* 1987

Margaret J. Ehrhart. *The Judgment of the Trojan Prince Paris in Medieval Literature.* 1987

Betsy Bowden. *Chaucer Aloud: The Varieties of Textual Interpretation.* 1987

Felipe Fernández-Armesto. *Before Columbus: Exploration and Colonization from the Mediterranean to the Atlantic, 1229–1492.* 1987

Michael Resler, trans. *EREC by Hartmann von Aue.* 1987

A. J. Minnis. *Medieval Theory of Authorship.* 1987

Ute-Renate Blumenthal. *The Investiture Controversy: Church and Monarchy from the Ninth to the Twelfth Century.* 1988

David Anderson. *Before the Knight's Tale: Imitation of Classical Epic in Boccaccio's Teseida.* 1988

Robert Hollander, *Boccaccio's Last Fiction:* Il Corbaccio. 1988

Charlotte A. Newman. *The Anglo-Norman Nobility in the Reign of Henry I.* 1988